White Wine Guide

A complete introduction to choosing white wines

Written by Jim Ainsworth

**Fully updated and revised by
Simon Woods**

The Mitchell Beazley White Wine Guide

by Jim Ainsworth, fully updated and revised
by Simon Woods

First published in Great Britain in 1990 by
Mitchell Beazley, an imprint of Octopus
Publishing Group Ltd, 2–4 Heron Quays,
London E14 4JP.

Revised editions 1999.

A CIP catalogue record for this book is
available from the British Library.

ISBN 1 84000 197 6

Commissioning Editor: Rebecca Spry
Managing Editor: Hilary Lumsden
Editor: Jamie Ambrose
Design: Lovelock & Co
Production Controller: Karen Farquhar

Typeset in Stone Serif, MetaPlus

Printed and bound by Toppan Printing
Company in China.

Contents

Top left: La Badia, a medieval abbey in the Italian region of Orvieto.
Top right: New oak barrels in an Oregon winery.
Bottom: Lagrasse, in the heart of France's Languedoc-Roussillon region.

Introduction

The best way to learn more about wine is to drink it. You can read books, pore over vintage charts and memorise lists of famous châteaux until the cows come home, but until you actually taste the stuff, your words are hollow. What's the point in knowing which grape variety Condrieu is made from if you've never seen a bottle? What's the point in knowing who makes the best Chardonnay in Western Australia if you never intend tasting it? And what's the point in being able to spell Pacherenc du Vic-Bilh – never mind pronounce it – if you ignore it when you see it on a wine list?

This book is aimed at practically minded folk who already enjoy wine but would like to know more about it. Life used to be far easier when the choice of wine was limited to offerings from France, Italy, Spain and Germany. Who could have predicted then that at the start of the third millennium we would routinely be pulling the corks on Chilean and Australian bottles? Or that Austria, Argentina and Canada would all be able to offer world-class white wines?

Faced with the wall of bottles from several different countries which even the humblest of wine shops has today, many people go into overload mode and end up simply plumping for an old favourite. There's nothing wrong with old favourites, and you'll find many of them in the following pages, with descriptions of where they come from, what they're made from and who makes the best versions. But you'll also find suggestions for which other countries and regions to head for in order to discover similar wines, finer wines or better-value wines. By expanding your experience, appreciation and knowledge of wine, you'll become more and more confident in your own judgment. Very soon that wine wall won't seem quite so daunting.

How to use this book

The book is organised in an A–Z fashion, giving details of all the major white wine styles, regions and grapes. Wine-producing countries are described in a separate section. Sparkling and rosé wines are also included, even though some are made exclusively from red grapes. Red grapes can be found in the companion *Red Wine Guide*. In the next few pages you will find simple guides to matching wine with food.

Each entry in the directory follows a similar pattern, beginning with a brief *resumé*: a regional listing gives the best-known wines, the main grape varieties and the general style of the wines; a grape variety listing gives the general style of the wines it produces and the regions where the variety is grown; a specific wine listing gives the region of origin, the grape varieties used and a brief description of the typical flavour. Where relevant, the entry will also have a quality/price rating as follows:

	Quality		Price
*	Mediocre	£	£4
**	Simple quaffer	££	£4–6
***	Good	£££	£6–10
****	Excellent	££££	£10–15
*****	The best	£££££	£15+

The quality bands assess each wine on a worldwide, rather than a regional, scale of worth. The price bands reflect approximately the retail cost of a wine, rather than its cost in a restaurant, where it will usually rise in price to a higher band.

Following the main body of the entry, where relevant there are details of the tastes to expect from the wine/grape/region/country. In addition, where relevant there is a box of recommended producers and, in certain cases, entries for the larger countries also give details of the main wine laws.

At the end of each entry is a subsection entitled "Where next?" This suggests taste paths to follow, directing the reader towards other entries in the directory – highlighted in bold – where information on similar styles of wine can be found. The recommended wines may be slightly lighter or heavier, a little oakier or less oaky, cheaper or more expensive, but each recommendation is designed to encourage confident experimentation.

Wine with food

Entire volumes have been written about matching food and wine, as if the subject were a precise science. It isn't, it never will be and it only makes wine unnecessarily complicated. If people concentrated on serving wine they love with food they love, they would be happy 99 per cent of the time. Having said that, here are ten guidelines which will either increase your pleasure or help you avoid the few disastrous combinations that do exist.

1   **Body talk** Weighty food needs weighty wine and light food needs light wine. So Aussie Shiraz with your steak-and-kidney pie, and Muscadet with your oysters.

2   **Who is showing off?** Meaning which is more important to you: the dish you're making or ordering in a restaurant or the bottle of wine you're going to have with it? Whichever comes first, the other should be content to play a minor role. Great food, uncomplicated wine; great wine, uncomplicated food. Uncomplicated in either case doesn't mean tasteless. A first-class organic chicken, simply roasted, is an excellent choice with a fine, mature red from any part of the world, or a good white burgundy. Similarly, Gavi will never be the world's greatest white wine, but fine examples can happily partner a variety of ornate dishes.

3   **The acid test** Acidity is what keeps a wine fresh, and all wines have it to some degree. Sweet wines often have a very high level to prevent cloying. If a wine is lower in acidity than the food it's served with, it will seem flabby. This is seldom a problem, as apart from fruit, few foods are high in acidity. If you find yourself with a wine that is just too acidic for the food, try sprinkling a little vinegar or lemon juice on the dish and the wine will calm down and behave better. Acidity in a wine is useful for counterbalancing the richness of fatty foods.

4   **Sweets for my sweet** If a wine isn't as sweet as the food it's served with, it can seem bitter, acidic and astringent. There's not much you can do about this except take note of it for next time. Remember that certain vegetables such as carrots and onions are actually sweet, and this

character is especially noticeable after long, slow cooking. With savoury dishes and even lighter desserts, you don't have to go for something that is out-and-out sweet, providing it has plenty of ripe, fruity flavour.

5   **The Italian job** If in doubt, try a bottle of Italian wine. High acidity and not much flavour is a hallmark of many Italian whites, but it means you won't have any disastrous clashes.

6   **Sauce for the goose** If a dish has a strongly flavoured sauce, it's more important to think of this than the meat/fish/whatever underneath. If you've used wine in the sauce, serve a similar wine with the dish.

7   **Bun fight at the Oaky Corral** Too much oak in a wine is a killer, unless you have some smoked fish or meat on hand.

8   **Red or white?** Is red wine really better with meat and white wine with fish? Swap them around and see for yourself. You'd be surprised how well rich Chardonnays go with steaks and how well less-full-bodied reds such as Pinot Noir and lighter Chiantis partner salmon.

9   **Say cheese** Cheese and wine is supposed to be a classic combination, but which wine and which cheese? If you do some experimenting with a selection of cheeses – hard, soft, goat's, blue and smoked – you'll be surprised how unpalatable some of the combinations are. Red wine is what many would choose for the entire cheeseboard, but you might find that whites, especially sweet wines, perform better. Serving just one very good cheese with an appropriate wine may be the best solution.

10   **Bread and water** Occasionally, some combinations are either truly vile – *fino* sherry and chocolate profiteroles – or simply do no favours to either the food or wine, for example, mature red burgundy and Brie. Okay, we all make mistakes. Have a drink of water, nibble a piece of bread in between mouthfuls and remember for next time.

The 11th guideline is to ignore any or all of the above if it conflicts with your own experience. Put a variety of wines and plates in front of a panel of "expert" tasters and, at the end of the nibbling and sipping, there will often be little agreement as to which are the best combinations. So if you do find that *fino* sherry and profiteroles is your thing, then go for it – just don't invite us to your dinner parties.

A–Z of white wine

Grosset
Henschke
Lenswood Vineyards
Nepenthe
Petaluma
Shaw & Smith
Geoff Weaver

Adelaide Hills

Finesse in Australia? Shome mishtake shurely ...
Best-known wines Lenswood Sauvignon Blanc,
Grape varieties Sauvignon Blanc, Chardonnay, Riesling
Style Refined, silky, and not fruit-driven Chardonnay;
rich yet pungent Sauvignon Blanc
Quality/Price ***·····⟩****/£££·····⟩££££

Slopes? Cool climate? Strewth, you could almost be in Europe, although in fact you're less than an hour from Adelaide. The vineyards here are dotted among the hills up to around 1,200 feet (365 m), and are some of Australia's coolest. Even northern Europeans, hardened by cold showers and cross-country runs, have been known to don a thick woolly or two while visiting them.

Adelaide Hills is also the source of some of the country's finest white wines. The few Rieslings made are good, but the best come from slightly further north in the Eden Valley, now officially designated as part of the Barossa. For Chardonnay, however, stay put. In the 1980s, Brian Croser at Petaluma led the way with his wine from Piccadilly; since then, several other producers have either set up here or acquired vineyards in the region. This is also the only place in Australia where Sauvignon Blanc consistently produces wines that can compete with – and often outclass – those from New Zealand.

The Adelaide Hills taste Take your stereotypical Kiwi Sauvignon Blanc – slightly catty and herbaceous but quite weighty, with pea-pod and gooseberry flavours; add just a little extra weight around the midriff and you'll have an Adelaide Hills version. Chardonnays are rather more at the mercy of the individual producers, but the winemakers here strive to tone down overt fruit and oak characters, preferring to make a more complex, tighter, barrel-fermented style of wine that can age well. Riesling is zesty and zippy, and capable of even longer ageing. Petaluma's rich, toasty Croser shows the region's vast and still largely untapped potential for sparkling wines.

Where next? Go for **New Zealand**'s **Sauvignon**s (from the North Island as well as **Marlborough**). **Australia**'s good, cooler climate **Chardonnay**s include **Yarra Valley**, Mornington Peninsula and **Margaret River**.

Albariño

Spain's answer to Viognier
Style Heady and aromatic, with peach and apricot flavours
Grown in Rías Baixas in northwestern Spain, Northern Portugal

Albariño is so interesting that it's surprising to think no New World countries have had a stab at producing it. And no doubt there are arguments with the Portuguese as to where the grape originated; in Portugal, after all, Alvarinho makes some inspiring Vinho Verde. Yet stray from this northwestern corner of Iberia, and you'll be hard-pressed to find any Albariño at all. Shame.

The Albariño taste Peaches and spice are most common, with nuts and cream in heavier versions. Lightly oaked versions can be successful, but most producers prefer to let those wonderful aromas sing out.

Where next? **Viognier** is the obvious first. **Alsace** competes in aromatic terms, plus try **Spain**'s Verdejo from **Rueda** and **Portugal**'s **Vinho Verde**.

Aligoté

Humble peasant in the fiefdom of the regal Chardonnay
Style Tart, lemony and tends to need a dash of cassis
Grown in Burgundy most famously; also Bulgaria and Romania

Burgundy's other white grape is something of a poor relation to the aristocratic Chardonnay, never aspiring to greatness and typically served as a kir with a dash of *crème de cassis* to make its often rapier-like acidity more palatable. The best examples come from the village of Bouzeron, in the Côte Chalonnaise, which has its own appellation: Bourgogne Aligoté de Bouzeron.

The Aligoté taste Most Aligoté is lemony, tart, tangy and flinty with (at best) medium body – fine for a refreshing slurp at the end of a day among the vines, but hardly the stuff of greatness. However, given a decent year and old vines, competent producers turn out something fleshier, with a touch of the light, creamy nuttiness of Burgundian Chardonnay.

Where next? Dry **Chenin Blanc** and Gros Plant from the **Loire** both fit the bill.

Alsace

Fabulous and definitely French wines in Germanic disguise
Best-known wines Gewurztraminer (spelled, in this region, without the umlaut)
Grape varieties Gewurztraminer, Pinot Blanc, Tokay-Pinot Gris, Riesling, Sylvaner, Muscat, Chasselas
Style Depending on the sweetness, the weight of burgundy or Sauternes with rather more exotic aromas
Quality/Price **⋯⟩*****/££⋯⟩£££££

Alsace produces some of France's best white wines. They are skilfully made, cool-climate wines, varied in style, drinkable without having to be cellared for yonks – and affordable.

It is best to forget that Alsatian wines have ever had anything to do with Germany. This is difficult, given some of the names, but anybody looking for light, flowery, bland Liebfraumilch or delicate, ethereal, sweet Rieslings will not find them here. Alsace is in France, and the wines taste like it.

The Alsace taste Alsace's grape varieties are transformed into wines which are fuller-bodied than their German counterparts, with alcohol levels in line with the rest of France. Direct fruit flavour is the main draw; oak is irrelevant. Alsace is a good place to start tasting varietals because the wines here are uncontaminated by extraneous flavours. At one time, they were unusual in being France's only varietally designated wines; now half the world sells its wines this way.

Gewurztraminer may well be the best place to begin. It comes at you with rich, exotic, tropical-fruit flavours of lychee and mango. It does not knock on the door and wait politely; it barges in and creates a strident, larger-than-life hurly-burly you cannot ignore. Even when dry, it never seems bone-dry: the richness of fruit and fatness of texture see to that. It is a lack of obvious acidity that gives buxom Gewurztraminer its broad, ripe, leisurely style, and the feeling that it has never heard of girth control. The best dry Alsatian Gewurztraminers are light- to medium-bodied, crisp and restrained rather than powerful. Sweeter versions can be top-heavy, descending into caricature and providing something that is fascinating to taste but not always to drink.

Muscat is one of the few grapes that tastes just as squishily, juicily fresh whether made into wine or stuffed into your mouth in its raw, spherical state. Alsace Muscat is slightly different: it still has the freshness and the glorious

Muscat fruit, but it is one step removed from fresh-grape feeling because it is dry. It is not austere, and it is still light, but it is just a weeny bit more serious than most other Muscats. Because it is not blanketed by sweetness, the wine's acidity is free to make itself felt; perhaps it is for this reason that many people find Alsace Muscat perfect as an *apéritif*.

Pinot Blanc has probably been underrated in the past. It does not produce wines with ostentatious, gaudy, swaggering, look-at-me flavours, but makes those with everyday, nine-to-five tastes. You could easily overlook it – and many people have – but that is no reason to dismiss it. Whip off the bowler, throw away the furled umbrella, and underneath is a clean, sharp, fresh-faced, likeable, dependable, salt-of-the-earth, appley and definitely upwardly mobile sort of wine. It is bright, attractive and undemanding and, unlike, say, Gewurztraminer, it will partner a wide range of dishes.

The dark horse of grape varieties here is Tokay, or Pinot Gris. Picture a cross of the fleshy peaches and cream of Pinot Blanc with the spice of Gewurz and you won't be far off the flavour. The curious thing about it is that, at whatever stage of its life you drink it, it always seems to be forward and friendly but lacking the acidity to age further. Yet it goes on and on, acquiring honeyed hints along the way. Wines bearing the words *vendange tardive* (VT, *see* page 12) or *sélection des grains nobles* (SGN, *see* page 12), made only in the ripest years, are virtually indestructible. As for the name, Tokay sounds unusually exotic for France, whereas Pinot Gris sounds like it might be Burgundian. Alsatians prefer Tokay, but Brussels insists on Pinot Gris, so the accepted compromise is to call it Tokay-Pinot Gris. This, however, does not affect the taste.

A selection of classic cuisine from Alsace, matched perfectly with the region's variety of white wines

Riesling is the most regal of the region's seven permitted varietals, though not the most approachable. Inexpensive Alsace Rieslings can usually be drunk young; at that age, they already possess a style, weight and decisive cut that set them apart from other wines. But, they show best with bottle age. Riper, fuller, richer Rieslings develop from a steely beginning through a honeyed adolescence into a kerosene- and petrol-like maturity. The grape's acidity can keep the wine alive for decades. Again, VT and SGN wines are the real stayers.

Sylvaner, the French spelling of Silvaner, is rarely worth getting worked up about. It is usually basic drinking wine, the sort you might put on the table with the salt, pepper and ketchup; part of the furniture rather than a painting to display and admire. Chasselas (sometimes called Fendant in Switzerland, Gutedel in Germany) is extremely ordinary and in Alsace is only used with other varieties, *Edelzwicker* being the name for these bucket-shop blends. Alsace's sparkling wine, Crémant d'Alsace, is made mainly from Pinot Blanc, although Riesling and Chardonnay can be used, too. The appellation was introduced in 1976, and wines are still variable but improving.

A final warning: one problem with Alsace wines is that you have no idea precisely how sweet a wine is going to be from its label. There are dry VT wines and distinctly off-dry basic *cuvées*, while those labelled SGN can be dripping with the apricot and marmalade of noble rot, or only mildly affected. The only way of knowing for certain is to pull the cork and take a slug.

Where next? **Oregon** is the only region currently close to matching Alsace. Weissburgunder and **Pinot Blanc** can be very good in **Austria** and the warmer parts of **Germany** such as **Baden**. Head to the same places and **Australia** for dry but fleshy **Riesling**. **Gewürztraminer** from other parts of the world (where its umlaut is reinstated) struggles to attain the Alsace style, so look to exotic varieties such as **Viognier** and **Albariño**.

READING ALSACE LABELS

The name of the producer and the grape variety will be prominent on the label of an Alsace bottle; it is worth deciphering some of the other information, too.

• Most wine, whether varietal or blended, is entitled to the Alsace AC. Alsace *grand cru* AC covers specific vineyards for certain grape varieties or blends; only Gewurztraminer, Riesling, Muscat and Pinot Gris varietals will be considered. If the wine comes from just one vineyard, it will be named on the label.

• *Vendange tardive* (VT) means that the grapes were picked late, giving them a high sugar level and consequently a high level of potential alcohol.

The wine may not necessarily be sweet, but it will be full and fairly alcoholic.

• *Sélection des grains nobles* (SGN) means that individual grapes (some of them infected with noble rot) were picked to make a rich and (usually) sweet wine.

• Words such as *réserve, réserve exceptionelle, cuvée spécial* and, *sélection spéciale* have no legal force: they will generally indicate a producer's best wine.

Anjou-Saumur

From the sublime to the ridiculous
Best-known wines Rosé d'Anjou, Coteaux du Layon, Sparkling Saumur
Grape varieties Chenin Blanc, Chardonnay, Grolleau, Cabernet Franc
Style Chenin Blanc in all its fascinating guises plus some of the world's most mediocre rosé
Quality/Price *⋯⟩*****/£⋯⟩£££££

East of Muscadet, the vineyards of Anjou sprawl across the River Loire, encompassing Saumur and producing gallons of uninspiring rosé wines, the lesser-known reds of the region, and several exciting whites. The great grape of Anjou is the "difficult" Chenin Blanc, often known locally as Pineau de la Loire. The strident acidity of this grape can make for short, sharp and shocking wines, and when these are then given over-enthusiastic doses of sulphur, the results can be Old World whites at their most dreadful. Yet in those vintages when the grapes ripen fully (not everywhere by a long chalk), that acidity also acts to preserve the best wines (be they dry, medium or sweet) for years, nay, decades. At a more humble level in the AC of Anjou itself, Chenin is rendered slightly more user-friendly by the inclusion of up to 20 per cent Chardonnay and/or Sauvignon Blanc.

The region also makes sparkling wines, the best and best known of which come from Saumur. A good-quality white Saumur Mousseux (the producers often drop the "Mousseux" because of its downmarket connotations) will typically be Chenin Blanc with healthy dollops of Chardonnay and Cabernet Franc. Pinot Noir can form up to 60 per cent of the blend, but few wines take advantage of this. The rosé versions tend to be largely Cabernet Franc, and can be very good.

Ah, yes: pink wine. It was marketing campaigns rather than inherent flavour which propelled Rosé d'Anjou to popularity in the 1970s. This slightly sweet and insipid pink wine made (usually) from the lacklustre Grolleau/Groslot grape is still available if you insist. But without a Mateus-style image to sustain it, it has largely been abandoned in favour of other slightly sweet and insipid wines, and no one is too displeased. Real rosé fans always knew that the best Loire pinks were those based on Cabernet, usually Franc but sometimes Sauvignon, such as Cabernet de Saumur and especially Cabernet d'Anjou.

The Anjou-Saumur taste Chenin Blanc needs something to soothe its rasping, savage nature; otherwise, it is reluctant to reveal its inner core of apples, nuts and honey. In the basic Anjou and Saumur appellations,

Chardonnay or Sauvignon Blanc provide the foil, giving a welcome lift of fruit. An alternative balancing tool is sweetness, be it with the lighter, medium-dry wines of Coteaux de Saumur and Coteaux de l'Aubance, or the heady botrytis-affected concoctions of Coteaux du Layon, Bonnezeaux and Quarts de Chaume (*see* **Coteaux du Layon**).

But what about dry Chenin Blancs? The only thing that will mollify the brooding, even unpalatable character these savage beasts can have in their youth is time in bottle. Savennières, the epitome of dry Chenin, demands at least a decade in bottle, and the great single-vineyard wines, Coulée de Serrant and La Roche aux Moines, even longer. The rewards of patience are graceful wines with a creamy nuttiness, unparalleled in the world of wine.

By contrast, Cabernet d'Anjou and other rosés drink well from their release on the third Thursday of November following the vintage. The best have a touch of toffee-ish sweetness and plenty of supple strawberry flavour. Good examples are capable of ageing surprisingly well. The same cannot be said of the sparkling wines. The often harsh, green-appley flavours of most of the whites are not rendered any more palatable by bottle age. Richer, riper wines with Chardonnay in the blend are better, although there is very little to worry the producers in Champagne.

Where next? Head to **Touraine** for more **Chenin Blanc**. The same grape is grown elsewhere in the world, but just doesn't taste the same. Contrast with wines of similar sweetness from the **Rheingau** and **Pfalz**.

Asti

Bottled joy
Region Piedmont
Grape variety Moscato Bianco, aka Muscat Blanc à Petits Grains
Style Frothy, heady, musky and – unusually for a wine – grapey
Quality/Price *·····⟩***/££·····⟩£££

RECOMMENDED PRODUCERS
Cinzano
Fontanafredda
Gancia
Martini

Asti Spumante, or simply Asti, as it is now officially known following promotion to DOCG status in 1994, suffers from the same image problem as rosé – real men just don't drink sweet sparkling wine. Fortunately, there are enough wimps and women to get through the ocean of the stuff that is made each year in Piedmont.

Unlike most sparkling wines, Asti gets its fizz from the initial fermentation, which takes place in a sealed tank, thus trapping the escaping carbon dioxide. Once the producer has achieved the balance he is looking for between alcohol and residual sugar, the fermentation is stopped by rapid cooling, and the wine is bottled.

The industrial scale of production means that the wines are hardly the most complex. Those in search of more character should choose the less fizzy, less alcoholic and even more grapey Moscato d'Asti. However, for any sort of celebration, Asti will bring a smile to the faces of all but the most dour of folk. It's also great stuff to serve at weddings, as it's much more at home with a piece of stodgy fruit cake than dry, acidic Champagne.

Vineyards of Rochetta Palafea in the south of the Asti province

The Asti taste Asti is one of the few wines that actually tastes of grapes – freshly crushed ones with a pervading musky perfume. Try to buy from places that have a speedy turnover of stock, as it's not really a wine that should be allowed to linger once bottled.

Where next? Moscato d'Asti is Asti with knobs on. No other region makes such joyous sparklers, but Clairette de Die comes as close as any (see **Rhône**). Prosecco fizz from northeast Italy, with its pungent character, offers an interesting Italian alternative (see **Veneto**), while in its sparkling form, the rare Brachetto d'Acqui (also from **Piedmont**) has much in common with Asti – apart from the fact that it's red.

Baden

Source of Germany's least Germanic wines
Best-known wines ZBW's Baden Dry
Grape varieties Müller-Thurgau, Weissburgunder (Pinot Blanc),
Ruländer (Pinot Gris), Riesling
Style More flesh and less fruit than the German norm
Quality/Price *····⟩****/£····⟩££££

Baden used to be the place people were directed for German wines that weren't
too, well, Germanic. For years, the wines had a simple label and an equally
simple flavour. They were a great success. It's warmer here than in much of the
rest of Germany, thanks to shelter from the Black Forest and the mountains to
the west, so ripening grapes isn't a great problem.

Then other regions got in on the act, making attractive and simply labelled
wines. So far, Baden hasn't known how to reply. And, with a few notable
exceptions, the region's growers still have not found life after Baden Dry.

The Baden taste The finest Baden wines, those from the Bereich Kaiserstuhl,
are usually based on Pinot Gris, or Ruländer as it is known here. They are
fat and spicy, rather than overtly fruity, and often influenced by oak. Pinot
Blanc makes similar if slightly less spicy styles. Müller-Thurgau abounds,
and re-labelling it as Rivaner doesn't make it taste any better. Riesling is rare,
but can be good, with rather more flesh than elsewhere in Germany.

Where next? **Alsace** makes wines made under similar conditions, or
Franken in **Germany**'s heartland makes dry and austere styles.

Barossa

Little and Large
Best-known wines Eden Valley Riesling, Barossa Valley Semillon
Grape varieties Riesling, Semillon, Chardonnay
Style Plump and juicy in the Barossa Valley, steely in terms of
Eden Valley Riesling. "Attractive Semillon wishes to meet
Chardonnay with GSOH."
Quality/Price **····⟩****/£····⟩££££

If you're a lonely batch of wine looking for a partner with
which to make beautiful music, the Barossa Valley is the place
for you. Batches of grapes, grape juice or wine come from far

A view across
the charming
and diverse
landscape of
the Barossa
Valley

and wide to be blended in this region, and many of Australia's largest companies such as Yalumba, Orlando (of Jacob's Creek fame), Wolf Blass and Penfolds have major wineries here. There is nothing wrong with this, either legally or oenologically; indeed, it is an integral part of the Australian way of winemaking. If a company owns vineyards in Coonawarra, Padthaway and McLaren Vale, there is no point in building three expensive wineries when one expensive winery and a truck will do the job just as well.

If you're looking for a recognisable Barossa style with these blends, you won't find one. However, this is also home to many small wineries, and these are now coming out from under the shadow of the Big Boys. What they make depends on where their vineyards are in the region. The Barossa Valley floor is warm and, to an outsider, patently red wine country. However, the Silesian immigrants who first settled the area thought otherwise, so white grapes – especially Riesling – outnumber reds.

In fact, it is too warm here to make great Riesling, and the plump, fleshy Semillons and Chardonnays are generally the best wines. Head southeast into the cooler Barossa Ranges and the Eden Valley, and Riesling comes into its own, making long-lived, powerful, steely wines. You'll also find Chardonnay, Semillon, Gewürztraminer, Sauvignon Blanc and the odd patch of Viognier.

The Barossa taste The region first made its name for the Rieslings, and these remain its finest whites. The best (from Eden Valley) are greeny-gold, flowery but full-flavoured, big and weighty by German standards, but with good, balancing, lemon-lime acidity, concentrated fruit, and a long, spicy finish. With age (and it can take as little as three years), they develop a honeyed richness with the hallmark kerosene note, but are still bright, lively and well-defined thanks to the acidity. When botrytis strikes, the results can be intense, floral, honeyed and delicious. Barossa floor Chardonnay is rich and ruddy and, thanks to barrel-fermentation, not as oaky as was once the case. Semillon comes in oaked and unoaked forms, and the wines are rather more forward than their Hunter Valley counterparts, with broad, citrus-fruit flavours. They age well – far better than the Chardonnays – developing toasty hints along the way. Wines from the cooler regions are more subtle, crisp and elegant.

Where next? **Adelaide Hills** producers say their wines are finer and less obvious than the Barossa's; try them and see, and throw in a few wines from **Clare**, **Margaret River** and **Yarra Valley** at the same time.

RECOMMENDED PRODUCERS

Court-les-Mûts
De la Jaubertie
Le Raz
Richard
Tour des Gendres
Montravel

Bergerac

Bordeaux satellite in all but name
Region Southwest France
Grape varieties Sauvignon Blanc, Sémillon, Muscadelle
Style Crisp, dry and slightly herbaceous
Quality/Price **⋯⟩****/£⋯⟩£££

Bergerac is a sad case of an "also-ran" in the wine world. Despite the similarities of soil, climate, grape varieties and styles of wine, it is not part of neighbouring Bordeaux. Bergerac has been discriminated against in the past, having to send its wines down the Dordogne via Libourne, and paying extra taxes for the privilege of using somebody else's backyard in order to reach the outside world.

Châteaux de la Jaubertie and Tour des Gendres show that the region is capable of making wines that can outclass Entre-Deux-Mers and even some loftier Bordeaux appellations. However, with no shortage of competitors (either locally or around the world) in the crisp, dry white department, Bergerac's producers still have room for improvement.

The Bergerac taste Bergerac Sec and Montravel, appellations within the Bergerac boundaries, are made principally from Sauvignon Blanc, often with some Sémillon and Muscadelle thrown in. Typically fresh, green, nettley and with hints of blackcurrant leaves, they are best within two years of vintage. More ambitious wines, often with oak influence, have the structure to keep going for a further year or two. The sweet wines of the region – Monbazillac, Saussignac and Bergerac – vie with the lesser sweet wines of Bordeaux. None is as good as great Sauternes, but the best can be excellent value.

Where next? Try Côtes de Duras, another Bordeaux wannabe, or head straight for **Bordeaux** itself, beginning with the **Entre-Deux-Mers**. Alternatively, taste what **New Zealand** does with the same grapes.

Blanquette de Limoux

Venerable southern French fizz

Region Languedoc-Roussillon

Grape varieties Mauzac, Chardonnay and Chenin Blanc

Style Rustic and appley

Quality/Price *···⟩***/££···⟩£££

Prepare to be confused. Not one but three different sparkling wines are allowed to be made in the Limoux region, south of Carcassonne. Granddaddy of them all is Blanquette Méthode Ancestrale, formerly known as Vin de Blanquette. Supposedly invented at the Abbey of St Hilaire in 1531, it thus lays claim to the title of the world's most venerable sparkling wine. There is no secondary fermentation. Instead, the wine is bottled when its initial fermentation is halfway through, meaning that it undergoes the remainder of the process in bottle, which gives it its fizz.

Blanquette de Limoux and Crémant de Limoux, on the other hand, are both made by the Champagne method. While Blanquette Méthode Ancestrale must be 100 per cent Mauzac, Blanquette de Limoux can have up to ten per cent Chardonnay and Chenin Blanc. Crémant de Limoux is Mauzac plus a minimum of 30 per cent Chardonnay and Chenin Blanc, but with neither variety allowed to exceed 20 per cent. Got all that, then?

Crémant de Limoux was introduced in 1989 in order to see whether producers preferred to adopt a more "international" style of wine or whether they'd stick to the more traditional Blanquette. Very few have opted for the Crémant approach, although it seems that both appellations will co-exist for the time being. Good as the wines are, especially coming from so warm a region, they are never going to excite, due largely to the lack of character of the Mauzac grape. This is demonstrated by the fact that the best wine of the region, Domaine de l'Aigle's Pinot Noir/Chardonnay, falls outside all three appellations and includes no Mauzac.

The Blanquette de Limoux taste Blanquette de Limoux has a sharp, appley freshness and bite that follows up the faint grassy, cidery aroma, while Crémant de Limoux is a slightly more refined and complex version, with a hint of biscuit. Best of all is Blanquette Méthode Ancestrale, an Asti look-alike: sweet and light in alcohol, with refreshing, appley fruit.

Where next? Cross the Pyrénées to **Catalonia** for the similarly earthy **Cava**, or look to **Loire** Crémants for a bit more taste and a slightly higher price. New World fizz is often better value.

RECOMMENDED PRODUCERS

(Dry Whites)
Alpha
Carsin
Chasse-Spleen
Doisy-Daëne
Haut-Bertinerie
Lamothe
Loudenne
Lynch-Bages
Mouton Rothschild
Margaux
De Plassan
Reynon
Roquefort
De Sours
Thieuley

Bordeaux

Second fiddle to the reds, but capable of playing just as sweetly
Best-known wines Sauternes, Pessac-Léognan, Graves,
Entre-Deux-Mers
Grape varieties Sémillon, Sauvignon Blanc, Muscadelle
Style Everything from crisp and dry to heady,
unctuous and sticky
Quality/Price *·····⟩*****/£·····⟩£££££

Unless there is a revival, Bordeaux whites will soon be joining the why-aren't-they-more-popular club, whose other members include Riesling, Alsace wines and sherry.

It is several years now since Bordeaux began to clean up its act and its wineries, installing proficient winemakers, gleaming stainless steel and the odd new-oak barrel or two, and learning how to make Sauvignon Blancs and Sémillons that aren't dull, flat, oxidised and over-sulphured. Yet despite the vast improvements in quality at all levels, demand for the wines remains stolid. Even with the very finest from Pessac-Léognan and Sauternes, there is seldom the frenzied excitement which accompanies the region's reds.

The Bordeaux taste The flavour of white Bordeaux can range through every shade and style from the driest of dry to the unctuously sweet. Dry whites are based around Sauvignon Blanc and Sémillon, with Muscadelle in attendance if required. Other varieties are permitted to get in on the act in some appellations – for example, it is theoretically possible to have a 100 per cent Chenin Blanc wine in Côtes de Blaye – but they are little used.

The driest wines are the whites made with a high proportion of Sauvignon Blanc. The flavour is grassy and vegetal, a little like a green pepper, but not so powerful as a California Fumé Blanc or a flinty Pouilly-Fumé from the Loire. The presence of Sémillon in most of these dry wines adds a hint of honey, while judicious use of oak brings a smoky note. The best come mostly from Graves and Pessac-Léognan, but conscientious producers in lesser appellations such as Bordeaux Blanc, Premières Côtes de Bordeaux and Entre-Deux-Mers can make excellent wines. In particular, a few châteaux in the Médoc make some white wine to go alongside their reds, yet these can only be labelled Bordeaux Blanc (or Bordeaux Blanc Supérieur for those with a higher level of alcohol).

The same is true of producers in Sauternes and Barsac, who use identical varieties for their dry and sweet wines. Some of the dry wines have a touch of botrytis, which makes for "interesting" rather than great wine. Sauternes and Barsac represent the summit of sweet Bordeaux. However, the wines from Cérons *see* **Graves**), Ste-Croix-du-Mont, Loupiac and Cadillac (*see* **Entre-Deux-Mers**) offer cheaper alternatives – the influence of botrytis will generally be less obvious, even in the great years, but the best are soft and attractive with honeyed, waxy, fruit flavours.

Bordeaux rosé is rare but, if pushed, those from châteaux such as Bertinerie, de Sours, Thieuley and Clarke can be attractive styles, with refreshing, toffee-ish, blackcurrant fruit. Rarer still is the region's sparkling wine – Crémant de Bordeaux – unfortunately, none of the wine made so far has been worth making a detour for.

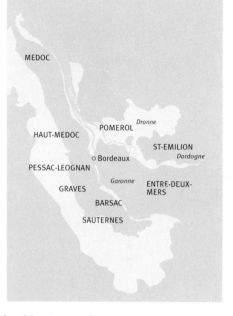

Where next? For nearby comparisons, try Côtes de Duras and **Bergerac** for dry whites, **Monbazillac** for sweet ones. Further afield, **Sémillon** or **Sauvignon Blanc** are grown in many countries, with oaked versions from **California** and **New Zealand** having much in common with the classier Bordeaux whites. For sweet wines, those from **Austria** make good alternatives. See also specific entries for **Entre-Deux-Mers**, **Graves**, **Pessac-Léognan** and **Sauternes and Barsac**.

British Columbia

Beautiful and potentially brilliant
Best-known wines Watch this space
Grape varieties Riesling, Chardonnay, Kerner, Bacchus, Ehrenfelser
Style International
Quality/Price *····⟩****/££····⟩£££££

RECOMMENDED PRODUCERS
Blue Mountain
Calona
Hawthorn Mountain Vineyards
Inniskillin Okanagan (CHK)
Mission Hill
Quail's Gate
Sumac Ridge

Ontario may have led the way for the modern Canadian wine industry, but thousands of miles away in British Columbia, the locals are doing an excellent job at catching up. Like Washington State to the south, the most important vineyards and wineries lie to the east of the Cascade mountain range. The variation in climate throughout the 160-km-long (100 miles) Okanagan Valley – which has its own version of the Loch Ness monster called the Ogopogo – means that there are conditions to suit virtually every type of grape variety.

Curious, then, that several of the locals rather perversely stick to varieties such as Kerner, Bacchus and Ehrenfelser instead of concentrating on better (and more commercial) grapes.

The British Columbian taste British Columbia is still finding its vinous feet, so there is little to speak of yet in terms of regional style. Some Chardonnays are quite lean, but this may be a result of producers picking their fruit too early. Despite the possibilities for grapes such as Riesling, producers focusing on the Germanic varieties tend to be more erratic than those concentrating on Chardonnay. Icewine is not produced to the same extent as it is in Ontario – good ones are impressively rich, sweet and full of flavour, although sometimes you wish for a little less intensity.

Where next? **Ontario** is a long way away, so a more valid comparison is with the wines from further south in **Washington** and **Oregon**. **Austria** also offers glimpses of a region with great potential in the early stages of development.

Burgenland

Sweetness by the See
Best-known wines Ruster Ausbruch
Grape varieties Chardonnay, Weissburgunder, Welschriesling, Bouvier, Muskat Ottonel, Sauvignon Blanc
Style Classic sweet wines, heady yet elegant
Quality/Price **⋯⟩*****/££⋯⟩£££££

Enthusiasts for the great sweet wines should treat themselves to a holiday on the banks of Austria's Neusiedlersee, the shallow lake at the heart of the Burgenland region to the southeast of Vienna. The mists rising from the lake provide the perfect conditions for the development of botrytis (*see* **Noble Rot**) in the vineyards of towns such as Rust, Illmitz and Apetlon. A growing band of passionate (and occasionally potty) producers are taking full advantage of this, producing wines as good as anything made in Germany or Bordeaux, or any other sweet wine region in the world.

There is more to Burgenland than just sweetness, however. Away from the lakeside, the mists disappear and, as well as several red varieties, Chardonnay and Sauvignon Blanc are becoming popular choices for the vineyards. But good as these can be, for the moment the main reason for plumping for Burgenland is for those superb botrytis wines – a few of which can rival some of the world's most famous.

The Burgenland taste Burgenland's finest botrytis wines are luscious, heady, sweet affairs, laden with botrytis character and full of creamy pineapple, apricot and peach fruit. But perhaps their best attribute is balance. Sweet as they are, there is acidity to balance, and your mouth is left refreshed and wanting more rather than feeling like it has been assaulted with a sugar cricket bat. In addition, Ausbruch wines, the speciality of the town of Rust and made in the fashion of Tokay, often have an overtone of coffee.

Where next? Anywhere where great sweet wine is made – **Germany** for *Beerenauslesen* and *Trockenbeerenauslesen*, **Sauternes** and **Alsace** for SGN wines, the **Loire**, **Bordeaux**... you choose.

Burgundy

The place that launched a thousand Chardonnays
Best-known wines Meursault, Chablis, Corton-Charlemagne, Pouilly-Fuissé, Puligny-Montrachet
Grape varieties Chardonnay, Aligoté, Pinot Blanc, Pinot Gris (Pinot Beurot)
Style Complex, rich, dry and succulent
Quality/Price *⋯⟩*****/£⋯⟩£££££

RECOMMENDED PRODUCERS
Bouchard Père & Fils (since 1995)
Joseph Drouhin
Louis Jadot
Louis Latour
Olivier Leflaive
Verget

Burgundy the region produces some of the greatest white wines in the world – Chablis, Puligny-Montrachet, Meursault – from what many people consider to be the greatest white grape, Chardonnay. Quantities are small (or at least too small to satisfy a thirsty populace), and prices can be high, so burgundy the wine has been copied, emulated and reproduced around the world. At one time, it was the names that were borrowed, leading to claims that as much "Chablis" was consumed in a single day as was produced in the village of Chablis in a whole year. Now, Chardonnay has established itself worldwide, and most respectable winemakers aim to make a wine that reflects their own circumstances rather than just another burgundy look-alike.

Yet Burgundy remains the source of inspiration. Its best wines still achieve a remarkable degree of elegance and balance that many others can dream about. Not all burgundy is like that, of course. The region stretches from chilly Chablis in the north to the edge of Beaujolais in the warm south, a distance of 200 km (125 miles); only a small fraction of that area is occupied by white vines. After Chablis, there is a gap of nearly 112 km (70 miles) before the Côte de Beaune, heart of white burgundy production, and home to Meursault and Puligny-Montrachet. OK, there is a handful of very good white wines produced in the Côte de Nuits, but the Côte de Beaune is really where it's at.

A short hop southwards from there brings you to the Côte Chalonnaise, and then it is another break of some 24 km (15 miles) before you reach the Mâconnais.

Buying burgundy is as fraught with danger as buying a second-hand car. It is not so much the make of car that matters as the man who sells it to you. If he is reputable, you could walk away with a bargain: a genuine low-mileage Ford that won't give a moment's trouble. If he is not, then you might end up with an expensive and duff Mercedes that spends more time in the garage than on the road. So it is with burgundy. The makes or names and the appellations offer the nearest we can get to a cast-iron warranty that the wine does come from where it says – the village of Puligny-Montrachet, for example. But there are lots of Puligny-Montrachet wines, and not all are equally good. It is the producer, the *négociant* who blended it, or the merchant who stocks it we need to get to know.

The practical complexity arises from a few simple principles. Foremost among these is the AC system (*see* **France**) which, as throughout France, varies in degree of specificity. The best vineyards, designated *grand cru*, can produce sublime wines, depending on the producer. *Premier cru* does not refer, as in the Médoc, to the top wines, but rather to the second tier. These are, or again can be, brilliant and exciting wines. Village wines come from vineyards within a village boundary and may be either from a single plot of land, or a blend of wines from several. Regional appellations, such as Hautes-Côtes de Beaune, cross village boundaries and may extend to whole regions (eg Bourgogne Blanc AC).

By itself, the appellation system is fairly straightforward. Yet it is complicated by an inheritance system which, by dividing the estate equally among all children, has progressively segmented the whole of Burgundy into smaller and smaller plots. This could mean that a grower now has, say, one row of vines in each of four vineyards in Puligny-Montrachet, and a couple in each of two vineyards in Meursault. His options are to make and bottle the wine from each vineyard separately; to make two village wines by combining the separate vineyards within each; to make a generic white burgundy; or to sell it all to a *négociant*, who will combine it with the wines of other growers. There is no simple way for the consumer to tell which is best.

The Burgundy taste Styles may differ, but the one thing all the top wines have in common is the grape variety. Chardonnay's international stardom has confirmed two things: first, its adaptability to different conditions – pale, light and refreshing here; golden, unctuous and rich there. Although not reaching such extremes in Burgundy, it does help to explain differences between the leaner style of Chablis and the intensity and complexity of Montrachet. The second thing that Chardonnay's missionary work has brought home is that there is still nowhere quite like Burgundy for elegance or sheer class at the top of the range. It still produces wines that are balanced, complete and integrated, with acidity restraining any natural exuberance. It remains the model that most New World producers have in their heads when they plant their first Chardonnay vines. If you want to taste the best Chardonnay in the world, this is where you come, cheque-book in hand, to join the queue.

Whether you begin at the bottom of the quality ladder or higher up depends on how healthy that cheque-book is. Paupers should avoid Bourgogne Grande Ordinaire (the second adjective is the relevant one) and begin with Bourgogne Blanc or the Mâconnais. If you're slightly better heeled, go for Chablis, the Côte Chalonnaise and some of the lesser appellations of the Côte de Beaune, such as St-Romain and Auxey-Duresses. The Rupert Murdochs among you should spring straight into Meursault, Puligny-Montrachet and Chassagne-Montrachet and the *premiers* and *grands crus* of these villages.

If you tire of Burgundian Chardonnay, some producers maintain a few rows of Pinot Gris and Pinot Blanc. The curious thing is that wines from these grapes taste more like burgundy than like Pinot Gris and Pinot Blanc from elsewhere. Look out, too, for Aligoté, especially from the Côte Chalonnaise. Burgundy's sparkling wine, Crémant de Bourgogne, is made from Chardonnay and Pinot

READING BURGUNDY LABELS

• The term *grand cru* applies to particular vineyards, such as Chevalier-Montrachet (in the village of Puligny-Montrachet) or Corton-Charlemagne (in Aloxe-Corton). Each of these has its own appellation independent of the village.

• The term *premier cru* covers slightly lesser vineyards – for example, Les Perrières (in the village of Meursault) or Les Pucelles and Clavoillon (in Puligny-Montrachet). These vines are usually labelled with both village and vineyard name but, if made from several *premier*

cru vineyards, they may simply be labelled with the name of the village, plus *premier cru*.

• Other wines from within the village boundary can use the village appellation only, but a specific vineyard may still be mentioned on the label.

• Other vineyards will have a more general appellation such as Hautes-Côtes de Beaune or Bourgogne Grande Ordinaire. These less specific ACs cover a wider area, obscuring fine differences but making less expensive wines.

Noir, plus Pinot Blanc and Aligoté. It can come from anywhere between the northern Yonne and Mâcon. The warmer climate means the wines are fuller and softer than Champagne, although still quite dry. Among the best producers of Crémant de Bourgogne are Caves de Bailly, André Bonhomme, André Delorme, Cave de Lugny, Simmonet-Febvre and Caves de Viré.

Négociants Burgundy has dozens of villages and hundreds of producers. If you're not sure how to start off on the burgundy trail, you might want to begin with the *négociants*. These are companies which buy grapes, juice or finished wine from a number of different sources and then blend wines to their own liking. Some can be excellent, some can be mediocre. As always with burgundy, the only watertight guarantee as to a wine's quality is to pull the cork and drink the stuff.

Where next? Assuming you don't want just A N Other **Chardonnay**, burgundy look-alikes are not too widespread. **California** leads the pack for those wanting more than just fruit, with **New Zealand** and **Australia** close behind, while a few examples from southern **France** and **Austria** show great promise for the future. For sexy white wine with oak influence, the best from **Pessac-Léognan** are good bets; given bottle age, Australian **Semillon** (with or without oak) can be superb. See also entries for **Aligoté, Chablis, Chassagne-Montrachet, Côte Chalonnaise, Côte de Beaune, Mâconnais, Meursault, Pouilly-Fuissé** and **Puligny-Montrachet**.

California

Best of the New World – and don't they know it
Best-known wines Classy Chardonnay – and White Zinfandel
Grape varieties and **Style** Infinite range and diversity
Quality/Price *····⟩****/£····⟩£££££

Unlike in Chile, Australia and New Zealand, it wouldn't be the end of the world for the producers in California if they were to never export any more wine. A rapidly growing number of America's 250 million people are discovering the pleasures of wine, and are exercising their patriotic sentiments by plumping for their country's products seven times out of ten. This means two things. Firstly, the Yanks get to cherry-pick their best wines, so many never even leave the country. Secondly, the Californians cater for the tastes of domestic drinkers rather than those of Europeans. Sadly, the people that find this most galling are the Brits. London is supposed to be the centre of the fine wine trade, and some take the absence of California's greats as a personal insult. At the cheaper end of the market, the British wine trade has been accustomed to taking New World producers to one side and saying, "Now listen here, laddy. You're a good sort and we admire your spunk. But we think your wine would be rather better if you were to use more oak/use less oak/add a little Chardonnay/change your labels, etc. Tell you what: knock $20 off the price per case and we might have a deal." But telling a successful Californian producer that his wine is too sweet or too expensive has absolutely no effect at all, and the Brits shouldn't expect it to.

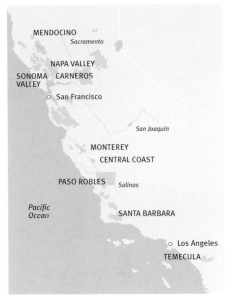

But, well, many California wines *are* too sweet or too expensive. At the cheaper end of the market, where the "fighting varietals" rule, Chardonnay, Sauvignon Blanc, Colombard and others, usually made with fruit from the vast Central Valley region, routinely come with higher sugar levels and lower flavour levels than similarly priced wines from other countries.

At the opposite end of the scale, fashion rules, and "collectors" rush to grab the few available bottles from the latest cult producer. Any new winery employing the right winemaking consultant, the right marketing expertise and producing wine in minuscule quantities can command an extortionate price for its wines. And if Robert Parker or the *Wine Spectator* like it, you can add 50 per cent for the follow-on vintage. Fortunately, between these two extremes, there are sane human beings who make decent wine and charge a fair price for it.

The California taste Chardonnay remains the state's favoured grape by a long way, and the general style has evolved from the overblown rip-snorters of the 1970s through the underblown and often under-ripe style of the 1980s to the just-right-blown wines of today. Oak is being used with greater sensitivity and, thanks to processes such as barrel-fermentation and lees stirring, the one-dimensional fruit characters are giving way to greater complexity. Carneros and Sonoma County are the source of many of the best, but there are also pockets of excellence in regions further south. Few of the wines are built to last, although the best often need five years from vintage to fully unravel.

Sauvignon Blanc performs well, although in a richer, fuller and rather more food-friendly style than in the Loire and New Zealand. The barrel-fermented and aged versions, often labelled Fumé Blanc, compare favourably with wines from the Graves region of Bordeaux. A band of producers, collectively known as the "Rhône Rangers", has planted Viognier, Marsanne and Roussanne. These Rhône varieties are particularly successful in the cooler areas of the Central Coast – try the wines from Alban and Au Bon Climat. Look out, too, for whites made from Malvasia, Muscat (especially in the hands of Andrew Quady), Chenin Blanc, Pinot Gris, Pinot Blanc, Tocai Fruiliano, Colombard and a host of other varieties.

California's best-known pink wine is that marketing man's dream, white Zinfandel. Chilled on a picnic in a San Francisco park, it can be delicious in its simple, sweet and berryish fashion. Served warm in a Birmingham bedsit, the same is, sadly, not true. Some producers such as Bonny Doon do make more serious rosés, but they are few and far between.

As producers learn which regions provide the best fruit, California's sparkling wines are getting better and better. The most ambitious ones are *méthode champenoise* wines based on Pinot Noir and Chardonnay sourced from the cooler regions such as Carneros, and finesse has appeared where once there was just fruit.

Where next? Search out the Old World prototypes of California styles – **Burgundy** for **Chardonnay**, the **Loire** and **Bordeaux** for **Sauvignon Blanc**, the **Rhône** and **Italy** for others. And see what **New Zealand** and **Australia** do with the same grapes. Look for wines from the Central Coast and see the specific entries for **Carneros**, **Monterey**, **Napa Valley** and **Sonoma**.

Carneros

RECOMMENDED PRODUCERS
Acacia
Domaine Carneros
Gloria Ferrer
Saintsbury

Beaune in the USA
Grape varieties Chardonnay
Style Full-bodied yet crisp
Quality/Price ***⋯⟩****/£££⋯⟩£££££

In the northern hemisphere, it's supposed to get warmer the further south you go. Carneros hasn't realised this. The region straddles the bottom of Napa and Sonoma, and its proximity to San Francisco Bay makes it cooler here than further north in both regions – there is a 4 °C (39 °F) difference between Carneros and the upper end of Napa.

It is from here that much of California's finest Chardonnay comes, and vines are gradually displacing grazing cows from the region. Good as the quality is now, we can expect even better things in the future as new plantings of improved clones of Chardonnay – known as Dijon clones – come on stream.

If you visit the region, however, don't expect heaps of wineries. Most of the producers who make Carneros Chardonnay are based further up the Napa Valley and either own vineyards here or buy in fruit from contract growers.

The Carneros taste Carneros Chardonnay seldom reaches the heady alcohol levels which some California wines can have. As with all Chardonnay, each winery puts its individual stamp on the variety, but you can expect sleek, complex, well-balanced wines.

This is also prime fizz country, a fact endorsed by the presence of Taittinger (Domaine Carneros), Freixenet (Gloria Ferrer) and Codorníu (Codorníu Napa). Pinot Noir and Chardonnay, occasionally aided by Pinot Blanc and others, are used to create ripe but elegant wines.

Where next? Other ambitious **California Chardonnays** come from further north in **Sonoma** County, Santa Barbara and pockets of the Central Coast. And you could always try some of that stuff from **Burgundy**...

Wind machines prevent the risk of frost in the vineyards of the Carneros region

Catalonia

Not just Cava country
Best-known wines Cava
Grape varieties Macabeo, Parellada, Xarel-lo, Chardonnay, Muscat, Gewürztraminer
Style Easy, earthy, sparkling wines; improving table wines
Quality/Price ** ⋯⃗****/£⋯⃗£££££

RECOMMENDED PRODUCERS
Can Feixes
Concavins (Santara)
Jean León
Marqués de Alella
De Müller
Puig & Rocca
Miguel Torres

Although the regulations don't insist that Cava comes only from Catalonia, in practice, virtually all of it does. Most of this is made in Penedès, the district stretching down the coast immediately west of Barcelona. However, if wine-drinkers are familiar with Penedès today, it is more likely to be through still wines, and in particular the still wines of Miguel Torres. The Torres company has existed since 1870, but it only began to spring to prominence a century later, when Miguel Torres began to make a range of wines using both Spanish

Ampurdán-
Costa Brava –
one of the
most northerly
wine-producing
regions in
Spain

and imported varieties. These rapidly gained a following throughout the world. Before Torres, much of the white table wine in Catalonia was made with the grapes used for Cava – Macabeo, Parellada and Xarel-lo – and it was pretty dull. Even today, it is surprising that more people haven't followed Torres' lead in planting Chardonnay, Sauvignon Blanc and others.

Apart from Cava and Penedès, there are three other Catalonian DOs (*see* **Spain**) of interest. Alella, just north of Barcelona, makes good Chardonnay and rather ordinary fare from Xarel-lo. Further inland, Chardonnay is also the top performer in both Costers del Segre, where Raïmat makes fine still and sparkling versions, and in Conca de Barberà. The DOs of Tarragona and Terra Alta are less impressive, although the occasional good wine, such as De Müller's Moscatel Seco, can surface.

The Catalonia taste It is largely the producer and the grape variety that call the shots in Catalonia. If the traditional Macabeo, Parellada and Xarel-lo are used to the exclusion of all others grapes, the wines will seldom rise above simple quaffer level. Bring in Chardonnay, and you're usually talking about someone who is more ambitious in his or her winemaking, so ripe, fruity wines with an oak influence are the norm. Other varieties have so far been less successful, although Torres uses Gewürztraminer and Muscat grapes to make the wonderfully aromatic and slightly sweet Viña Esmeralda.

Where next? Contrast with **Rueda** and more modern styles of **Rioja**.

RECOMMENDED PRODUCERS

Can Feixes
Codorníu
Freixenet
Marqués de Monistrol
Mont Marçal
Raventós i Blanc
Segura Viudas

Cava

Strives to do better
Region Predominantly in Catalonia
Grape varieties Macabeo, Xarel-lo, Parellada, Chardonnay, Garnacha, Monastrell
Style Soft, earthy
Quality/Price *⋯⟩****/£⋯⟩£££££

The Cava industry dates back to the 19th century, when Champagne was enjoying a worldwide boom. The reason for Cava's existence, then and now, revolves largely around price. Demand for sparkling wines is high, but

Champagne's price puts it out of reach for many of us. With the advent of New World (and especially Australian fizz) Cava is finding the competition tough going, and is resorting to newcomers such as Chardonnay to add a bit more zip to its wines.

The Cava taste Nobody could accuse the generally sound, but a little pedestrian, Cava wines of being too zippy and bitingly fresh. The flavours are broad, earthy and sometimes fat, although they are becoming livelier by degrees. Cava suffers from being made with not terribly exciting grapes. The party line is that Macabeo has the fruit, Xarel-lo provides acidity and structure, while Parellada polishes the hard edges and adds aroma. In the care of a good winemaker, Cava can be ripe, fresh and citrussy and great value for money. Debate is hot as to what part Chardonnay should play in Cavas of the future. The 100 per cent Chardonnay Gran Brut from Codorníu offshoot Raïmat ranks as one of the finest wines of the *genre* – although it is atypical.

Where next? For equivalent value in the fizzy world, there is only one direction to go: Down Under. So try a sparkler from **Australia**'s Yalumba, Seaview or Seppelt Great Western.

Chablis

Much maligned
Region Burgundy
Grape varieties Chardonnay
Style From steely and flinty to rich and creamy, with a common appley thread
Quality/Price **⋯⟩*****/££⋯⟩£££££

RECOMMENDED PRODUCERS
Billaud-Simon
Boudin
JM Brocard
La Chablisienne
Dampt
Dauvissat
Defaix
J-P Droin
J Drouhin
Jean Durup
William Fèvre
A Geoffroy
J-P Grossot
M Laroche
Louis Michel
Raveneau
Simmonet-Febvre
Testut
Verget
Vocoret

First off, Chablis comes from Chablis – a small village beside a small river called the Serein – and from the green, hilly countryside that surrounds it, in northern France, between Paris and Dijon. It is white (the wine, not the village) and it is made from Chardonnay. Anything else labelled "Chablis" – be it from Spain, Australia, the Americas, or wherever – is bogus. Thanks to extensive lobbying by the good folk of Chablis, such frauds are also disappearing (gradually).

Because of its popularity, there has been pressure on Chablis to expand. Most of the outlying land that was formerly classed as Petit Chablis has now been incorporated into Chablis proper, which today accounts for over half the production. Land that fell under the designation of plain Chablis has, not always with justification, joined the ranks of the famous *premiers crus*. There are now now fewer the 40 *premiers crus*, although some of them are so small as to be irrelevant, while others have still to prove that they deserve the *premier cru* designation. For the moment, it is probably safer to stick to the originals – Côte de Léchet, Fourchaume, Mont de Milieu, Montée de Tonnerre, Montmains and Vaillons are among the best – and most importantly, always remember that the producer's name is paramount.

Grand cru Chablis is really a cut above the rest, being bigger, richer, more intense and characterful, with more finesse about it. There are seven vineyards which qualify for *grand cru* status: Les Clos, Valmur, Vaudésir, Les Preuses, Grenouilles, Blanchots and Bougros.

The Chablis taste Textbook Chablis (and this is a textbook of sorts, so pay attention) is greeny-gold, appetising, bone-dry, lean with appley fruit (Granny Smiths in some years; Cox's Orange Pippins in others) with a hint of cream, but it never develops the rich, full, fat, tropical-fruit style of Chardonnay from warmer climates. Chablis has a bright, glinting, cutting edge that keeps it refreshing, keen and lively, and brings you back for more and more sips.

There is also a mineral component, attributed to the Kimmeridgian limestone soil, and often described as steely or flinty, which seems to give the wine backbone. Grape and soil together produce a feeling of tautness in the wine, with the tension of a coiled spring. Chablis isn't a laid-back, relaxed sort of wine; it is rather on edge, as if restlessly looking at its watch and wondering if it shouldn't be on its way. Some producers have tried to soften this by using oak and/or malolactic fermentation (*see* **Chardonnay**). This has divided opinion in Chablis, but even those in the oak camp seem to be moving towards reducing its flavour impact.

Move up the quality scale to *premier* and *grand cru* and the wines become bigger, more concentrated, and taste as if the apples have had vanilla cream poured over them, with a sprinkling of lightly toasted nuts on top. They will require more time before they are ready to drink (five years instead of two), and they will last longer once they are. They develop the complexity of apples, nuts, butter, toast, spice and cream.

Where next? **Burgundy** has many other **Chardonnay**s, but none quite like Chablis. Try Chardonnay from **South Africa**, northern **Italy**, **New Zealand**, cooler spots of **Australia** and **California** – and let us know if you find anything like Chablis.

Champagne

Too good to save just for celebrations
Region Champagne
Grape varieties Pinot Noir, Pinot Meunier, Chardonnay
Style Refined and elegant, fruity but never too exuberant
Quality/Price **⋯⟩*****/£££⋯⟩£££££

Proper Champagne comes from northern France and is made from three grape varieties: the white Chardonnay and the red Pinot Noir and Pinot Meunier. The first two are the classic grapes of Burgundy 240 km (150 miles) to the south. Up here, though, in Champagne's rolling, featureless wheat fields, they are rather out of their depth: the still wine they make is pinched and mean because of the high acidity. But this acidity is exactly what makes sparkling wine so exciting. It has to have that incisive cut; otherwise, once the bubbles have been added, it can seem fat, heavy and dull – hardly the ideal *apéritif*.

The well-drained chalk soils on which the grapes are planted are responsible for Champagne's delicate flavours and thus for the overall quality. Reims and Epernay are the centres of production, separated by the valley of the River Marne (mostly red grapes) and the Montagne de Reims, where Pinot Noir does especially well. South of Epernay, the Côte des Blancs is devoted almost entirely to Chardonnay. Around 100 km (60 miles) away to the southeast in the Aube, most of the grapes are red.

It may seem strange that such an aristocratic wine as Champagne should be a blend not only of grape varieties, but alos of wines from far-flung vineyards. This *assemblage* of wines, sometimes as many as 70 different wines from different years, grapes and vineyards, is one of the top jobs in any Champagne house. It determines the house style; in the case of non-vintage wines, it must also be consistent from batch to batch and year to year, evening out the vagaries of vintage variation. It is the *assemblage* of a balance of flavour, freshness, body, fruit and finesse that is one of Champagne's hallmarks – allowing it to stand out above its competitors from other parts of the world.

The Champagne taste If you want to feel ripped off, buy a bottle of still wine from the Champagne region under the Coteaux Champenois or Rosé de Riceys appellations. It comes in red, white and pink versions, often in a rather pretty bottle, and wears a price tag similar to that of the fizzy stuff. Which,

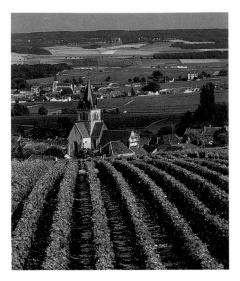

Endless vineyards and beautiful small towns are scattered around the countryside of Champagne

of course, is what the region is all about. While all Champagnes are made by the *méthode champenoise* (*see* **Sparkling Wine**) and from the same three grape varieties, the style and quality of the wines can vary enormously. Drinkers are divided over their preferred style of Champagne. It can vary from pale lemon to deep gold in colour; from a green, stinging freshness overlaid with baker's yeast, to a mellow, biscuity richness; from a light, young Champagne that might open the batting before lunch, to a mature and gentle evening's entertainment; from white to pink; from bitingly bone-dry to rich and creamy. And unless you're familiar with the many producers, you won't know what to expect until you pop the cork.

Non-vintage (NV), which accounts for something like 85 per cent of all Champagne, should be perfectly drinkable straight off the shelf, although most won't mind – and may even benefit from – a year or two under the stairs. Vintage Champagne is made in particularly ripe and fine years, using only the best grapes. It is a more individual wine than NV, generally richer and fuller because of having spent more time on the lees; and less uniform because it should express the character of that particular vintage. Ten years is about the age to drink a vintage, by which time it is creamy and soft. Some wines will last longer, losing some of their fizz on the way, but becoming richer and toastier.

The 100 per cent Chardonnay Blanc de Blancs, which appears in both vintage and non-vintage form, is the longest-lived style; indeed, it can be rather austere in its youth. Blanc de Noirs, which contains precisely zero per cent Chardonnay, differs little from a standard *cuvée*. Rosé Champagne is unique in being the only rosé in Europe that, legally, can be a blend of red and white wines. Colours vary from barely pink through *oeil de perdrix* (when did you last look a partridge in the eye?) to light red, while notes of raspberries and strawberries appear in addition to the standard flavours of Champagne.

Top of the tree are the *prestige cuvées*. These are generally vintage wines (although Krug's NV Grande Cuvée bucks the trend) and are

CHAMPAGNE STYLES

(See Sparkling Wine for methods of production.)

• *Extra brut* is sometimes seen; this has no added sugar.

• *Brut* is what most people see as Champagne; with less than 15 grams of sugar per litre (g/l), the style varies from dry to very dry.

• *Extra sec* (extra-dry) is less dry than brut!

• *Sec* (dry) has an often perceptible sweetness.

• *Demi-sec* (semi-dry) is distinctly sweet.

• *Doux* (rich or sweet) is rare and sweet.

(or should be) the best wines a Champagne house produces. They are luxury products with price tags to match. Expensive, yes, but not overpriced when you compare them with the very finest wines from other classic regions.

A word of warning concerning vintage Champagne. A wine labelled 1982 Brut could have been bottled as early as 1985, as recently as a few months ago or, indeed, at any time in between. In order to temper the youthful acidity, early bottlings generally receive a high level of *dosage*; later bottlings, softened by extra time on the lees, have a lower *dosage*. The result is that two wines with identical labels may end up tasting very different. The earlier bottling will be sweeter and will also have aged very differently from the later one. Bollinger sells a wine labelled RD – *Récemment Dégorgé*, or recently disgorged. But buy a case of 1976 RD at auction and chances are that it will not be recently disgorged at all. It could have been in bottle for 15 years. Bottling dates do appear on a few labels, but still not enough. Be warned.

Where next? Champagne look-alikes are few and far between. Some of the best, however, are those made by offshoots of Champagne companies in **Carneros** and Anderson Valley in **California**, **Yarra Valley** and **Adelaide Hills** in **Australia**, and **Marlborough** in **New Zealand**, but few would pass as Champagne. And why should they? A handful of producers – and we're talking a hand missing a finger or two – in **England** have shown that they can make wines which can easily pass for Champagne.

Chardonnay

Still the world's favourite white grape
Style Always fruity, but largely subject to the producer and the *terroir*
Grown in Well, Greenland *doesn't* have any...

Chardonnay is not the world's most widely planted white grape variety; that honour goes to Spain's lowly Airén. It may not even be the world's best white variety; Riesling could take up that challenge. But, by golly, if the Burgundians, who started the whole Chardonnay craze, had one *franc* for every time anybody talked about it, planted it, or drank a bottle of it, they would be so rich they would be able to give their Puligny-Montrachet away free. The problem is that many people would refuse to accept it since, although the wine is made from 100 per cent Chardonnay, it doesn't actually have the magic word "Chardonnay" on the label. Chardonnay is at the forefront of a revolution which has seen wine-drinkers move from choosing their wine according to the place it comes from to buying by varietal. On the one hand, this is good: anything that makes wine easier to understand for those who are new to it is to be welcomed. On the other hand, this is bad: it brings wine down to the lowest common denominator, erasing any concept of origin.

Cynical producers know that if they include a smidgen of Chardonnay in a bottle of a less popular variety, they can say so on the label and the wine will sell, hence blends such as Sémillon/Chardonnay, Chenin/Chardonnay and Colombard/Chardonnay (dominant grape variety named first). For many people today, there are just two white wines: one is Chardonnay, the other isn't. The result is that Chardonnay has been trampling through the world's vineyards in recent years, eating up less fashionable varieties in its path.

The late 1980s and early 1990s saw massive amounts of Chardonnay vines being planted all over the world. Then came a surge in popularity for red wine as news spread about its health benefits for the heart and for relieving stress. (Absolutely right, of course; 6.30 am board meetings go a whole lot better with half a bottle of Cabernet on top of a fry-up and a double espresso.) Producers began to wish that they'd planted more red grapes instead, but have we seen the Chardonnay being rooted up or grafted over to red varieties? No, and we won't in the future. It's the other white grapes that may well disappear, and we'll just see the blends becoming Chardonnay/Chenin, Chardonnay/ Colombard and so on.

You see, virtually everyone in the wine industry loves Chardonnay. Unlike its Burgundian other half, Pinot Noir, it's a breeze to grow in a wide variety of locations and conditions. In cooler regions, it can be a tad sensitive to frost in early spring – but then, who isn't? Winemakers love it because they can put their thumbprint on it through various practices in the cellar (more of which later). Accountants love it because it sells. And consumers love it because it makes their life easy. A British supermarket shopper could drink a different Chardonnay every week and still not exhaust the range on the shelves. Let's move on and see why they drink it in the first place.

The Chardonnay taste The precise taste is hard to pin down. What is often thought of as the Chardonnay flavour is actually the flavour of mass-market New World Chardonnay. In particular, it was Australian Chardonnay that first got many people hooked: it's splendidly buxom, oaky and laden with tropical fruit-cocktail flavours. But that is largely the flavour of an oaked wine made in a certain fashion from very ripe fruit, rather than the flavour of the grape itself.

We need to discuss winemaking in order to get more of a handle on the taste, so let's look at a couple of wines that are Chardonnay stripped down to the bone, namely an unoaked Chablis and an unoaked Australian Chardonnay. Neither, in this instance, has been anywhere near a barrel, neither has gone through malolactic fermentation, a process which takes place after alcoholic fermentation and which converts the harsh malic acid to softer, creamy lactic acid. The Chablis is light, crisp and appley with a green tinge and leaves your mouth refreshed. The Aussie is full-bodied, slightly golden in colour – almost sweet with a flavour like pineapples in syrup. There doesn't seem to be a common thread, although each reflects the climate in which the grapes were grown – coolish for the Chablis, hot for the Aussie.

What can a producer do to modify the flavours of his Chardonnay grapes? He could leave the grape skins in contact with the juice for a period after the grapes have been crushed. A short skin-contact, as it is known, can add flavour to a wine meant to be drunk young, although too much can add bitterness. He could start the fermentation using special cultured yeasts, or he could rely on those wild yeasts which are on the grape skins and in the air around the winery.

He could put his wine through malolactic fermentation which, as well as adding a slight toffee flavour, will make the wine softer and creamier, and reduce the impact of the acidity. In cool climates, this can be beneficial, but in warm regions, he may want to preserve the acidity. He could age the wine on the lees (the residue after fermentation has ceased). This adds biscuity characters, more so if the lees are stirred up regularly.

Then there's oak. An oak barrel has three effects on a wine. Firstly, it adds tannin and flavour – coconut, vanilla, spice, especially cloves, almonds, caramel. Vary the source and species of oak, where, how and for how long it was dried, how heavily the wood is charred on the inside and how many times the barrel has previously been used, and the impact on the wine also varies. Secondly, it modifies flavours. A Chardonnay that has done its alcoholic and malolactic fermentations in a stainless-steel tank before being transferred to a barrel to age is less interesting and more gawky than one where those processes took place in the barrel in the first place. Thirdly, there is the ever-so-slow oxygenation process, by which the wine "breathes" through the tiny pores in the oak, which again adds complexity.

But oak doesn't have to come in barrel form. You can buy shavings (chips as they're known), and chuck these into a wine when it's fermenting or ageing in a steel tank. Alternatively, you can suspend wooden staves in the tank. If done well, the only difference between a wine made with chips or staves and one made in barrels will be the oxygenation effect. These are only some of the things our chap can do in the winery to influence the taste of his Chardonnay – or of any other variety for that matter. The problem with many modern Chardonnays is that they taste only of what has gone on in the winery. There may be some indication of whether the wine came from a cool or a warm climate, but in most Chardonnays made today, you taste the cooking methods rather than the main ingredients. And if all you want from a wine is for it to be fruity, easy-drinking and inoffensive, there's nothing wrong with that.

So it is with Chardonnay. Burgundy does not make the finest Chardonnay in the world just because of what the growers do with their grapes, but more importantly because of where and how those grapes are cultivated in the first place. This fact has hit home among winemakers throughout the world. Everyone who is looking to produce serious Chardonnay wants to talk about their vineyards. Aside from selecting an appropriate site, matters such as how to prepare and maintain the soils, which clones to plant, how to train the vines, how to prune for optimum yield, and how and when to harvest all have a huge effect on the flavours in the grapes. Good Chardonnay occurs when producers are scrupulous in the vineyards and sensitive in the winery, and it doesn't come cheap.

In addition, Chardonnay often needs time in bottle to appear at its best, especially wines from cooler climates, as white burgundy and Blanc de Blancs Champagne amply testify. Real Chardonnay is a wonderful experience, beautifully textured with a myriad flavours and aromas. The best places to look for it are in Burgundy and California, but Australia, New Zealand, Oregon and many other places are showing that they can make Chardonnay that transcends the merely fruity, or the input of the winemaker.

Where next? **Semillon** from **Australia's Hunter Valley**, given bottle age, can be a match for Chardonnay in weight and interest, as can the top **Bordeaux** whites from **Pessac-Léognan**, and **Pinot Blanc** and **Pinot Gris** from **Oregon** and **Alsace**. Finally, **Riesling** is as underrated as Chardonnay is over-hyped: just as interesting, just as various.

Chassagne-Montrachet

RECOMMENDED PRODUCERS

Blain-Gagnard
Colin-Deléger
Fontaine-Gagnard
Jean-Noël Gagnard
Jacques Gagnard-Delagrange
Jean-Marc Morey
Bernard Morey
Michel Niellon
Fernand Pillot
Ramonet

Great wines by any standard
Region Burgundy
Grape varieties Chardonnay
Style Firm, full-bodied, long-lived and classy
Quality/Price ***⋯⟩*****/£££⋯⟩£££££

For some reason, Chassagne-Montrachet doesn't quite have the same cachet as those other great white-wine villages of the Côte de Beaune, Puligny-Montrachet and Meursault. Maybe this is due to the fact that, until recently, Pinot Noir vines outnumbered Chardonnay in the village – or maybe not. Whatever the case, the wines are excellent and frequently cheaper than those of neighbouring Puligny. Chassagne shares the *grand cru* vineyards of Montrachet and Bâtard-Montrachet with Puligny, and has its very own *grand cru*, Criots-Bâtard-Montrachet. There are no fewer than 51 *premier cru* vineyards, the best of which are Morgeot, Les Caillerets, Les Embrazées, La Romanée, Les Ruchottes and Les Champs-Gain.

The Chassagne taste Any reputation the wines of Chassagne Montrachet have had in the past for rusticity has been erased by improved winemaking. Firm and full-bodied, they need longer than most to reveal their nutty, toasty and appley flavours.

Where next? Start off with other **Côte de Beaune** wines, then move on to New World pretenders from places such as the **Adelaide Hills**, **Marlborough** or **Carneros**.

Chenin Blanc

Pale and interesting
Style Apples, nuts and honey
Grown in The Loire, South Africa, Western Australia, California, Argentina

Chenin Blanc is the Jekyll-and-Hyde of white grapes, the ugly cygnet that can turn into a magnificent swan. And anyone whose experience has been restricted to the ugly cygnets of the Chenin Blanc repertoire could be forgiven for challenging its claim to be a "major" grape variety. Made into a range of styles from dry to sweet, its wines can also vary in quality from the delicious to the downright charmless.

In France's Loire Valley, any sane modern viticulturalist would never plant Chenin, as the climate is on the worrying side of marginal. Cropped too high, Chenin only ripens fully in the very best vintages. Wines made in lesser years are not so much pinched as squeezed heavily with industrial pliers, and scream with the acidity that is a hallmark of the variety. No wonder some winemakers in the region are resorting to adding a dollop of Chardonnay or Sauvignon Blanc to soften the acidic blow (*see* **Anjou-Saumur**). However, good growers will prune their vines to reduce the yield – meaning not only will the flavour be more concentrated, but the chances of the grapes ripening will be much higher. The acidity will still be there, of course, but there will now be extra substance to counterbalance. Whether the wines are dry or – thanks to the influence of botrytis – headily sweet, they will be capable of lasting for decades and are substantially undervalued.

Take Chenin out of the Loire to somewhere where it ripens with ease, and the picture changes considerably. In South Africa, where it is known as Steen, it is the most widely grown variety, making up over 30 per cent of the vineyard area. There are some cracking late-harvest and botrytised versions such as Nederburg Edelkeur, but few producers take it seriously for dry wines, consigning it to the role of the cheap and cheerful. The same is true in California and other New World countries. Those making real efforts with the grape, such as Collards in New Zealand, Dry Creek in California and Houghton in Western Australia, are few and far between.

The Chenin Blanc taste At its best, young Loire Chenin Blanc is lightly floral and sweetly perfumed, has good weight and body, and is reminiscent of melons, apples, quinces and wet hay or wool. But when it is picked before the grapes have had a chance to ripen properly, there is almost no fruit to back up the screaming acidity. The apple taste turns sour, and drinking the dry and even medium-dry versions can be about as much fun as having your teeth drilled.

The lack of well-defined "primary" grape and fruit aromas is what makes the "secondary" aromas so important. These are the complex smells that transmute and develop in bottle: the reward for keeping the right wine for the right length of time. Dry Chenin Blanc becomes nutty; sweet Chenin Blanc becomes first apricotty and then delightfully honeyed. But it takes time – decades, even. Loire Chenin Blanc, especially in its dry form, is not for beginners. The best wines need cellaring for 20 to 30 years or more, and require remarkable patience.

In contrast, New World versions are drinkable from the word go. In cheaper wines, the taste is often indistinguishable from that of other varieties: vaguely fruity but not much else. More ambitious versions have pithy citrus fruit in addition to the appley fruit of the Loire. While not as pronounced as in the Loire, the acidity is still there, and the wines keep remarkably well, developing honeysuckle and toasty characters.

Where next? Lesser German **Riesling**s, especially *trocken*, or dry, versions, can have the rasping acidity of young **Loire** Chenin. If it is the richer, sweeter, more mature style that appeals, then Rieslings of *Auslese* quality (*see* **Germany**) and above, whether from Germany or elsewhere, make an interesting comparison. As an alternative to the better New World Chenins, try Australian Marsanne or Verdelho.

Clare

If this is red-wine country, why are the whites so good?
Best-known wines Riesling from Polish Hill River and Watervale
Grape varieties Riesling, Semillon, Chardonnay
Style Powerful, limey Riesling, chubby Semillon
Quality/Price ***⋯⟩****/££⋯⟩££££

If you want proof that Australia has life after Chardonnay, the Clare Valley is the place to come. This is South Australia's most northerly vine-growing region, some 96 km (60 miles) north of Adelaide, and it is quite hot. Although Chardonnay does appear here, it is Semillon (without the é) and (in particular) Riesling which dominate. The Watervale region has traditionally been the source of many of the best, but wines from the cooler Polish Hill River are just as impressive.

The Clare taste Clare Rhine Rieslings have plenty of lime-juice and mineral flavour, but stop short of coarseness on account of the crisp, citric acidity, and many manage to achieve an attractive, delicate fragrance. Botrytis versions are rare but can be impressively powerful and luscious. Similarly, Semillon is gutsy and packed with flavour, but pithy, lemony acidity prevents it from becoming too wobbly. Good examples of both varieties age far better than all but the very finest Australian Chardonnays.

Where next? Barossa **Rieslings**, especially from the Eden Valley, vie for the title of **Australia**'s finest. For **Semillon**, head for **Margaret River**, the **Hunter Valley** or the **Barossa**.

Colombard

Understudy to Sauvignon Blanc
Style Crisp, fresh, lightly aromatic
Grown in Southwest France, California, South Africa, Australia

Has Colombard's day been and gone? Quite why it became California's most widely planted grape in the 1980s is hard to fathom, but it did, with some wineries even treating it to an oaky overcoat. In France, it enjoyed fame as the flavour behind Vin de Pays des Côtes de Gascogne. The growers in Cognac and Armagnac had found themselves with a surplus of the stuff, so luminaries such as Yves Grassa and the Plaimont co-op took it off their hands and turned out one of the success stories of the 1980s. Then, in both instances, Chardonnay and other, sexier varieties began to muscle their way in, and Colombard just wasn't man enough (grape enough?) to fight back.

Colombard has now been overtaken by Chardonnay in the Californian league table, and no serious winery wants to put its name on the label. It's the same story in France, with buyers preferring a big name over a less familiar one. Shame, really. What Colombard does well is retain flavour and acidity when cropped at fairly high levels – which means that it's ideal for cheap-and-cheerful wines with a bit of crispness to them. The South Africans effortlessly make remarkably pleasant versions which knock spots of many Sauvignon Blancs at twice the price. Similarly, Vin de Pays des Côtes de Gascogne, much of which is based on Colombard, is still far more satisfying than the average *vin de pays* Sauvignon – or Chardonnay, for that matter. But that's fashion for you.

The Colombard taste   Easy-drinking, lemony, fresh, dry, zingy and lively. More ambitious versions, such as that of the Primo Estate near Adelaide, gush with gooseberries and herbs.

Where next?   **Sauvignon Blanc** does a similar sort of thing and usually with a bit more style – but not at this price.

Condrieu

More than a hint of the "Come hither"
Region Northern Rhône
Grape varieties Viognier
Style Heady, fragrant apricots and peaches
Quality/Price ***⋯⟩*****/££££⋯⟩£££££

Ah, fashion. There was a time – quite recently, in fact – when the only people who knew anything about Condrieu and the Viognier grape from which it was made were those doing wine exams. Ask them what it was like and they "ummed" and "erred" and finally confessed that they'd never actually tasted any. Today, Condrieu could sell its production several times over, and is able to command prices comparable with classy white burgundies.

This does not mean that the region's growers are now wealthy, however. Viognier can be a sod to grow, and a sod to turn into wine, and not every Condrieu is a stunner. With only around 22,000 cases of the stuff produced in a typical year, much of it from Rhône *négociants* such as Guigal, Jaboulet, Delas Frères and Chapoutier, the smaller producers have precious little to sell.

Notwithstanding its difficult nature, other wine-producing parts of the world anxious to get in on the act are planting Viognier faster than you can say *Trockenbeerenauslese*; there has even been talk of the grape becoming the next Chardonnay – and all because of one minute appellation in the northern Rhône. Well, two appellations, actually: the three-hectare Château Grillet lies within the boundaries of Condrieu but has its own appellation. In recent times, it has been outclassed by many Condrieus, although all agree that it has the potential for greatness.

The Condrieu taste The prime position of Condrieu's vines, overlooking the River Rhône and facing the sun, undoubtedly contributes to the heady, fragrant, peachy, dried-apricot flavour of the wine and the rich, oily texture that is spread over a distinctly dry and earthy base. This is wine to serve at a seduction. Oak can work, but as Condrieus are best drunk young, it often gets in the way. There are also sweet versions made from very ripe and sometimes botrytised grapes; these can be too much of a good thing. And, as we know, too much of a good thing is absolutely wonderful.

Where next? **Viognier** is cropping up more and more around the world, but **California** does it better than anyone else. Slightly less heady, but still very aromatic, is **Albariño** from **Rías Baixas**.

Coonawarra

Threatened by reds on all sides
Grape varieties Chardonnay, Sauvignon Blanc, Riesling
Style Full-flavoured but never vulgar
Quality/Price ***⋯⟩****/££⋯⟩££££

RECOMMENDED PRODUCERS
Katnook
Penley Estate
Rymill
Wynns

The reputation of Australia's most famous wine region rests on its success with red wines, but that is not to say that there are no decent whites to be found. The sea, which is only some 80 km (50 miles) away, helps keep the region cool, so Chardonnay does well. So, too, does Sauvignon Blanc, although it is far less widespread. Riesling used to be the most widely planted variety here, but its loss of popularity, combined with the clamour for Coonawarra reds, means that there is now little to be found. Indeed, with Australia's major large companies exploring other regions, it would come as no surprise to see all whites displaced from Coonawarra in the future.

The Coonawarra taste As elsewhere in Australia, the big, rich, oaky, buttered-toast style of Chardonnay of circa 1986 (as exemplified in Coonawarra by Wynns) has given way to wines of more finesse – still intense and rich, but not as vulgar. Riesling is ripe and rich with orangey fruit, but never as classy as versions from other South Australian regions. The pleasant surprise is Sauvignon Blanc, which, in the hands of Katnook, is a dead ringer for good Marlborough wines from a warmer year.

Where next? Try other wines from the Limestone Coast, particularly Padthaway or **Margaret River** in **Western Australia**.

Côte Chalonnaise

It's tough being in the shadow of the great Côte d'Or
Best-known wines Montagny, Rully
Grape varieties Chardonnay, Aligoté
Quality/Price **----⟩****/££----⟩££££

The limestone outcrops of the Côte de Beaune (*see* overleaf) reappear haphazardly in the Côte Chalonnaise, and it is on these that white grapes thrive best. The villages of Montagny and Rully have them in greater abundance than, for example, Mercurey and Givry, and hence produce rather more white wine. Wines from outside these villages which gain the approval of a special panel can call themselves Bourgogne Côte Chalonnaise.

Other geographical and climatic characteristics (altitude and cool temperatures) combine to make the wines of the Côte Chalonnaise less authoritative than those of Meursault and Puligny; they have much less definition and know-where-I'm-going flavour. This used to be the source of good value, but prices now are not much cheaper than those of lesser villages in the Côte de Beaune, and reliability still leaves much to be desired. However, if it's Aligoté you're after, then this is definitely the place to come.

The Côte Chalonnaise taste The wines may not be as pricey as in the Côte de Beaune, but the Burgundian rule of only going for top growers is equally, if not more, relevant here. Good examples, especially those from Rully and Montagny, can have the fat, buttery texture of the Côte de Beaune, with apple-crumble fruit and the occasional hint of spice. Lesser versions are more like basic Mâcon. The addition of a *premier cru* vineyard name means little here – Mercurey, for example, has 53 of them – although some, such as, Les Cloux in Rully, do seem to regularly make better wine.

Where next? Contrast with more ambitious **Mâconnais** wines such as St-Véran: same grape, different soil. And see how they stand up against the rapidly improving **Chardonnay**s of southern **France**.

Côte de Beaune

If only all Chardonnay tasted like this...
Best-known wines Le Montrachet, Meursault, Corton-Charlemagne
Grape varieties Chardonnay, bits of Pinot Blanc and Pinot Gris
Style Powerful yet graceful, juicy, bone-dry and complex
Quality/Price **·····⟩*****/££·····⟩£££££

Apart from a large coronary artery at Chablis and a few major vessels down in the Mâconnais, the heart of white Burgundy is the Côte d'Or, a thin strip of hillside running south from Dijon for some 65 km (40 miles). The northern half, the Côte de Nuits, is, with the exception of rarities such as Musigny (de Vogüe), Nuits-St-Georges (Domaine de l'Arlot) and a few others, very much red-wine country. But by and large, great white burgundy is the province of the southern part of this area – the Côte de Beaune.

The best vineyards, where fine differences in soil and drainage interact with microclimatic blips and foibles to produce incomparable wines, are designated *grands crus* (*see* **Burgundy**). In the north of the region lies the village of Aloxe-Corton, overlooked by the famous hill of Corton. Corton-Charlemagne is entirely white wine, and is for some the summit of white burgundy. The most popular vote for top dog goes to Le Montrachet, which straddles the border between Puligny-Montrachet and Chassagne-Montrachet. It is surrounded by four other *grands crus,* which can often match (but seldom exceed) the class of Montrachet itself.

The *premier cru* vineyards of Puligny and Chassagne can be almost as impressive, as can those of nearby Meursault, which has no *grands crus*. And even village wines – those labelled simply as "Meursault" or "Puligny-Montrachet" – can be complex, thrilling and delicious. Taste a few and you'll soon realise what has prompted quality-minded producers the world over to stick a few Chardonnay vines in the ground.

Yet while these three villages dominate the top end of burgundy production, their wines are in short supply, and often cost an arm, a leg and a major part of a torso. Fortunately, there are other parts of the Côte de Beaune that are very capable of delivering the burgundy experience at a more pocket-friendly level. An excellent way to find the best wines is to discover who is making the finest Meursault, Chassagne and Puligny, and then to try what the same growers are doing in the villages of Auxey-Duresses, Beaune, Pernand-Vergelesses, St-Aubin, St-Romain, Santenay and Savigny-lès-Beaune. Some of the real bargains are the humble Bourgogne Blancs, as these are often declassified from loftier appellations and will have been made with the same meticulous care.

The rugged, wilderness and solitude prevail in the more remote parts of the Côte d'Or

The Côte de Beaune taste Great white burgundy is archetypal, copybook stuff: well-bred, well-proportioned, graceful and elegantly dressed. It is not thin and overcropped, not heavy and gawky, but balanced: there is buttery richness, but the wines are not greasy and fat; there is restraint, but the wines are not pinched and tart; there is juiciness, but the wines are not mere thirst-quenchers. Fruit and oak harmonise into whole wines that are greater than the sum of their parts. Drink them before they're ready, however, and you will miss out on the magic. Some of the top wines require ten years minimum to reach their peak, and even more lowly bottles will be all the better for five years' age from vintage.

Meursault, Chassagne and Puligny are covered elsewhere in this book. Corton-Charlemagne from the upper slopes of the hill between Aloxe-Corton and Pernand-Vergelesses are more reserved than their Puligny cousins – tighter, less ripe, more closed, but with a generous pinch from the spice box. Of the other appellations, St-Aubin, lying behind Chassagne and Puligny, is perhaps the best sited. However, the variety of aspects and soils in this area means that it is difficult to speak of typical styles. The good wines can rival those from more famous villages, while others are leaner and less impressive. The Hautes-Côtes de Beaune vineyards, on the higher ground overlooking the Côte de Beaune, are cooler, but capable of making crisp, demanding wines in better vintages.

Where next? Ambitious **Chardonnays** from **California, New Zealand** and **Australia** seek to emulate Côte de Beaune wines: check if they do. Within **France, Chablis** *grands crus* can be very close in style in the best vintages.

Coteaux du Layon

Sweet wine bargains of the world
Region Loire
Grape varieties Chenin Blanc
Style Honey, apples, apricots, quince and citrus fruit
Quality/Price **┄┄⟩*****/£££┄┄⟩£££££

The most luscious sweet wines of the Loire come from vineyards adjoining the River Layon, a tributary which joins the Loire a short distance downstream from Angers. The production of such wines, however, presents difficulties for growers. In good, ripe years, autumn warmth and humidity create ideal conditions for the Chenin Blanc grapes to be affected by botrytis, and the grapes rot and shrivel, concentrating sweetness and preserving acidity. They will make excellent rich wines for long-keeping – but in tiny quantities. When conditions are unfavourable in this region (and routinely in less-favoured parts of the Loire), growers have to be content with a more general late-picking rather than a selective berry-by-berry collection, resulting in less-concentrated wine.

Within the Coteaux du Layon boundaries are Quarts de Chaume and Bonnezeaux, where the south-facing situation and the shelter combine to produce wines which represent the *crème de la crème* of sweet Chenin Blanc. Seven other villages stand out from basic Coteaux du Layon. Best of these is Chaume, which has its own AC of Coteaux du Layon-Chaume, while the other six – Beaulieu, Faye, Rablay, Rochefort, St-Aubin and St-Lambert – can append their names to the Coteaux du Layon-Villages appellation.

The Coteaux du Layon taste There is a big difference between wines that have been smitten with botrytis and those that have not. Without it, they are pleasant, fragrant and appley with hints of honey, nuts and nettles, and if the wrong sort of rot has set in, there can be somewhat earthy notes reminiscent of cheese rind.

With botrytis, those same flavours are concentrated and joined by others of pineapple, peach, quince, liquorice, mint, herbs and more. Bonnezeaux and Quarts de Chaume take these flavours to a higher degree of intensity, although they seldom attain the lusciousness of Sauternes. All are underpinned by that characteristic Chenin acidity, which means that most wines produced today are capable of outlasting you, dear reader. With extra time in bottle, the sweetness becomes less obvious, and flavours of vanilla, nuts and honey come more to the fore. Don't bother with food: these are wines for sipping by themselves.

Where next? The only other country succeeding with sweet **Chenin Blanc** is **South Africa**. Head off to the Rhine for **Germany**'s response to similar conditions (*see* **Rheingau, Rheinhessen, Pfalz**), or to **Sauternes and Barsac**.

Côtes de Gascogne

Tasty proof that not all *vin de pays* has to be varietal
Region Southwest France
Grape varieties Ugni Blanc, Colombard, Manseng (Gros and Petit), Sauvignon Blanc
Style Crisp, tangy and fresh as a daisy
Quality/Price **⋯⟩***/£⋯⟩£££

RECOMMENDED PRODUCERS
Yves Grassa
(du Tariquet and others)
Du Joy
De Maubet
Plaimont Co-op
De San Guilhem

In the Gers *département* of southwest France, traditional wisdom was that the Ugni Blanc (*see* **Trebbiano**) and Colombard grapes made such thin, sharp, acidic and undrinkable wine, that the only thing to do was to distil it for Armagnac. But when spirits consumption began to dip, growers found themselves with plenty of extra grapes on their hands. A few smart thinkers began to look towards table wine as a solution. If the grapes were allowed to ripen more, and the wines were made using stainless-steel tanks and temperature-controlled fermentation, maybe something good would result. It did.

Farm birds in The Landes area of Gascony, where the wines complement local delicacies such as *foie gras*

The Côtes de Gascogne taste Typical Côtes de Gascogne is fragrant, well-textured and rich enough to let you know you're drinking it, but not too substantial as to ever get too serious. The flavours of lemon, apple and gooseberry, often tinged with herbal hints, are refreshing and keep you coming back for more. You would swear that Sauvignon was behind the wines, but most of the time you would be wrong. Oaked versions are richer, although the wood can dampen that youthful enthusiasm. A few producers make wines from 100 per cent Gros Manseng, and these can be splendid, fleshy, peachy concoctions.

Where next? Providing it isn't too old, South African **Colombard** can be just as fresh and zippy, and the cheaper **Chenin Blanc**s ring similar-sounding bells.

The sprawling support system used to train vines in Emilia-Romagna

Emilia-Romagna

Glimmers of hope in a sea of mediocrity
Best-known wines Lambrusco, Albana di Romagna
Grape varieties Albana, Trebbiano
Style Very little at present
Quality/Price *····⟩****/£····⟩££££

Sadly, the region that is home to Parma ham and Parmesan cheese is not a great source of white wine. Trebbiano abounds, and where it doesn't, the equally lethargic Albana holds sway. How many *lira* must have changed hands in order for Albana di Romagna to be the first Italian white wine to attain DOCG status is hard to imagine. For sparkling wine, Emilia-Romagna has that perennial favourite, Lambrusco.

Yet there are pockets of more exciting wines. The DOCs of Colli Piacentini and Colli Bolognesi allow varieties such as Riesling, Sauvignon, Pinot Grigio, Chardonnay and Malvasia to be used. Others are following the IGT/*vino da tavola* route (*see* **Italy**) to produce the styles they want, with some success.

The Emilia-Romagna taste Good as the new wave of varietal wines are, it is still too early to speak of a regional style. Like most Italian whites, the traditional wines of Emilia-Romagna typically have reasonable texture but little in the way of actual flavour. Lambrusco, of course, is an exception.

Where next? The closest neighbouring style has to be Albana di Romagna, and the rest of **Italy** has plenty of **Trebbiano** to offer. But do you *really* want it?

Entre-Deux-Mers

Much-improved source of Bordeaux whites
Grape varieties Sémillon, Sauvignon Blanc, Muscadelle
Style From the crisp and dry to the honeyed and sweet
Quality/Price *····⟩****/£····⟩££££

The *"deux mers"* in question are the rivers Garonne and Dordogne. Between them lies a region that used to be the source of some of Bordeaux's most dismal wines, but that is now increasingly impressive with each new vintage. The innovation that woke up the producers was temperature-controlled fermentation. Ferment the grapes cool, and the fresh, grassy aromas stay fresh; they don't turn to stale, damp hay like they used to. The grape varieties used in the region are the familiar Bordeaux trio of Sémillon, Sauvignon Blanc and Muscadelle. The wines do not have the stature or weight of Graves, but can better straight Bordeaux Blanc (*see* **Bordeaux**).

The Entre-Deux-Mers appellation itself only covers dry whites, but there are also several sweet wines made in the region. The villages of Loupiac, Cadillac and Ste-Croix du Mont lie just across the Garonne from Sauternes and Barsac. The relatively low price such wines command means that few producers are able to lavish as much care on their wines as they do across the river. Yet in good years, when botrytis is widespread, the wines can be very good and excellent value, with Loupiac being the pick of the trio.

The Entre-Deux-Mers taste The dry wines are unpretentious and easy-drinking, light, apple-fresh and slightly grassy. They should, in general, be drunk as young as possible, although a higher proportion of Sémillon in the blend and a dab of creamy oak will help the wine age for two or three years from the vintage. The style of the sweeter wines is very much dependent on the ambitions and bank balance of the producer. Rich ones who can afford the expense of picking only botrytised grapes and perhaps the odd new barrel or two can make apprentice Sauternes. Most of the sweet wines, however, are simple, honeyed and floral, pleasant but not great.

Where next? Try **Graves** and **Bergerac** for another go at the same style. **Sauternes and Barsac** are the obvious comparisons for the sweeter wines.

Franken

No, it isn't a Mateus bottle
Best-known wines Würzburger Stein
Grape varieties Müller-Thurgau, Silvaner, Riesling
Style Dry and full-bodied
Quality/Price *⋯⟩****/£££⋯⟩£££££

Like Baden, Franken is predominantly dry-wine country. Correction: it is predominantly *beer* country, on the edge of Bavaria, east of the Rheingau, where the climate begins to turn severe and Continental. Those who take time off from beer-drinking understandably enjoy wines of a weighty, earthy and dry disposition. Franken seems concerned with the distinctiveness of its containers: you pour from a flat flagon, or *Bocksbeutel* – allegedly modelled on a goat's scrotum – into a Franken Stein. The most famous vineyards lie in Iphofen and Würzburg, with Würzburger Stein being the best of the region. Riesling is grown, but Silvaner and Müller-Thurgau are more popular.

The Franken taste Like Baden, Franken goes in less for the ethereal, aromatic styles, and more for the full, dense, textured styles, with fruit often taking second place to earthy, mineral flavours. Franconian Silvaner is earthy and vegetal – sometimes a bit green and sappy, sometimes a bit smoky – but usually the wines are among the best examples of the grape anywhere. Müller-Thurgau digs deeper than the superficial floweriness that characterises it elsewhere. Riesling from warm, sunny years can be honeyed and immensely satisfying.

Where next? **Baden** is the nearest German equivalent. **Austria** has more sun to coax more sugar into the grapes but, like **Franken**, makes dry wines.

Frascati

When in Rome...
Region Latium
Grape varieties Trebbiano, Malvasia
Style Often bland and flabby, but can be far better
Quality/Price *⋯⟩****/£⋯⟩£££

RECOMMENDED PRODUCERS
Casale Marchese
Castel de Paolis
Colli di Catone
Fontana Candida
Villa Simone
Conte Zandotti

Made in the hills south of Rome, Frascati has traditionally supplied the city with dry, everyday jug wine. It combines the high-yielding, light Trebbiano with the more serious and more difficult to handle Malvasia. The latter's

High-trellised vines in the lush Latium region, home to the Frascati DOC

tendency to oxidise and become flabby is rescued by Trebbiano's fresh acidity. Unfortunately, too few producers have the patience to bother with Malvasia, and innocuous Trebbiano often dominates. The less Trebbiano in the blend, the more interesting the wine. Some even go so far as to exclude Trebbiano altogether. Vigna Adriana from Castel de Paolis sees Malvasia being very successfully vinified, given a helping hand by Viognier.

The Frascati taste While it's a struggle to find flavour in most Frascati, good versions with lots of Malvasia in the blend are creamy and nutty, sometimes with peach and citrus-fruit flavours.

Where next? For lighter Italian wines, try **Trebbiano**; for more interesting wines, try **Malvasia**.

RECOMMENDED PRODUCERS

Abbazia di Rosazzo
Borgo Conventi
Livio Felluga
Marco Felluga
Josko Gravner
Vinnaïoli Jermann
Livon
Miani
Puiatti
Rocca Bernarda
Ronco del Gnemiz

Friuli-Venezia Giulia

Not all Italian whites are bland
Best-known wines Collio Pinot Grigio and Pinot Bianco
Grape varieties Chardonnay, Sauvignon Blanc, Pinot Grigio, Pinot Bianco, Verduzzo, Picolit
Style Aromatic, fresh and stylish, whatever the variety
Quality/Price *···⟩****/£···⟩£££££

With the exception of Asti, all Italy's famous wines are red. Why should the country which the Greeks called *Enotria*, "The Land of Wine", be so deficient in the white department? One of the regions seeking to redress this balance is Friuli-Venezia Giulia. It lies along the border with the former Yugoslavia in the eastern part of the hip of Italy's misshapen leg, and – unlike the rest of the country – it has remained impervious to the charms of the otherwise ubiquitous and dull Trebbiano.

RECOMMENDED PRODUCERS
CONTINUED
Russiz Superiore
Mario Schiopetto
Venica & Venica
Vie di Romans
Villa Russiz
Volpe Pasini

The main DOCs here are Friuli-Grave (formerly Grave del Friuli), a rather large and sprawling region, and the three smaller zones of Collio, Colli Orientali del Friuli (COF) and Isonzo. Each permits a wide range of red and white grape varieties. Chardonnay and Sauvignon Blanc are widespread, but the wines made from Pinot Bianco and Pinot Grigio can be just as impressive – as can their price tags. Grapes such as Tocai Friuliano, Verduzzo and Ribolla Gialla show that the local colour is very colourful indeed. Also, the indigenous Picolit is loudly fêted by producers in the region for the dessert wines it can make, although the liquid in the glass often fails to live up to the reputation.

The Friuli-Venezia Giulia taste   It's cool here, so the wines always have the necessary acidity to bolster them. How they perform largely depends on the intention of the producer. The best growers manage to preserve the flavours of each grape while instilling a cool, spicy, slightly earthy character into their wines. On the few occasions when oak is used, it is rarely intrusive.

Some of the best wines are blends of different grapes. A great example is Jermann's Vintage Tunina, a blend of Pinot Bianco, Chardonnay, Sauvignon Blanc and Picolit. Sweet wines from Picolit and Verduzzo are good rather than great, and are the results of late-harvesting rather than botrytis.

Where next?   **Trentino Alto Adige** offers an Alpine variant with German flavour. **Tuscany** and **Piedmont** are increasingly sophisticated.

The soft slopes of Capriva del Fruili give rich flavour to this region's white wines

Gaillac

The wines that time forgot
Region Southwest France
Grape varieties Mauzac, Ondenc, Len de l'Elh,
Sauvignon Blanc, Sémillon
Style Apples and citrus fruit
Quality/Price *····⟩***/£····⟩£££

Gaillac's grapes probably pre-date the Romans, and some of their names seem to be descended from a lost language: Mauzac, Ondenc, and the out-of-sight Len de l'Elh. Growers in the region turn them into every style of wine imaginable: dry to sweet, still to sparkling. The sparkling wines are probably the best wines of the region, although outside Southwest France, you are far more likely to encounter the perky dry whites.

The Gaillac taste The still dry wines are sharp and tangy, occasionally a little pinched with hints of green apples, liquorice and lemon juice; riper grapes and sweeter wines give off an aroma of cider. The *méthode champenoise* sparklers are simple and fragrant. More interesting are the wines made in the *méthode Gaillaçoise* – the wines get their fizz and any residual sweetness from completing their first (alcoholic) fermentation in bottle.

Where next? The drier **Vinho Verde** wines have a similarly sharp attack and light prickle. **Muscadet** has a family resemblance. Acidity levels can compare with **Chenin Blanc**, so try sparkling Chenin Blanc-based wines from the **Loire** (*see* **Anjou-Saumur, Touraine**).

Gavi

Not white Barolo
Region Piedmont
Grape varieties Cortese
Style Weighty, with lemon overtones
Quality/Price **····⟩****/££····⟩££££

Piedmont does have some excellent white wine, but for the most part, it's not Gavi. Quite why this stylishly packaged but ultimately ordinary wine (made from the Cortese grape) sprang to prominence over wines made from Arneis, Favorita and Muscat, is hard to fathom. Still, perhaps you need something undemanding to go with the fish course before you get into those reds.

The beautifully serene and enchanting countryside near Parodi, in Piedmont's Gavi DOC

The Gavi taste It's hard to pin a precise flavour on Gavi – even on the best versions. There is something vaguely lemony, perhaps peachy, with occasional hints of smoke. Underpinning all this is noticeable acidity and what wine folk call "vinosity" – meaning that there is real substance to it. Certainly the texture is often more remarkable than the flavour. Good Gavi can age happily for five years from vintage, gaining weight and a little more character as it does.

Where next? For something of similar weight from **Italy**, try the better Trebbiano-based wines such as Lugana from **Lombardy**. Or head to the northeast, where fine **Soave** and almost anything from **Friuli-Venezia Giulia** will outclass most Gavi.

Gewürztraminer

A voluptuous, come-hither type of grape
Style Pungent and oily, floral with ginger, lychee and rose water to the fore
Grown in Alsace, Italy, New Zealand, Australia, California and Chile

Gewürztraminer remains one of the world's most easily recognisable wines. There is certainly something wonderfully vulgar about that aromatic assault: the cheap scent 12-year-olds spray on their first Valentine cards, decaying flower water, a tart's boudoir – well, allegedly. Gewürz, as lazy wine folk often call it, is most closely identified with Alsace (minus the umlaut ü), along France's northeastern border with Germany. The word Gewürz means "spice" in

German, and the related Traminer grape is believed to have originated in the village of Tramin, in Italy's Südtirol (*see* **Trentino-Alto Adige**). Gewürztraminer is still popular in the region. Eastern Europe has plenty of Traminer, but it seldom achieves the depth of flavour of its spicier relative.

No other region has, as yet, achieved the wholesale success with Gewürz enjoyed by Alsace. However, judging by impressive versions from places as far apart as Chile's Casablanca Valley, Marlborough in New Zealand and the Willamette Valley in Oregon, this is only because the variety is not as fashionable as Chardonnay, Sauvignon Blanc and others.

The Gewürztraminer taste All Alsace wines are aromatic but, with its heady, floral scents combined with others of ginger, rose water and lychees, Gewürz takes aromatic to a new level. Making decent Gewürz is something of a balancing act. Successful versions are picked late enough for the full aromas and flavours to have developed, yet not so late that the little acidity in the grape has disappeared. The best climates allow long, gentle ripening in weather that is sunny but not too warm. Many producers overdo the amount of skin contact (*see* **Chardonnay**) in an attempt to extract more flavour, and this can result in bitter, oily characters in the wines.

There can be quite a variation in weight and intensity of flavour. Lighter, dry versions are refreshing and brisk, while fuller and more alcoholic wines can have an unctuous richness. The better sweeter versions, whether nobly rotten or not, held together by depth of flavour, can be capable of long ageing.

Where next? Other Alsatian varieties, especially **Pinot Gris**, can taste uncannily like Gewürz at times, whether from Alsace or elsewhere.
Viognier, **Albariño**, and **Argentina**'s Torrontés, also inhabits this domaine.

Gisborne

More than just jug wine
Best-known wines Chardonnay
Grape varieties Chardonnay, Müller-Thurgau, Chenin Blanc, Riesling, Gewürztraminer, Sauvignon Blanc
Style Rich, ripe, peachy Chardonnay, balanced and aromatic Gewürztraminer
Quality/Price ***⋯⟩****/££⋯⟩££££

Gisborne is thought of as the high-yielding grape-basket of New Zealand's North Island. While that may be generally true, it over-simplifies the case. It is wetter here than 160 km (100 miles) down the east coast in Hawke's Bay and,

although much of the wine is extremely ordinary, with Müller-Thurgau still
going strong, it is at least decently made. Yet there are treasures here, too, from
particularly well-endowed vineyard sites, and the Chardonnays can be as good
as any. While there are few producers based in the region, many of New
Zealand's major companies source fruit from this area.

The Gisborne taste Rich, exotic, tropical fruit has been a common thread
of Gisborne Chardonnay, but the wines are becoming more subtle and complex
as the producers alter their winemaking styles. The sweet and dry Chenin
Blanc and Riesling from Millton Vineyard, and the opulent Gewürztraminer
of Montana and Matawhero, show that there are other strings to the
Gisborne bow.

Where next? Hawke's Bay, **Martinborough** and **Marlborough** are the
other contenders for the title of **New Zealand**'s best **Chardonnay** region.

Graves

Return from the Graves
Best-known wines Pessac-Léognan, Sauternes
Grape varieties Sémillon, Sauvignon Blanc, Muscadelle
Style Crisp, stylish dry whites; complex, honeyed sweet whites
Quality/Price *·····>*****/££···>£££££

Graves stretches south from the suburbs of Bordeaux in a wide
swathe of land occupying the south bank of the Garonne as far
as Langon. At the beginning of the 1980s, Graves was a byword
for some of the most cack-handed white-winemaking
imaginable. Something had to happen, and perhaps the
catalyst for change was the establishment in 1987 of the
Pessac Léognan appellation. This took in virtually all the best
land and the serious châteaux of the region, and meant that
the finest wines now no longer bore the Graves name.

Those left as Graves realised that they needed to pull their socks up and
move with the times. Many switched to red wine production, while the
remainder began – slowly at first, but then with more urgency – to embrace the
need for cleaner, fresher white wines. Today, the use of oak can often be
excessive, and there are still too many indifferent or grotty Graves. However,
many châteaux have been successful, and now make wines that compare with
their more noble relatives in Pessac-Léognan. Within the boundaries of Graves,
although curiously forbidden to produce wines labelled as such, are the

RECOMMENDED PRODUCERS
Archambeau
De Cérons
Clos Floridène
Constantin
Pierre Coste
De la Grave
Grand Enclos du Château
de Cérons
Landiras
Magence
Montalivet
Rahoul
Respide-Médeville
Roquetaillade-La-Grange
St Georges
Du Seuil

appellations of Sauternes and Barsac – sources of the world's greatest and most famous sweet white wines. These are not the only sweet wines of the region. Graves Supérieures and Cérons never manage to rise to the heights of Sauternes, but are considerably cheaper – and occasionally they can be very good.

The Graves taste Unlike the lumpen, over-sulphured wines of yesteryear, the best of the new breed of white Graves is clean, fruity and crisply refreshing, yet with the stylishness for which France is renowned. Sémillon provides the substance, the honeyed, nut-kernel nuttiness and the ability to improve in bottle, while Sauvignon contributes the grassy freshness and lively cut that makes these wines attractive to drink young. Proportions vary from wine to wine. Most are at their best between two and four years of age, although the ambitious ones can be kept for longer. Some are matured or (better still) fermented in oak, and have a full, creamy, vanilla-like texture with a lick of spice.

The style of the sweet wines of Cérons and Graves Supérieures depends on the degree of botrytis infection and the care lavished on the wine, but the best have the same honeyed-nut character and waxy apricot fruit that are found in Sauternes.

Where next? Californian and Western Australian blends of **Sauvignon Blanc** and **Sémillon** can impress. **Hawke's Bay** Sauvignon is more Graves-like than its **Marlborough** compatriots. Try **Austria's Burgenland** for some sweet alternatives.

Hawke's Bay

RECOMMENDED PRODUCERS
Babich
Church Road
Clearview Estate
Collards
Crab Farm
Delegat's
Linden Estate
Matariki
Mills Reef
Morton Estate
Ngatarawa
Te Mata
Trinity Hill
Vidal
Villa Maria

As good for whites as reds
Best-known wines Babich Irongate and Te Mata Elston (both Chardonnays)
Grape varieties Chardonnay, Sauvignon Blanc
Style Full-bodied with ripe fruit and smoky oak influence
Quality/Price ***⋯⟩****/££⋯⟩££££

After Marlborough, Hawke's Bay on the east coast of the North Island is New Zealand's largest wine region. It is a warm, sunny and sheltered spot, with a wide variety of soils, some of which rank as the youngest winegrowing soils in the world, since they are the residue from the large earthquake that hit the region in 1931. Ripening most grape varieties here is not a great problem, and because of this, Hawke's Bay's reputation is based more on red wines than white. But the Chardonnays from the region can be as good as any in the country. The Sauvignon Blancs, too, can be excellent, although the style is markedly different from that of Marlborough.

The Hawke's Bay taste The Hawke's Bay Chardonnay style is fuller and fatter that that of Marlborough, with fruit ranging from ripe citrus through peaches to melon and passion-fruit. Butterscotch and nutty notes crop up, and oak makes its presence felt – occasionally too strongly. Sauvignon Blancs have pithy citrus-fruit flavours, and are often either fermented or aged in oak, to yield wines more in line with those of Bordeaux than the Loire.

Where next? Try **Marlborough** or **Martinborough** for the local contrast, **Burgundy** and **Bordeaux** for the inspiration, and **California** and **Australia** for the competition.

Hunter Valley

RECOMMENDED PRODUCERS

Allandale
Brokenwood
Evans Family
Lake's Folly
Lindemans
McWilliam's
Peterson
Reynolds Yarraman Estate
Rothbury Estate
Rosemount
Saxonvale
Simon Whitlam
Tyrrell's

Who says Australian wines won't age?
Best-known wines Hunter Valley Semillon
Grape varieties Semillon, Chardonnay
Style Tight and limey but developing to glorious toastiness (Semillon)
Quality/Price ***⋯⟩****/££⋯⟩££££

It's hot; it's humid; it often rains at harvest time – you would have to be slightly mad to plant vines here. Fortunately for wine-lovers (and for the folks of Sydney just two hours' drive away) there are enough madmen around to make the Hunter Valley one of Australia's best-known wine regions. Its fame has little to do with its size: only around four per cent of Australia's wine comes from the Hunter Valley.

More important is the region's proximity to Sydney, which encouraged a number of people to set up small wineries in the Hunter during the 1960s and early 1970s. The wines of Lake's Folly, Hungerford Hill, Brokenwood, Petersons and Rothbury Estate soon began to attract attention beyond Sydney, and their success encouraged those in other parts of Australia to set up wineries for themselves. The region is unique in Australian terms in that it has a style of white wine in the shape of Hunter Valley Semillon that is regarded as a benchmark. The Chardonnays are good – indeed, Australia's first commercial version was a 1971 Tyrrell's wine.

The stunning new-wave architecture of the Rothbury Estate in the Hunter Valley

The Hunter Valley taste Taste Hunter Semillon young and you wonder why everyone raves about it. At a tender age it is a light, lemony, fresh but undistinguished wine with around ten per cent alcohol. This is ideally the kind of wine that you might swig as an *apéritif* or, on the other hand, gulp to chase down a barbied prawn.

But taste it again in ten years' time and the transformation is astounding. It has broadened into a rich and oily wine – waxy, like honeycomb fresh from a hive – but quite dry and still remarkably fresh. And it's so toasty that it seems as if it has spent months in oak, even though it has never been near a barrel.

That's Semillon from the Lower Hunter. It is also grown in the warmer, drier Upper Hunter, where it seldom performs as well, producing wines which mature earlier and are not as complex. Chardonnay, however, thrives in the valley's upper reaches, and it yields rich, creamy wines with vanilla and pineapple flavours that have traditionally not been afraid to flaunt their oakiness (although the style is becoming less woody). Rosemount Roxburgh is the pinnacle of this style.

Lower Hunter Chardonnays tend to be more peachy and less tropical than those from the Upper Hunter, and with age the wines acquire something of the toastiness of the region's Semillon.

Where next? Western Australia's **Semillon** has the potential to age as well as Hunter versions, as do French dry whites such as those from the the **Rhône** and **Pessac-Léognan**. **New Zealand**, **California** and **Burgundy** offer **Chardonnay**s of similar weight.

Jura and Savoie

The wines that time forgot

Best-known wines Jura's *Vin Jaune*

Grape varieties Savagnin, Chardonnay and Chasselas, Roussette (Altesse), Jacquère, Molette, Roussanne

Style Bizarre... and crisp and light

Quality/Price *····⟩****/££····⟩£££££ and **····⟩***/££····⟩£££

RECOMMENDED PRODUCERS

D'Arlay (Jura)
Jean Bourdy (Jura)
Jaques Puffeney (Jura)
Rolet (Jura)
Pierre Boniface (Savoie)
Mercier (Savoie)
Varichon et Clerc (Savoie)

The Jura is one of France's most traditional winemaking regions, producing the peculiar *vin jaune* and the rare *vin de paille*. *Vin jaune* is France's answer to *fino* sherry. Made from Savagnin, it is left in the barrel for at least six years, developing a surface mould called *flor* which allows a very gentle oxidation. Unlike sherry, however, it is not fortified. The tiny AC of Château-Chalon makes the best – bottled in dumpy 62 cl clavelins, it will last for decades. The rare, expensive *vin de paille* is made by drying grapes in racks, rather like *vin santo* in Italy.

Savoie specialises in snappily crisp, ultra-light, dry and refreshing Alpine wines. Their only problem is that most are devoid of flavour, and are similar to neighbouring Swiss styles. Crépy is made from the Chasselas grape (Fendant in Switzerland) and Seyssel from Roussette, which also makes good *mousseaux* (slightly sparkling). Chardonnay is a permitted variety and Jacquère is also highly thought of locally. Wines labelled Chignin-Bergeron are 100 per cent Roussanne and are perhaps the only Savoie wines that don't require drinking as young as possible. Vin du Bugey is a neighbouring VDQS, where Chardonnay can be surprisingly successful.

The Jura and Savoie taste The Jura's rosés, made from Pinot Noir, can be tasty in a solid yet fragrant way. Savagnin is decidedly odd, developing strange, powerful, earthy flavours. *Vin jaune* is closer to a sherry style – a curious blend of old fruit and barrels, with a strong smell of damp hay – definitely an acquired taste. The creamy, nutty *vin de paille* is rather more user-friendly.

Savoie's Chardonnays occasionally can be crisp and fruity, Jacquère and Roussette tend to have a tangy bite, while the peppery, yeasty Seyssel Mousseux is a very acceptable sparkler. But apart from crispness and freshness, it is a struggle to find flavour in most of Savoie's wines

Where next? For the Jura, start off with a quick look over the border at **Switzerland**'s wines. Then compare *vin jaune* with *fino* and *manzanilla* **Sherry**. Finally, compare *vin de paille* to Hermitage from the **Rhône** and **Vin Santo**. In Savoie, for Crépy, try **Muscadet** and for Seyssel, try a southern **Rhône** white; also try wines from **Trentino-Alto Adige**.

Jurançon

The other great sweet wine from Southwest France
Region Southwest France
Grape varieties Gros Manseng, Petit Manseng, Courbu
Style Apricots and apples, with honey and cinnamon
in the sweeter wines
Quality/Price **⋯⟩****/££⋯⟩££££

With Bordeaux as such a venerable neighbour, it is no surprise that even seasoned wine-drinkers know very little about these excellent sweet wines. Botrytis is seldom a feature of the *moelleux* wines; instead, the long, dry autumns allow the grapes to ripen and partially shrivel on the vines. Petit and Gros Manseng are the main varieties used (Petit Manseng is more noble).

Jurançon Sec is the dry wine of the region, the grapes are harvested earlier, and are thus less subject to worsening weather conditions. While not in the same class as the *moelleux* wines, Jurançon Sec guarantees a steady income while grapes for sweeter wines are concentrating their sugar.

The Jurançon taste Jurançon Sec has an aroma of apricots (fruit, kernel and all) and the occasional hint of grapefruit. Sweet Jurançon is deliciously honeyed, ripe and exotic, with the taste of mangoes sprinkled with cinnamon. It has a clean, refreshing streak of acidity, making it a great wine for fruity desserts. Some producers make barrel-fermented versions which adds an extra dollop of vanilla cream to the fruit cocktail.

Where next? The **Chenin Blanc**-based wines of the **Loire**, dry and sweet.

Languedoc-Roussillon

You can have your gâteau and eat it
Best-known wines Muscat de Rivesaltes
Grape varieties Muscat, Clairette, Bourboulenc,
Chardonnay, Sauvignon Blanc, Viognier, Grenache Blanc,
Marsanne, Roussanne, Rolle...
Style Everything under the Mediterranean sun
Quality/Price *⋯⟩****/£⋯⟩££££

While the progress made by the wine industries in countries such as Australia, New Zealand and Chile in the last 30 years has been remarkable, what has been happening in Languedoc-

Roussillon is just as astonishing. This vast region, stretching from the mouth of the Rhône westwards and southwards to the Spanish border was, until very recently, condemned as suitable only for wines sold in labeless litre bottles. The collapse in demand for such wines forced the producers to move onwards (ie sell up) or upwards. The result is a leaner and far healthier region, refered to by some as France's "New World".

**RECOMMENDED PRODUCERS
CONTINUED**
Puech Haut
Des Quatre Sous
Hugh Ryman
Sieur d'Arques
De Terre Mégère
Val d'Orbieu
Vaquer

The advent of the *vin de pays* system has seen familiar varieties such as Chardonnay and Sauvignon Blanc take hold in many vineyards. New technology, especially machine-harvesting and the cooling apparatus, has brought about a huge improvement in quality and freshness. In the initial stages, the wines from these internationally known grapes, and from the newly sexy Viognier, were often uninspiring, but flavour and character are increasing with each vintage.

At the same time, growers in traditional appellations of the region have also been pulling their socks up. Seeing the success of the *vins de pays*, they have upgraded their cellars, perhaps buying a few new oak barrels, and taken more care in their often quite ancient vineyards. The resulting wines have been a huge step up from the previous leaden-footed offerings, and have shown that the south does not have to rely on Chardonnay and Pals to make decent white wine. Perhaps the most exciting thing about the area is that by no means all of the decent vineyard areas have yet been found. Limoux has already shown that it can make classy Chardonnay, both still and sparkling.

The Languedoc-Roussillon taste

Given the huge diversities of *terroirs*, winemaking skills, grape varieties and styles of wine, it makes little sense to talk of a regional style for Languedoc-Roussillon. Chardonnays can taste of very little, or they can be similar to top-notch burgundy. Chardonnay from Limoux is fresh and zesty, with a subtle, oaky sheen. With varieties such as Sauvignon and Viognier, yields form a major factor, with high-cropped vines of both providing wines that can be rather insipid. Certain large Australian companies have major interests in the region, and their input is apparent in the wines. Flying winemakers also exert their influence extensively here.

Even with the traditional appellations, the producer is more important than the village a wine comes from. Flavours range from crisp and quite sour or bitter through fat, fleshy and peachy to intense, complex and almost savoury wines capable of considerable bottle age. Rosés are similarly varied. Only with the *vins doux naturels* (sweet fortified wines) does a distinct style appear.

Where next?

Start with **Burgundy** and the **Rhône**. **Provence** is lagging behind slightly, but still has some fine whites in a similar vein. See specific entries for **Blanquette de Limoux** and **Vin Doux Naturel**.

Liebfraumilch

It's a wine – just
Regions Pfalz, Rheinhessen, Rheingau, Nahe
Grape varieties Minimum of 51 per cent Riesling, plus
Silvaner, Müller-Thurgau, Rivaner
Style Sweet, vaguely floral
Quality/Price *⋯⟩***/£⋯⟩££

The name of this infamous wine, which amounts to a good half of its appeal, derives from the Liebfrauenstift-Kirchenstück vineyard near Worms, but there is no longer any connection between the two.

Liebfraumilch took on a life of its own long ago. It is a *Qualitätswein bestimmter Anbaugebiet*, or QbA wine, which means that the grapes (or 85 per cent of them, at any rate) must come from within a single *Anbaugebiet*, or designated wine region. Four such regions are permitted to make it, including Rheinhessen, Pfalz, Rheingau and Nahe. It is Rheinhessen and Pfalz that make the lion's share. Don't look for deluxe Liebfraumilch; it's like trying to find flavour in tofu.

The Liebfraumilch taste At best, Liebfraumilch is light, flowery, sweetish, and "of pleasant character" (as the law insists it must be). There are no complicated nuances of taste – indeed, there is often very little taste at all – though every now and again you can be surprised. All you really have to remember is to cool the wine.

Where next? The only way is up. Erase the Lieb word from your vocabulary and try the real stuff. A German **Riesling** *Spätlese*, perhaps from the **Mosel-Saar-Ruwer**, is an excellent place to start.

RECOMMENDED PRODUCERS
Bailey's
Campbells of Rutherglen
Chambers' Rosewood
Morris
Stanton & Killeen
Yalumba

Liqueur Muscat and Tokay

Every bit as imposing as Ayer's Rock
Region Northeast Victoria, Australia
Grape varieties Muscat, Muscadelle
Style Liquid Christmas pudding; Tokay has a hint of fish oil
Quality/Price ***⋯⟩*****/£££⋯⟩£££££

Some of Australia's most distinctive wines come from hot, dry northeast Victoria, close to the Murray River around Corowa and Rutherglen. This is real "sticky" country, where climatic conditions favour high sugar levels in the grapes, and sweet, fortified wines have long been a traditional product of this rather hostile environment. As recently as 1960, something like 70 per cent of the wine that Australians drank was fortified. There is no end of "sherry" and "port" produced in these regions, but Liqueur Muscat and Liqueur Tokay are genuine originals – not copies of European styles.

The grape used for Liqueur Muscat is the Muscat à Petits Grains Rouges – here called Brown Muscat. Tokay has nothing to do with either the Tokay-Pinot Gris grape of Alsace or with Hungarian Tokáji. It is made with Muscadelle, third fiddle to Sémillon and Sauvignon Blanc in Bordeaux, but here featuring in a starring role.

The wines are fortified to stop fermentation and retain their natural sweetness (similar to how port is made), and then aged in old wood in a sherry-like *solera* system (*see* **Sherry**). The casks are often kept in primitive sheds with corrugated tin roofs, and the baking sun results in a high evaporation rate, making the wines more and more concentrated with every passing year. In some wineries, such as Morris, you can find tiny barrels full of wine that is over 100 years old and has the consistency of molasses. Most of the wine sold is considerably younger and less gloopy, although it could never be accused of lacking concentration.

The Liqueur Muscat and Tokay taste First impressions of Muscat suggest that it seems to be made from treacle toffee, raisins, figs and many other dried fruits, coffee and chocolate. You might find a hint of Muscatty grapiness, but the Christmas pudding impression usually overwhelms it – especially in the older wines. Despite all this sweetness, the wines do manage to retain an essential freshness.

The rarer Liqueur Tokay wines share the dark-chestnut or mahogany colour of the Muscats, although sometimes you will find a tinge of green. They have an amazing range of flavours – toffee, chocolate, caramel, butterscotch, honey, marmalade, roasted and burnt coffee, Tía Maria liqueur and – believe it or not – a savoury edge of green olives and fish oil. But don't let that put you off.

Buy the most venerable wine you can afford in order to get the richest and most complex flavours, although it may be better to begin with a younger, less expensive version to gradually acclimatise your mouth.

Where next? These wines are unique in their style, but sweet *oloroso* and Pedro Ximénez **Sherry**, Malmsey **Madeira** and a few **Vins Doux Naturels**, such as Vieux Rivesaltes, come the closest in style.

Loire

A river runs through it
Best-known wines Sancerre, Vouvray, Muscadet
Grape varieties Chenin Blanc, Sauvignon Blanc, Muscadet
Style Dry, medium, sweet, sparkling, rosé – everything, in fact
Quality/Price *·····⟩*****/£·····⟩£££££

The River Loire runs north for 1,020 km (635 miles) from the Massif Central at the heart of France, then west into the Atlantic. Its upper reaches are home to some rarely seen Gamay wines, and there are some fine wines further downstream made from Pinot Noir and Cabernet Franc. These apart, the Loire is very much white-wine country, with white grapes making up nearly 90 per cent of total production.

The central Loire is home to Sauvignon Blanc. The best-known appellations of the region are Sancerre and Pouilly-Fumé, but Reuilly, Quincy and especially Menetou-Salon (from producers such as Henri Pellé, Domaine du Châtenoy and La Tour St Martin) show that other villages are capable of making fine Sauvignon Blanc. Sauvignon extends westwards into the vineyards of Touraine, and good Touraine Sauvignon gives Sancerre and Pouilly a run for their money. Here is where Chenin Blanc begins to take over, with wines such as Vouvray and the underrated Montlouis. Chenin's real stronghold, however, is Anjou-Saumur. Here, it makes top-notch stuff, such as the dry Savennières and the sweet Coteaux du Layon, plus rather more mediocre fare of varying sweetness.

Crémant de Loire, the sparkling wine made using grapes from Touraine and Anjou-Saumur, can be some of the Loire's best fizz. Despite being permitted to

Château de Coulaine, a stunning Chinon estate, in the heart of the Loire region

use both Chardonnay and Pinot Noir, few producers have so far sought to copy the wines of Champagne, and Chenin Blanc tends to dominate the blends. Gratien & Meyer and Langlois-Chateau are the best-known proponents, and their finest *cuvées* rank among the best of the region. This stretch of the Loire is also famous (perhaps infamous) for its rosés. The best, usually based on Cabernet Franc, are very good. The relevant word for the worst is: avoid.

Last stop before the Atlantic is the Pays Nantais, home of Muscadet. This well-known wine is made from the eponymous grape, also known as Melon de Bourgogne. Less renowned (and rightly so) is the painfully tart and fruitless Gros Plant. Its few fans claim it is just the thing to serve with oysters. You may agree – if hair-shirts, beds of nails and five-mile runs are your thing.

Several other small appellations along the twists and turns of the Loire are less easy to pigeonhole. Among them (and always worth a try for curiosity's sake) are Cheverny VDQS (some of it made from the Romorantin grape, unique to Cheverny); Coteaux d'Ancenis (especially the wines made from Malvoisie, Alsace's Pinot Gris); Pouilly-sur-Loire (the same Pouilly where Fumé is made, but this is from the less-than-inspiring Chasselas grape), St-Pourçain VDQS (which uses the Tressalier grape), and Vin de l'Orléanais VDQS (made from Pinot Blanc and Chardonnay). Haut-Poitou from near Poitou is a VDQS capable of making decent Sauvignons and sparklers, especially when the local co-op is involved. Finally, wines from the Jardin de la France, one of the country's largest *vin de pays* regions, are seldom as pretty as the appellation's name.

Where next? New Zealand Sauvignon Blanc; sweet **South African Chenin Blanc**, and some southern French wines, such as **Jurançon** Sec, have similarities to dry Chenin. Instead of **Muscadet**, try **Aligoté** or **Vinho Verde**; for Gros Plant, try therapy. See also **Anjou-Saumur, Coteaux du Layon, Muscadet, Sancerre/Pouilly-Fumé, Touraine** and **Vouvray**.

Lombardy

Italian sparkling wine that isn't sweet?
Best-known wines Franciacorta, Lugana
Grape varieties Chardonnay, Pinot Bianco, Pinot Nero, Trebbiano
Style Champagne look-alikes, and Trebbiano which tastes of something
Quality/Price *·····⟩****/£·····⟩£££££

RECOMMENDED PRODUCERS
Bellavista
Guido Berlucchi
Ca' dei Frati
Ca' del Bosco
Ca' di Frara
Cascina la Pertica
Monsupello
Provenza
Uberti
Vercesi

It's not as noble as Piedmont to the southwest, and it is not as profligate as its eastern neighbours Veneto and Emilia-Romagna. It is easy to forget Lombardy when whizzing round the Italian wine

The rugged beauty of Valtellina in Lombardy, with the Alps towering behind

regions, yet this is home to some of Italy's finest wines. And they're fizzy. In 1995, the Franciacorta DOC was split into two. Today, the still wines of the region come under the Terre de Franciacorta DOC, while Franciacorta itself, now elevated to DOCG level, is for *méthode champenoise* sparklers only. Under the new regulations, the wines have to be made from Chardonnay and Pinot Bianco with up to 15 per cent Pinot Nero, and must be aged on the lees for a minimum of 25 months, 37 months if the wine is to be sold as a *riserva*.

Still whites of the region can be good, but they don't stand out as much as the Franciacorta sparklers. Much of the wine from Oltrepò Pavese (literally "over the Po from Pavia") ends up in fizzy form, but a few producers are making strides with Pinot Bianco, Riesling and Chardonnay. Also worth looking out for is Lugana, made along the shores of Lake Garda, especially as this seems to be one of the few places where Trebbiano can be coaxed into making something that rises above the humdrum.

The Lombardy taste The sparkling wines of Franciacorta have the fruit and biscuity complexity their compatriots usually lack – although their price often leads you to expect that they will be even better than they are. Top Lugana has creamy, buttery, nutty hints, and as Ca' dei Frati's Il Brolettino shows, they can cope very nicely, thank you, with a lick of oak.

Where next? For the sparkling wines, **Champagne** is an obvious starting place. For still wines, **Trebbiano** doesn't get much better than Lugana, so go for quality and try top **Soave** or the wines of **Friuli-Venezia Giulia**.

Mâconnais

Burgundy with a southern accent
Best-known wines Pouilly-Fuissé
Grape varieties Chardonnay
Style Ideally rich, ripe and nutty, but frequently bland
Quality/Price *·····⟩*****/££·····⟩£££££

RECOMMENDED PRODUCERS
Barraud
Bonhomme
Cordier
Corsin
Deux Roches
J Drouhin
Guffens-Heynen
Guillemot-Michel
Manciat-Poncet
Gérard Martin
Merlin
Talmard
Thévenet
Verget
Vincent

Nowhere else in Burgundy is the gulf between the best and the worst quite so wide as it is in the Mâconnais. At this southern extreme of Burgundy, the climate is warmer, and unscrupulous producers take advantage of the conditions to take as large a crop from their Chardonnay vines as the appellation laws allow. The result is bland wine that isn't cheap. Mâcon Supérieur is not superior at all, just more alcoholic. Chardonnay fans would be much better off in the Languedoc.

But to dismiss all Mâcon is a big mistake. There are 43 villages in the region entitled to the appellation of Mâcon-Villages, and dedicated growers in the best of these – Viré, Clessé, Chaintré, Uchizy, Davayé, Lugny, La Roche Vineuse, Prissé – make some of the best-value wines in Burgundy. The co-ops at Chardonnay (from whence the grape could well have originated), Clessé, Lugny, Prissé, St-Gengoux and Viré are all capable of making wines to match those of the finest growers. The best-known wine of the region is Pouilly-Fuissé which, when on form, can hold its own with top Côte de Beaune wines. Pouilly-Loché and Pouilly-Vinzelles never rise to the same heights, but St-Véran (when on form) can be almost as good as Pouilly-Fuissé – at half the price.

A common sight along the wine routes of Burgundy: an invitation to drop in and taste wine

The Mâconnais taste Basic Mâcon Blanc should be crisp, refreshing and undemanding, best swigged for quenching a thirst rather than sipped sedately. Good Mâcon-Villages is a distinct step up. This is burgundy with a sun-tan, nutty and buttery, making up in honest fruity flavour what it lacks in subtlety. In some cases, the wines are actually slightly sweet, especially in those parts of the region where botrytis occurs.

A few growers have even used noble rot (botrytis) to create fascinating sweet wines, although the conditions required to make these are rare.

Where next? The **Languedoc** does cheap-and-cheerful **Chardonnay** – cheaper and more cheerfully. Also look at what **South Africa**, **New Zealand** and the cooler parts of **California** and **Australia** are doing with Chardonnay.

Madeira

What's cooking?

Grape varieties Malvasia, Bual, Verdelho, Sercial, Tinta Negra Mole

Style The most intense wine experience in the world

Quality/Price **·····⟩*****/££·····⟩£££££

The invention of Madeira was one of those fortuitous accidents. Casks of wine from this Atlantic island, situated 483 km (300 miles) off the African coast, were traded around the world. And on their travels to and fro across the equator and the high seas, their contents became somewhat "cooked". The wine should have tasted foul, but instead, it was actually rather nice. Eventually it was shipped back and forth deliberately in order to achieve the right amount of cooking before being returned home and sold on to customers in northern Europe.

It would be a bit of a palaver to maintain such a means of production today, so the islanders have developed alternative systems of replicating the heating process. Cheaper wines are warmed through heating coils to around 40 °C to 50 °C (105 °F to 125 °F) and kept there for a minimum of three months. Higher quality Madeira is aged in 600-litre barrels and stored in warm rooms where the ambient temperature is 30 °C to 40 °C (85 °F to 105 °F). The finest wines are often just left in casks under the eaves, with no form of artificial heating – the longer and gentler the ageing, the better the wine.

Basic Madeira comes in a variety of sweetness levels: Dry, Medium Dry, Medium Sweet and Sweet. These categories used to be referred to as Sercial, Verdelho, Bual and Malmsey, but since 1993, any wine bearing one of these names must be made from at least 85 per cent of each of the respected grape varieties. Most basic Madeira tends to be made from Tinta Negra Mole, the grape which was widely planted in the island's vineyards after phylloxera struck at the end of the 19th century. Wines from Reserve level (five years old) upwards will normally be made from Sercial, Verdelho, Bual or Malmsey. Special Reserve is ten years old and Extra Reserve is 15 years old.

In all cases, the age refers to the youngest component in the blend. Vintage Madeira, made only in exceptional years, must spend at least 20 years in cask before being released. Terrantez and Bastardo are two other grape varieties; they are hardly used now, but venerable bottles may occasionally turn up at auction. The older the wine, the more intense the experience; Madeira is one of the few wines that lasts longer than the cork. Store a bottle on its side for half a century and the cork will begin to crumble, so unless the wine is to be drunk straight away, it is a good idea to keep it standing upright. In addition, the cooking and lengthy maturation make Madeira virtually indestructible. Keep it as long as you like before opening and, once opened, it will last very happily for months.

The Madeira taste Sercial is pale, rather sharp and tangy, sometimes with a light, attractive, cheesy whiff – like a mature parmesan. Despite the dryness, and the acidity that keeps it fresh, there can still be a chocolatey richness.

Verdelho is medium-dry with more colour and body, and a more pronounced nuttiness and cheesiness, with a great depth of flavour and a lively streak of cleansing acidity. Bual is medium-sweet, darker still, often with a greeny tinge at the edge, fuller-flavoured, rounded, supple, with a feel of chocolate caramel and a distinctively oxidised smell.

Finally, Malmsey, made from Malvasia Candida, the grape behind Frascati, is the richest and sweetest style, with a whiff of burnt caramel. It has a velvety texture but, like all Madeiras, is never cloying because of the balancing acidity.

Where next? Marsala, Málaga, Sherry, Montilla-Moriles, Australian Liqueur Muscat and Tokay.

Málaga

No, not the airport
Region Andalucía
Grape varieties Pedro Ximénez, Moscatel
Style Rich and treacly, with hints of nuts and raisins
Quality/Price **⋯⟩****/££⋯⟩£££

RECOMMENDED PRODUCERS
Larios
Perez Teixera

This sweet, fortified wine has been progressively elbowed out of its prominent 19th century role as a favourite tipple of the British and Russian empires. Torremolinos is just up the road, so it is more profitable to build hotels along the coast than it is to grow grapes. Anyway, tastes have changed: who wants to drink dense, sweet, sticky wines any more? The lack of demand caused the best producer in the region, Scholtz Hermanos, to close its doors in 1996.

Most Málagas are sweet, ranging in alcohol from 15 to 20 per cent, and are made principally from the grapes that provide the sweetening for sherry: Pedro Ximénez and Moscatel. They go through a *solera* system rather like that used for sherry, so they are blends, not vintage wines. Anyone paying nearly $200 per bottle at auction for Scholtz Hermanos' Solera 1885 should take note: the amount of wine from 1885 in the blend will be tiny. One of the best styles is Lágrima, made from only the free-run juice.

**Sunset in
Archidona,
Málaga, in
southern Spain**

The Málaga taste At its luscious best, Málaga is raisiny, toffee-like and treacly, sometimes with smells of roasting coffee and nuts – unfashionable, perhaps, but delicious nonetheless. Grab some before they build another runway over the few remaining vineyards.

Where next? Sweet *oloroso* **Sherry**, **Port**, **Madeira**, sweet **Marsala**, Australian **Liqueur Muscat and Tokay**.

Malvasia

Badly in need of revival
Style Rich, nutty; can be musky with apricot and pineapple hints
Grown in Italy, Spain and Portugal

Frascati is just one of many Italian wines in which Malvasia pays a distinctly quiet second fiddle to Trebbiano. It is a shame that it isn't the other way around. Wherever these grapes meet, Trebbiano's freshness balances Malvasia's potential flabbiness, but it is Malvasia that provides the interest.

However, Malvasia is disappearing from many vineyards in favour of Trebbiano (easy to grow) and Chardonnay (easy to sell). Malvasia appears by itself throughout Italy. The finest versions come from cool regions such as Friuli-Venezia Giulia, where the grape retains some acidity. Sweet Italian Malvasia can be excellent, although its decline in popularity is making it increasingly hard to find. In Tuscany, much *vin santo* is Malvasia-based, while in the south, Malvasia delle Lipari, made on the Lipari Islands north of Sicily, is a relic of ancient times (*see* **Sicily**).

In Spain, Malvasia is the grape behind the traditional rich, golden, oaky whites of Rioja. Here, too, it is being elbowed out of the way by Viura. It is, however, regaining a foothold on the island of Madeira, where it used to make Malmsey, the sweetest style of Madeira. If you encounter Swiss or French wines labelled Malvoisie, it is likely to be a different grape variety. Malvasia Nera is a red variant found in Piedmont, Tuscany and southern Italy.

The Malvasia taste   Unless carefully made, Malvasia oxidises easily to become flabby, and often needs the zip of a variety such as Trebbiano to hold it together. The wines are deep-coloured, full-bodied and strongly scented, with a flavour that is sometimes nutty, sometimes musky, sometimes reminiscent of apricots. The sweeter wines are even deeper in colour, and have honeyed, ginger overtones as well as the apricot flavour and hints of pineapple.

Where next?   Strongly scented and musky? Sounds like **Alsace** would be a good place to start for both dry and sweet wines.

Margaret River

The other side of Australia
Grape varieties Chardonnay, Semillon, Sauvignon Blanc, Verdelho
Style Sophisticated, whatever the variety
Quality/Price ***⋯⟩****/££⋯⟩£££££

RECOMMENDED PRODUCERS
Amberley
Cape Clairault
Cape Mentelle
Chateau Xanadu
Cullen
Devil's Lair
Leeuwin Estate
Moss Wood
Pierro
Sandalford

The quality of the average wine is arguably higher in this beautiful part of Western Australia than in any other Australian wine region. If Margaret River is not better known, it is partly because those on the other side of the country are slow to accept this fact. This, in turn, spurs the vintners onwards and upwards, and the wines keep on improving, despite weather conditions that are often challenging.

The nearby sea moderates temperatures, but it also causes salinity problems in some vineyards, plus gusty winds and a lack of rain mean the vines can get stressed in summer. Even so, Chardonnay is very successful here, and so, too are Sauvignon Blanc and Semillon – whether by themselves or blended. The few pockets of Riesling that exist are slowly disappearing, but Verdelho has been a surprise hit.

The Margaret River taste Margaret River manages to pack a lot of flavour into its wines while at the same time keeping them from becoming vulgar. They are not short on acidity, which gives them a good, sharp definition. The attraction of Chardonnay here is its classic fullness of flavour, with toasty oak and vanilla, spicy pepper and cinnamon, and a generous pineapple ripeness – yet without any hint of the overblown, too-tropical fruit that so often afflicts hot-climate Chardonnays.

Sauvignon Blanc is often given a veneer of oak to calm down its herbaceousness and accentuate its gentle smokiness. Semillons vary from the pungent, grassy style which could almost be Sauvignon to a richer, waxy, oily style. Whether made with or without oak, they are every bit as satisfying and age-worthy as any other Australian version. These two varieties are also blended to impressive effect. Where grown, Verdelho makes spicy, fleshy wines of great charm.

Where next? Try **South Australia** for the more traditional approach to Australian winemaking, **New Zealand** for a competing modernist. Head back to the **Loire**, **Bordeaux** and **Burgundy** for the inspirations.

RECOMMENDED PRODUCERS
Cellier Le Brun
Cloudy Bay
Corbans
Forrest
Foxes Island
Goldwater
Grove Mill
Hunter's
Isabel Estate
Jackson Estate
Lawson's Dry Hills
Montana
Nautilus
Allan Scott
Selaks
Seresin
Vavasour
Villa Maria
Wairau River

Marlborough

Home of the world's most distinctive Sauvignon
Best-known wines Sauvignon Blanc
Grape varieties Sauvignon Blanc, Chardonnay, Riesling
Style Pungent Sauvignon; firm, limey Riesling; opulent Chardonnay – and excellent fizz, too
Quality/Price ***····⟩****/££····⟩££££

Marlborough, at the north end of New Zealand's South Island, must have clocked up the fastest rise in viticultural history. Nothing much happened until the firm of Montana arrived in 1973. Now, Marlborough is New Zealand's largest wine region, and its still climbing.

It was Sauvignon Blanc that made Marlborough's fame and fortune, and that still makes the most distinctive wines. Producers said that if you stuck a Sauvignon cutting in the ground and made sure it got enough water, it would grow like a weed, developing the tell-tale blackcurrant leaf, asparagus and green-pepper characteristics. As it happened, this was true.

Today, however, it isn't always true. Marlborough's rise in popularity has been such that virtually all the best parcels of land – usually gravelly soils from ancient river beds – have now been planted. People are still coming to the region looking to plant vines, but they're having to settle for less suitable soils. They will still be able to use the Marlborough name on their wines, but these wines will never be as good as those from better sites.

One sign that Marlborough has passed beyond "new kid on the block" status is the emergence of sub-regions within the region. The Awatere Valley is the only one of these to receive official recognition, but the vineyards on either side of Rapaura Road are also highly regarded. Another sign is the way in which the wines have moved on. The good guys have realised that there's only so much cat's pee a wine-drinker can take. By lowering yields, fruit ripens more easily; by occasionally using oak and/or some Sémillon to add more body, the wines have become less angular, with the overt flavours toned down in favour of extra complexity.

The expansive Montana wine estate in Marlborough extends almost to the horizon

The success of Marlborough's Sauvignon Blanc has deflected interest from the Chardonnays of the region. The latter can be excellent, although some commentators think that the wrong clones were planted in the region, and high yields can also be a problem. When Chardonnay is used for sparking wines, often in conjunction with Pinot Noir, the wines are among the most exciting in the New World. The Riesling can also be wonderfully rich but steely, while the Gewürztraminer impresses, but fashion continues to exclude both from most of the region's vineyards.

The Marlborough taste As the producers become more accustomed to their Sauvignon Blanc, the raw, intense style of wine has given way to something slightly more mellow but without sacrificing the fruit intensity. Blackcurrant leaf, asparagus and green-pepper flavours still abound, occasionally enlivened by a note of cat's pee and nettles, but these flavours are now wrapped in a more succulent, opulent structure. As more flavour is coming through in the grapes, producers are cutting down on residual sugar in their wines, leaving an impressive minerally streak.

The tropical fruit-cocktail style of Chardonnay is giving way to a more complex and complete style. Riesling benefits enormously from the long, slow growing season – dry wines are rich and limey, while late-picked versions, in ridiculously short supply, can be sensational. Gewürztraminer is wonderfully underplayed, with good acidity and a delicate aroma that gives it remarkable finesse. And finally, there are the sparkling wines, for which Marlborough has great potential. Imagine Champagne with riper fruit and you won't be far off the mark.

Where next? Hawke's Bay and Martinborough are the rivals in New Zealand both for Sauvignon and Chardonnay. Outside the country, other New World Sauvignon competition comes from the Adelaide Hills, Casablanca and Constantia in South Africa, and in the Old World from Sancerre and Pouilly-Fumé.

Marsala

RECOMMENDED PRODUCERS
De Bartoli
Florio
Pellegrino

Not just for the kitchen
Region Sicily
Grape varieties Grillo, Catarratto, Inzolia
Style Toffee, nuts and raisins
Quality/Price *····⟩****/£····⟩££££

This sweet, fortified wine was "invented" in 1773 by an English wine merchant called John Woodhouse. Seeing the similarity between the wines of the region and the fortified wines of Spain and Portugal, he added some two gallons of alcohol to every 100-gallon barrel of wine and shipped it to England. The resulting wine achieved an early success when Admiral Nelson ordered large quantities for his Mediterranean-based fleet. Its name comes from the Sicilian port where Woodhouse set up his warehouse and cellars.

The grapes used are the local Grillo, Catarratto and Inzolia which, before picking, are allowed to shrivel on the vine until they look almost raisin-like. After fermentation, the wine has some 12 to 14 per cent alcohol, which is augmented by adding neutral alcohol and two syrups: *sifone* (made from a blend of dried grapes and wine alcohol) and *cotto* (made from grapes that have been "cooked" down to a caramelised syrup). Together, they give Marsala its pungent flavours and slightly rubbery taste.

Look for wines labelled *superiore* (aged for at least two years) or *vergine* (aged for a minimum of five). *Vergine* is unsweetened and often aged in barrel. With ten years' ageing, it is labelled *riserva* or *stravecchio*. Perhaps the best wine of the region, Marco de Bartoli's Vecchio Samperi, cannot be called Marsala as, although it weighs in at around 17 per cent alcohol, it is not fortified. There are, unfortunately, many candidates for the worst wine, with some disgusting concoctions flavoured with egg, strawberry and chocolate.

Blending wines of different years and wood ageing are crucial in the making of Marsala

The Marsala taste Like Madeira, much Marsala is destined for culinary use, especially in zabaglione, a deliciously frothy custard. And much of it deserves no finer fate. The best Marsala has toffee-and-nut depth and flavours of dried citrus fruit and vanilla, which makes it a pleasant *apéritif* or an unusual accompaniment to powerful cheeses.

Where next? Start with **Málaga**, *amontillado* and *oloroso* **Sherry** and tawny port. **Vin Santo** is an unfortified alternative.

Martinborough

More than just Pinot Noir
Grape varieties Sauvignon Blanc, Chardonnay, Riesling, Gewürztraminer, Pinot Gris
Style Burgundian Chardonnay; fleshy, full Sauvignon; stunning botrytis whites
Quality/Price ***····⟩****/££····⟩££££

RECOMMENDED PRODUCERS
Ata Rangi
Dry River
Lintz Estate
Martinborough Vineyard
Nga Waka
Palliser Estate
Te Kairanga

Martinborough (or to give it its correct but less pronounceable name, Wairarapa), is best known as the source of some of New Zealand's finest Pinot Noir. Don't, however, make the mistake of shunning the region's whites, as they are also among the best in the country. Martinborough is rather like the Margaret River of New Zealand, in that virtually all the producers have high quality at the front of their minds. Chardonnay is the most widespread grape variety, with Sauvignon Blanc in close pursuit. Gewürztraminer and Pinot Gris also put in an appearance at the excellent Dry River, while Riesling is used for several styles of wine, including (at Lintz Estate) sparkling.

The Martinborough taste Chardonnay from the best producers is like fat burgundy – rich and fruity – with good oak use and an underlying tightness which means it ages well. Martinborough Sauvignon Blanc has been described as "Marlborough in drag", meaning that there is no shortage of ripe flesh to back up the grassy flavours.

Where next? Martinborough lies between **Marlborough** and **Hawke's Bay**, both in terms of geography and wine style. The Australian equivalents are **Yarra Valley**, **Adelaide Hills** and **Margaret River**.

<table>
<tr><td>

RECOMMENDED PRODUCERS

D' Arenberg
Chapel Hill
Tim Gramp
Hardy's
Geoff Merrill/Mount Hurtle
Wirra Wirra

</td><td>

McLaren Vale

What you see is what you get
Best-known wines Hardy's Stamp Series
Grape varieties Chardonnay, Sauvignon Blanc, Semillon, Riesling
Style Honest and packed with fruit flavour
Quality/Price **·····⟩****/££·····⟩££££

</td></tr>
</table>

McLaren Vale lies about an hour south of Adelaide. The climate here is warm, but modified by the waters of the Gulf of St Vincent, and few would disagree that the region's best wines are its beefy reds. Whites typify the "honest Aussie bloke" school of wine. They may not be the most complex, they may not be the most subtle, but you cannot deny that they are full of flavour, whatever variety has been pressed into service.

The standard is generally good, but there are signs that the best wines are still to come. Chardonnay, Sauvignon, Semillon and Riesling are the principal varieties, but the success of Chapel Hill's fruit-salad-and-honeysuckle Verdelho shows the potential for other varieties.

The McLaren Vale taste Chardonnay is rich, forward and peachy – and usually all the better for a touch of oak. Some producers specifically make unwooded versions, but these can be rather ungainly, like Linford Christie without his jockstrap or Dolly Parton minus her bra. Sauvignon is packed with fleshy, gooseberry fruit – not classy but honest, and benefiting from the addition of some Semillon. Riesling manages to make up in ripe, citrus-fruit flavour what it lacks in finesse. Look out, too, for the Grenache-based rosés packed with strawberry fruit.

Where next? Nearby **Barossa Valley, Clare, Adelaide Hills** and **Coonawarra** compete to offer **South Australia**'s best wines.

Meursault

The ideal introduction to great white burgundy
Region Burgundy
Grape varieties Chardonnay
Style Rich and buttery, yet refined
Quality/Price ***·····⟩*****/£££·····⟩£££££

RECOMMENDED PRODUCERS

Robert Ampeau
Michel Bouzereau
Boyer-Martenot
Coche-Bizouard
Coche Dury
Jean-Philippe Fichet
Albert Grivault
Rémi Jobard
François Jobard
Comtes Lafon
Latour-Giraud
Matrot
François Mikulski
Pierre Morey
Jacques Prieur
Guy Roulot

Meursault comes very close to many people's idea of what white wine drinking is all about. This is where Chardonnay shows its buttery richness, and where it marries perfectly with oak. There are no *grands crus* in the village, although the *premiers crus* of Perrières and Genevrières are deemed by many to be worthy of *grand cru* status. Even simple village wine can be good, but it is worth saving up for a *premier cru* from a good producer to see what all the fuss is about.

The style of Meursault varies noticeably from the north of the appellation to the south, with wines from the southern end being leaner and having much in common with those of neighbouring Puligny. Many of the *premier cru* vineyards lie along the Puligny/Meursault border. The hamlet of Blagny straddles the western end of this border, and sells its white wines as Meursault-Blagny.

The Meursault taste Meursault is dry but not as lean and taut as Chablis further north; it fills out into a more ample, well-built shape. It is rarely fat or overweight, but has enough flesh to accommodate all the flavours of peaches, cream, nuts and honey. The best are succulent, balanced, undeniably aristocratic, and age gracefully for at least ten years.

Where next? Compare with the other two great **Côte de Beaune** villages, **Chassagne** and **Puligny**. Still in **Burgundy**, **Pouilly-Fuissé** can be similarly fleshy. Or try New World **Chardonnays** from **Carneros, Martinborough** and **Adelaide Hills**.

Monbazillac

In the shadow of Sauternes

Region Southwest France

Grape varieties Sémillon, Sauvignon Blanc, Muscadelle

Style The best have honeyed liquorice, apricot and pineapple notes

Quality/Price *----›****/££----›££££

Monbazillac is a sweet country cousin of Sauternes, based on the Sémillon grape, with Sauvignon Blanc and Muscadelle lending a helping hand. It has the same problems as the other immediate neighbours of Sauternes: to make real botrytis wine is risky and expensive. Even Sauternes has a job convincing people to pay a realistic price, so what chance does Monbazillac have? But pick a good vintage and a good producer, and you're on to a winner.

The Monbazillac taste Proper Monbazillac is richly honeyed, with a trace of liquorice and a shade less bite than Sauternes. It can last a decade or two, or – in rare cases – four or five. More often, however, commercial reality means that few producers wait to see whether or not botrytis will strike. Most wine is simply sweetish and best drunk within about five years.

Where next? Sauternes and Barsac are the inspiration, but Loupiac and Ste-Croix-du-Mont are nearer in price. Sticky **Jurançon** is also good.

Monterey and San Francisco Bay areas

Melting pot

Grape varieties Chardonnay, Viognier, Riesling, Sauvignon Blanc

Style Too diverse to specify

Quality/Price ***----›****/£££----›£££££

This is not so much one large region as a collection of mini-regions. The common thread that holds the producers together is that they're not in Napa and Sonoma. The best are doing their darnedest to show that they can make wines that are at least as good as those from more vaunted areas.

As in most of California, the quality vineyards are sited where there is a cooling effect of one form or another – coast or altitude. There are *terroirs* suited to every conceivable grape variety, and producers whose ambitions vary from

Vines look out over the diverse agriculture of the Monterey region

being content to make easy-drinking wines in fairly large quantities to wanting to produce the very finest Chardonnay and Viognier in the state.

The Monterey and San Francisco Bay taste There is no such thing as a definitive style for the region. With some of the designated AVAs (*see* **United States**) having only one or two wineries, it is impossible to say which flavours are due to the producer and which to the *terroir*.

Chardonnay produces most of the best wines, with elegance and complexity being hallmarks. Yet the Rhône varieties – Marsanne, Roussanne and especially Viognier – have also been used to impressive effect.

Where next? Carneros, Sonoma and the Central Coast.

Montilla-Moriles

When I grow up, I'd like to be a sherry
Region Andalucía
Grape varieties Pedro Ximénez, Lairén, Muscat
Style Depends on the style: sherry-like but never as good
Quality/Price *⋯⟩***/£⋯⟩£££

RECOMMENDED PRODUCERS
Toro Albalá
Alvear
Gracia Hermanos
Pérez Barquero

Montilla has been playing the role of cheap sherry substitute for so long that it has almost convinced itself there is no more to life than that. Why should we want a cheap substitute for sherry when the real thing is such good value

La Lengue (the tongue) rock – a landmark in the rolling countryside of Montilla-Moriles

anyway? Montilla, however, is subtly different from sherry, and the good ones are worth drinking for their own sake.

Montilla is made inland, just south of Córdoba. The hot sun brings natural alcohol levels up to around 14 to 15 per cent so, unlike sherry, it does not always need to be fortified. The principal grape variety is Pedro Ximénez, which is often used to make thick, rich sweet wines, but also makes the light, straight *fino* (dry Montilla) and the *amontillado* (medium Montilla). Elsewhere, the wines must go by names such as Pale Dry, Pale Cream and so on. Since the very term *amontillado* means "in the style of Montilla", this policy has a certain irony to it.

The Montilla-Moriles taste *Finos* are produced by the action of *flor*, just like sherry, and a limited *solera* system operates. The overall effect is generally of a simpler, blander product, without the tangy, zesty bite of *fino* sherry, or quite the depth of nuttiness of a good *amontillado* sherry. Not a criticism, because there are times when the gentler Montilla may be more appropriate.

The real gems of Montilla are the dry *olorosos*, which are deep, nutty, long and complex, sometimes tasting of prunes, sometimes of espresso. There is also a small quantity of impenetrably dark, very rich, sweet and sticky Pedro Ximénez wines that smell like a bag of raisins or a rich, just-baked fruit cake. They have a soft, luscious feel and length of flavour similar to Liqueur Muscat.

Where next? Sherry, Málaga, Madeira, Marsala, Australian **Liqueur Muscat** and **Tokay**.

Moscato D'Asti

The perfect breakfast wine

Region Piedmont
Grape varieties Muscat
Style Essence of musky grapes
Quality/Price ***⋯⟩****/££⋯⟩£££

Ask a wine bore what his or her perfect-desert island wine would be, and you will probably receive an answer of "Latour 1961", "Cheval Blanc 1947" or some such untouchable wine.

Given the conditions and the absence of decent lamb, any sane person would be advised to plump for Moscato d'Asti. This is Asti (Spumante) with a PhD in hedonism – less fizzy, sweeter and very moreish.

This is what the best Moscato grapes in Piedmont are reserved for, and it deserves to be thought of as great wine. It is an ideal accompaniment to Christmas pudding but, providing you have the youngest available, it's great at any time of the year.

The Moscato d'Asti taste Crush some ripe, heady and musky grapes, add a little sparkle and a touch of alcohol. Light in body yet full of flavour – if it is possible to taste a fragrance, Moscato d'Asti manages it.

Where next? There really is nothing comparable produced anywhere else in the world. Fizzier alternatives include **Asti** itself, plus the *méthode traditionelle* wines of Clairette de Die, **Gaillac** and **Blanquette de Limoux**.

The pretty Belbo Valley in the heart of the Moscato d'Asti zone

Mosel-Saar-Ruwer

Home of the great, the good and the grotty
Best-known wines Bernkasteler Doctor, Maximin Grünhäuser
Grape varieties Riesling
Style Delicate yet precise and full of flavour
Quality/Price *····⟩*****/£····⟩£££££

Germany's River Mosel loops calmly around great, sweeping bends, altering the aspect of the vineyards along its shores. Here, this bank of the river is perfectly exposed; just around the bend the opposite bank faces the full force of the sun. The best vineyards skip from one side to the other, producing the most thrilling wines when raking sharply up the precipitous undercut slope on the broad, outside sweep of a bend; they are less successful on the gently flat, inside slip-off slope. If these wines don't excite you, then very little from Germany will, but it is best to make sure you try a really good example, even if

RECOMMENDED PRODUCERS
Grans-Fassian
Friedrich-Wilhelm-Gymnasium
Fritz Haag
Karthäuserhofberg
Reichsgraf von Kesselstatt
Dr Loosen
Mönchhof
Egon Müller
Pauly-Bergweiler
J J Prüm
Richter
Schloss Saarstein
von Schubert
Selbach-Oster
Bert Simon
H Thanisch
Heinz Wagner
Wegeler-Deinhard
Zilliken

that means paying a bit extra. This is a region that needs to be approached with a little passion; some emotion which, as the word suggests, will keep us moving, searching for better wines. If, and only if, we are struck by the glories of Mosel Riesling will it then be worth mastering the difference between, say, Bereich Bernkastel and Bernkasteler Doctor *Auslese*. If not, then we may as well forget about the whole thing.

The reputation of the Mosel rests not on the familiar *Grosslagen* (areas formed by a number of vineyards) – the Schwarze Katz of Zell, Piesport's Michelsberg – nor on the even larger *Bereiche* (sub-region) such as Bernkastel, but on some of the smaller sites. Perhaps the style reaches its apogee in the Middle Mosel around Bernkastel, where classic Mosel Riesling is made in half a dozen villages.

Among the best villages are Piesport (Goldtröpfchen rather than Michelsberg), Brauneberg (Juffer vineyard), Bernkastel (the nearly vertical Doctor vineyard rises straight up from the half-timbered village), Graach, Wehlen (Sonnenuhr vineyard), Zeltingen and Ürzig. Yet there are those who feel that the quintessential Riesling style really comes from the slate valleys of the Saar and Ruwer rivers, which join the upper Mosel either side of the Roman town of Trier. Regional names to look for include: Ayl (Kupp vineyard), Serrig, Ockfen, Wiltingen (the best estate is Scharzhofberg), Maximin Grünhaus, Oberemmel, and the Karthäuserhofberg vineyard.

The Mosel-Saar-Ruwer taste The great appeal of Mosel wines is their harnessing of opposing forces. We can taste the struggle between richness and lightness; between racy acidity and honeyed sweetness, elegance and vitality; and between simple, brisk, appley freshness and ethereal subtlety and complexity. They have an edginess, even when ripe, that makes them vigorous, lively and exciting. And all this without recourse to more than nominal levels of alcohol.

To call the resulting wines "balanced" seems rather tame; the tension never eases. But after five, ten, sometimes 20 or more years in their elegant green bottles, they achieve a harmony that seems greater than the sum of their parts. The wines dig deep, mining an apparently inexhaustible seam of complexity. And they do all this because of two things: the Riesling grape and the steep, slate slopes the river has engineered.

Mosel Rieslings are somehow full yet light; delicate, but charged with a remarkable energy. They leave you feeling complete but not sated, and seem to express perfectly the meeting of cold, grey slate and sun-ripened, squishy fruit. In the Saar and Ruwer, Riesling ripens with difficulty, but when it does, what we can taste is steely, minerally, ultra-clean and light as a feather – the pure, raw, naked grape unencumbered by trills or flounces. It may seem fragile, but the piercing, racy fruit is hard-edged and real enough.

Where next? The **Rheingau** offers equivalent quality, but emphasises weight and flavour rather than delicacy and finesse; the **Nahe** offers something in between.

Müller-Thurgau

Designer grape, low-price flavour
Style Floral, err... that's it
Grown in Germany, England, New Zealand, Italy
and Eastern Europe

No one is sure of the parentage of Müller Thurgau grape variety. The question is: is it a cross between Silvaner and Chasselas, Riesling and Silvaner, or even Riesling and Riesling? Perhaps it would be a real matter of concern if the grape amounted to much, but sadly, it doesn't.

Its inventor was a certain Dr Müller, and he apparently sought to produce a grape which had the quality of Riesling but ripened early and gave good yields. Unfortunately, for all those involved really, he succeeded in the last two aims, but not in the first.

Sadly, a grape with such attributes found favour in Germany to such an extent that it is now the country's most widely planted variety, and it is the power (if that is the right word) behind many a Liebfraumilch. It has also spread east to Hungary and the Czech Republic, south to Italy, west to England, and halfway around the world to New Zealand.

The Müller-Thurgau taste The wines produced from the Müller-Thurgau grape variety tend to be light, soft and easy drinking. They are uncomplicated, undemanding and approachable. And there is no need to delve into a big bag of evocative and *recherché* associations to conjure up an idea of what they smell and taste of.

Some of them are lightly fruity, others are not; some are vaguely flowery, others are not. There is little more to it than that, and often considerably less. Crop it low and you may find a reasonably full-flavoured wine with a steely edge, but few growers bother to make the effort. Don't keep Müller-Thurgau wines; they will not improve.

Where next? Hopefully, you'll want to move up from this level of wine – in which case, start with New World **Riesling** from **Australia**, **New Zealand** or cooler prts of the **United States**, which often has a touch of sweetness and some of Müller-Thurgau's floral aromas. It also has considerably more flavour.

Muscadet

Where's that lobster?
Region Loire
Grape varieties Muscadet (aka Melon de Bourgogne)
Style Often neutral, but the best have creamy, yeasty notes
Quality/Price *⋯⟩***/£⋯⟩£££

Muscadet is no longer in the news as much as it once was, but this wine from the mouth of the River Loire, around Nantes, remains an ideal partner for seafood. It is dry, light- to medium-bodied and refreshing. Ordinary Muscadet derives this quality from its relatively high acidity, while the best has a slight prickle of carbon dioxide that performs the same function more gracefully. It is unusual in having a maximum permitted alcoholic degree of just over 12 per cent.

As well as basic Muscadet, there are three sub-appellations that should be of higher quality. In ascending order of quality, they are Coteaux de la Loire, Côtes de Grandlieu/Grand Lieu and Sèvre et Maine. Only in these three regions can the wine be labelled *sur lie* – meaning the wine has been left on its lees after fermentation until at least the March following the vintage. This practice results in more flavour, complexity and body.

The Muscadet taste Muscadet's neutrality of taste and slight prickle, combined with its specific role as a wine to drink with food, make it one of the most Italian of French white wine styles. The grape is an early ripener, which has the effect of ensuring good acidity while not allowing much flavour to develop in the skins. Rather too much Muscadet is thus merely refreshing without a lot of character. Later picking, although slightly riskier, solves both these problems at a stroke. Good Muscadet is not particularly high in acidity, but it does have a ripeness of flavour that many cheaper wines lack.

The process of ageing *sur lie* gives a slight but attractive yeasty taste that is similar to Champagne, which develops its yeastiness from maturing on the lees in bottle. By the same token, a little carbon dioxide dissolves in the Muscadet, which we experience as a slight prickle on the tongue.

Most Muscadet is simple stuff for drinking as soon as possible, but the best Muscadet de Sèvre et Maine Sur Lie won't mind three or four years in bottle, and it can last for longer. A few producers have experimented with new oak to ferment and age their wines. The results can be impressive, although it would be hard to pick the wines as Muscadet.

Where next? From the same region, Gros Plant is cheaper – and tastes it. Alternatively, try **Aligoté**, **Gaillac**, dry **Vinho Verde** or **Pinot Grigio**.

Muscat

The grape that tastes of grapes
Style From light and frothy to rich and treacly, fresh and always grapey
Grown in Most European countries, Australia, North Africa,
South Africa and California

Muscat is not so much a single grape variety as a family of varieties, ranging from yellow and pink to red, brown and black. Most Muscat wines are sweet, and many are fortified. The finest kind for winemaking is the small-berried Muscat Blanc à Petits Grains, known in various places around the world as White Muscat, Moscato Bianco, Frontignac, Muscat Canelli, Muskadel, Brown Muscat and by several other names. Among White Muscat's triumphs are fizzy Moscato d'Asti and Asti Spumante from northern Italy, *vins doux naturels* such as Muscat de Beaumes-de-Venise and Muscat de Frontignan from southern France, the Greek Muscat of Samos and Australian Liqueur Muscat. This is also the grape which, as Lunel or Sargasmuskotaly, forms part of the blend for Hungary's great Tokáji, along with Furmint and Hárslevelü. Different-coloured mutations include Moscato Giallo/Goldenmuskateller and Moscato Rosa/Rosenmuskateller, found mostly in Italy's Trentino-Alto Adige region.

Muscat of Alexandria, also known as Moscatel, Hanepoot, Muscat Gordo Blanco, Lexia and Zibibbo, is suited to hotter climates and is not considered to be quite as classy a grape. The Australians use it extensively in cask wine, although with plantings of more noble varieties on the increase, this could change. It can be coaxed to greater things, however, as Sicily's Moscato di Pantelleria, southern France's Muscat de Rivesaltes and Portugal's Moscatel de Setúbal all demonstrate.

Similarly, Muscat Ottonel is another poor relation which occasionally rises to greatness. It produces musky but bland wines throughout Eastern Europe but, when affected by noble rot, most notably in Burgenland in Austria, the wines can be very impressive. This is also the most widely grown Muscat in Alsace. An unusual member of the Muscat family is Fior d'Arancio. Hailing originally from Italy, it is better known in Australia and California as Orange Muscat. The black-skinned Muscat Hamburg is the lowliest Muscat of all, and is hardly ever used to make wine.

There are many other grapes which are probably related but whose parentage is uncertain. These include Romania's Tamaiîosa Romaneasca, which is used in Cotnari, and the Greek variety Moscophilero. Germany's somewhat loutish Morio-Muskat has some Muscat characters, but is actually a cross of Silvaner with Pinot Blanc.

The Muscat taste Given the diversity of Muscat styles – dry to sweet, still to fizzy, light to sumptuously fortified – it is surprising that the wines have anything in common. But they do, and it's called grapiness. Lighter Muscats have a soft, elderflower, melon and peachy smell; heavier ones are heady with oranges and other citrus fruits. Yet behind it all, there is this grapiness. Sometimes you could almost be stuffing handfuls of sweet grapes into your mouth; at other times, with the richer fortified wines, you have to fight past the treacle or marmalade flavours to find it.

Muscat is usually made as a sweet wine, but it can be surprisingly successful as a dry one. Alsace is the prime source of such wines, but with sweet wines falling from favour, many other regions are making dry Muscat. These can be delicious, crisp and occasionally quite austere, but they wear their grapiness with pride.

Where next? For dry wines, **Argentina**'s Torrontés has something of a grapey character, while **Albariño**, **Gewürztraminer** and **Viognier** are similarly aromatic. Sweet substitutes are hard to find, but surely there's enough Muscat out there to prevent you becoming bored?

RECOMMENDED PRODUCERS
Beaumes-de-Venise
Co-op
Chapoutier
De Coyeux
De Durban
Guigal
Paul Jaboulet-Aîné

Muscat de Beaumes-de-Venise

France's finest *vin doux naturel*
Region Southern Rhône
Grape varieties Muscat Blanc à Petits Grains
Style Liquid barley sugar infused with the perfume of fresh grapes and orange zest
Quality/Price ***·····⟩****/£££·····⟩££££

France's finest fortified Muscat may have had its heyday in the foodie fads of the late 1980s, but it still has few peers as a wine for richer, fruit-based desserts, and it is also a lovely *apéritif*.

The Muscat de Beaumes-de-Venise taste Muscat Blanc à Petits Grains, the classy member of the Muscat family, is the grape variety used, and the wine is stamped with its irresistibly fresh, grapey hallmark. It can be rich, too, and muskily ripe with the perfumed taste of sultanas and acidity that keeps the whole thing in balance.

Where next? Try Moscatel de Setúbal, Muscat of Samos, Moscato di Pantelleria and Quady's Essensia from **California**.

Nahe

Small and potentially perfectly formed
Best-known wines Schlossböckelheim Kupfergrube
Grape varieties Riesling, Müller-Thurgau, Silvaner
Style Ripe and floral, with a steely core
Quality/Price **⋯⟩*****/££⋯⟩£££££

The Nahe adjoins Rheinhessen, nods across to the Rheingau
and extends towards the Mosel – tempting to think that the wines made here
express something of all three regions. Perhaps some of the better Rieslings do.

Village names to look for include Bad Kreuznach, Traisen, Norheim,
Niederhausen and Schlossböckelheim. It is worth remembering that the *Bereich*
(the district, as opposed to the village) of Schlossböckelheim covers something
like 180 vineyards; while the Kreuznach *Bereich* (as opposed to the city of
Bad Kreuznach) covers nearly 150 vineyards. Much *Bereich* wine makes rather
unspectacular and conventional drinking.

The Nahe taste Nahe Rieslings at their best seem to combine the steely,
minerally thrust of the Upper Mosel with the ripe, aristocratic bearing of the
Rheingau, while wearing an attention-seeking Rheinhessen flower in their cap.

Where next? A subtle comparison is with Upper **Mosel** wines and
Rheingau wines of similar standing and vintage. Try also the less
well-known **Pfalz** for more weight and depth, but less subtlety.
Cross the border to **Alsace** for a French angle on **Riesling**.

Napa Valley

Whites in a red valley
Best-known wines Carneros Chardonnay
Grape varieties Chardonnay, Sauvignon Blanc,
Chenin Blanc, Riesling
Style Opulent, complex Chardonnay; rich, pithy Sauvignon
Quality/Price ***⋯⟩*****/£££⋯⟩£££££

Although it is perhaps the most famous wine region outside
Europe, the Napa Valley is still young. Vines may have been
planted here for over 150 years, but the boom times of today
began only in the 1960s, when Robert Mondavi and others set
up. Most of the wineries are still run by their founders.

Progress has been brisk. Napa always had a name for its red wines, but the 1960s and 1970s saw producers planting dozens of different varieties – some red, some white. As these vines matured, it became more and more clear which varieties were suited to which vineyards. For example, Chardonnay, once planted widely throughout the region, has slid slowly southwards, in particular to the Carneros region, where the influence of the San Francisco Bay and coastal ranges provides a cooling effect.

More importantly, it quickly became clear which varieties were able to command the highest prices. Napa land has soared in value since the 1960s and continues to soar. It makes sense, then, for producers to plant the biggest cash cows, and by and large that means Cabernet Sauvignon and Merlot.

In the past, Napa has made fine Rieslings, Chenin Blancs and Gewürztraminers, but today they are not economically viable. Some versions remain, and you will find the occasional Viognier (Phelps is excellent), but for the most part, modern Napa whites mean Chardonnay and Sauvignon Blanc. Given the comparatively low price of the average Sauvignon Blanc, however, it would come as no surprise to see this variety losing its foothold in the valley in the not-so-distant future.

Which leaves Chardonnays, and Carneros is the prime source of many of these. Even if a wine is labelled simply "Napa Valley Chardonnay", a large (and increasing) proportion will have come from Carneros. The hillside vineyards also provide some of the finest Cabernet Sauvignon and Merlot grapes – even Chardonnay takes second place to red wine in Napa.

A view through the trees from the Sterling vineyards in the Napa Valley

The Napa taste In the case of Chardonnay, more and more of this is coming from the cooler Carneros region, and the same is true of sparkling wines. The main aspect of the region's Sauvignon Blanc is that it actually has more in common with Bordeaux than New Zealand. Here, it is rich and pithy, with ripe, lemony fruit to the fore and often toasty oak adding a creamy layer. The rare Sauvignon Musqué clone is used by Cain Cellars to make a beautifully aromatic wine. Napa Viognier is bold and full of heady, peachy flavour – a stylish match for great Condrieu.

Where next? Contrast with **Sonoma**, or **Monterey** and the Central Coast. Refer to the **Côte de Beaune**, **Bordeaux** and the **Rhône** for the prototypes.

The visually stunning Navarra region is now producing top-class rosé wines

Navarra

Still finding its feet with whites
Best-known wines Navarra Rosé
Grape varieties Chardonnay, Viura, Garnacha, Muscat
Style Strawberryish rosé; rich, grapey Muscat; international-style Chardonnay
Quality/Price **⋯⟩***/££⋯⟩£££

RECOMMENDED PRODUCERS
Camilo Castilla
Castillo de Monjardín
Bodegas Julián Chivite
Bodgeas Guelbenzu
Nekeas
Ochoa
Virgen Blanca Co-op

Arguably the source of Spain's finest rosé made from Garnacha, Navarra has struggled with white wines, much in the same fashion as neighbouring Rioja. Producers are coming to terms with using modern equipment to make fresh, simple wines from Viura, but they are not the sort of stuff you would cross the street for. Chardonnay has shown more promise, yielding some excellent wines when the *bodegas* use their oak with sensitivity. However, the best wines are the sweet, golden glories made from Moscatel de Grano Menudo, or Muscat Blanc à Petits Grains – sadly, all too rare.

The Navarra taste Navarra rosé is moreish, brimming with sweet, strawberry fruit and occasional hints of toffee. The best Chardonnays have pear, guava and peach flavours plus a creamy oak influence, and are excellent value. Moscatel varies from light and grapey with hints of barley sugar to rich, mature delights that are not far removed from Australia's Liqueur Muscats.

Where next? Apart from **Rioja**, other Spanish regions making progress with whites are Somontano and **Rueda**.

New South Wales

State of the nation

Best-known wines Hunter Valley Semillon

Grape varieties Semillon, Chardonnay

Style Lots of interesting Chardonnay; heady, sticky botrytis Semillon

Quality/Price **⋯⟩****/££⋯⟩£££££

New South Wales, Australia's oldest wine-producing state, is renowned chiefly for the Hunter Valley, cradle of antipodean winemaking – and justly so, for this region has created the country's most distinctive white-wine style, Hunter Semillon (*see* **Hunter Valley**). But the Hunter is quite far from being the only wine-producing region in the state.

Mudgee (rhymes with "budgee") lies on a high plain among the hills west of the Hunter Valley, and is kept relatively cool by its elevation; thus, the grapes benefit from a long, slow growing season that produces balanced, ripe fruit flavours. This is the only Australian region to have an "appellation" for its wines, which started with the 1980 vintage. "Certified Mudgee Appellation Wine" aims for a specific regional identity.

South of Mudgee lies Orange, an emerging quality region best known, perhaps, as the source of fruit for one of Rosemount's Chardonnays, but it also has a handful of producers of its own. A number of companies also source grapes from Cowra, west of Sydney.

The other major wine-growing region is Riverina (also know as the Murrumbidgee Irrigation Area and Griffith and, allegedly, the dope capital of Australia). In this dry, inland region, the high temperatures and fairly plentiful irrigation water have traditionally led to wines that were high in alcohol and low in acidity and class – ideal for satisfying the demands of the cheap fortified market. When this market began to wane, producers turned to making table wines. Although these started off as rather primitive, they've since become better and better as wineries have become more quality-minded and the vineyards have been upgraded to higher quality varieties. The surprising success of the region has been botrytis-affected Semillon which, from producers such as De Bortoli, can be stunning.

The New South Wales taste There is no such thing as a state-wide style. Chardonnay seems to be universally successful, and Orange has made some impressive Sauvignon Blanc. The one coherent style is Riverina Botrytis Semillon. Coloured a deep, golden yellow, it shows a great intensity of flavour and is rich and powerful, with well-balanced sweetness and acidity – very close to Sauternes in style, and a wine to age.

Where next? Begin with **Chardonnay** from anywhere else in **Australia** to see what regional styles emerge. And try a botrytis **Semillon** alongside a decent **Sauternes**, preferably with some *foie gras* close at hand.

New York State

Foxes and grapes
Grape varieties Chardonnay, Riesling, plus hybrid and *labrusca* vines
Style Well-rounded, subtle Chardonnay
Quality/Price *⋯⟩****/£⋯⟩£££££

This is an intriguing area for the wine-lover, almost impossible to categorise since three distinct styles of winemaking occur side by side. There are wines made from the native *Vitis labrusca* vine (rather than the European *Vitis vinifera*) which have a "foxy" aroma, as well as hybrid wines which tend to be bland. Thirdly, there are "real" wines as we know them, made from familiar *vinifera* varieties such as Riesling, Chardonnay and Sauvignon Blanc. These can be very good.

There are four main grape-growing regions: Lake Erie, Hudson River, the Finger Lakes and, most promising, the North Fork AVA (*see* **US**) of Long Island.

The New York State taste Long Island Chardonnay is well rounded, subtle and satisfying enough for lovers of white burgundy. The best Finger Lakes versions are comparable, although the average standard is lower.

Where next? Head north to **Canada** to see the progress in another region which has traditionally relied on *labrusca* and hybrid vines.

Ontario

All this and Niagara Falls, too
Best-known wines Icewine
Grape varieties Chardonnay, Riesling, Vidal
Style Full-bodied, dry Riesling; improving Chardonnays
Quality/Price **⋯⟩****/£££⋯⟩£££££

Ontario is the home and heart of Canadian wine, with over 75 per cent of the entire country's vines planted in the state. Although the main vineyard regions are on the same latitude as Languedoc-Roussillon, they are considerably cooler. However, the extremes of climate are tempered by the presence of large bodies of water – namely Lake Ontario and Lake Erie.

The modern history of Ontario wines can be dated back to 1988. That was the year that the government banned the use of the inferior native *labrusca* vines for table wines, so producers had to concentrate on hybrid and *vinifera* varieties. In the same year, the Vintners Quality Alliance (VQA) was established to give the wine industry a means of assessing the quality of its produce.

Progress since then has been speedy. The best wines of the region are the dry Rieslings, especially those from the Beamsville Bench overlooking Lake Ontario. Riesling is also used for Icewine, although the hybrid Vidal is more common here. Chardonnay is displacing Riesling from many vineyards, and there are also odd examples of Viognier, Sémillon and Gewürztraminer.

The Ontario taste The best Rieslings have sweet-and-sour citrus fruit allied to fresh, clean acidity. Late-harvest versions are usually more successful and better balanced than the rather showy Icewines, which can be just too intense for some palates. Producers are still coming to terms with Chardonnay, but there is richness and a good depth of apple-crumble fruit in the best. The 1994 Temkin-Paskus Chardonnay from Thirty Bench is a great wine by any standards.

Where next? See what they're doing either south in **New York State** or over on the other side of **Canada** in **British Columbia**.

RECOMMENDED PRODUCERS
Adelsheim
Amity
Archery Summit
Argyle
Cameron
Cristom
Domaine Drouhin
Elk Cove Vineyards
Erath Vineyards
King Estate
Ponzi Vineyards
Rex Hill
Silvan Ridge
Troon
Willamette Valley Vineyards

Oregon

Where Chardonnay often takes second place
Grape varieties Pinot Gris, Chardonnay, Pinot Blanc, Riesling
Style Fresh, spicy Pinot Gris, well-balanced Chardonnay
Quality/Price **····⟩****/£££····⟩£££££

Not every New World wine region is obsessed with Chardonnay. In Oregon, several winemakers favour Pinot Gris for their white wines. A lot of them were attracted to Oregon so they could get away from mainstream life and make the types of wines that interested them most – and for many, this meant Pinot Noir. Chardonnay would have seemed the obvious counterpart, but the early pioneers needed something they could begin to sell early in order to generate some cash. Some chose Pinot Gris – the wines were such a success that others followed suit. Today, there is a shortage of Pinot Gris, and plantings increase year by year.

Curiously, the number of acres of Chardonnay seems to have remained reasonably constant. This needs some explanation. Given the success of Pinot Noir, Chardonnay should flourish. However, the first Chardonnay vines planted were from Californian clones and didn't ripen as well as the producers expected. There is currently plenty of activity in Oregon's Chardonnay vineyards, but it involves replanting with clones which are better suited to the state's cooler climate. Already the results are beginning to show – and impressive they are, too.

As well as Pinot Gris and Chardonnay, Riesling is also widely grown but underappreciated, although there are some fine late-harvest wines. There are also pockets of Gewürztraminer, Pinot Blanc and even Piedmont's Arneis. The main wine-growing area is the Willamette Valley south of Portland, with most of the vineyards in the northern half. Other regions further south are the Umpqua Valley and, finally, the Rogue Valley close to the California state line. Further north, the Columbia Valley and Walla Walla AVAs (*see* **US**) along the Columbia River are shared with neighbouring Washington State.

The Oregon taste Oregon Pinot Gris sits nicely between Alsace and Friuli-Venezia Giulia in style, having the weighty ginger and citrus fruit of the former and the crisp freshness of the latter. The Chardonnays are in a transition stage, but early wines from the new clones have been tight and minerally, with juicy fruit and plenty of *matière*, as the French say. Argyle's sparklers have fruit and finesse, but there are few other sparkling wines of note.

Where next? For **Chardonnay**, head for anywhere in the world, perhaps beginning with neighbouring **California**. **Alsace** is the home of **Pinot Gris**, so see how the **Oregon**ians measure up.

Orvieto

Umbria's best-known white wine – unfortunately
Region Umbria
Grape varieties Trebbiano and others
Style CFDN – crisp, fresh, dry, neutral; great, but rare, sweet wines
Quality/Price *⋯⟩****/£⋯⟩££££

The town of Orvieto and its viticulture dates back to Etruscan times. It is a place of seductive charm and, over the years, its wine has gained a fame based mostly on packaging: the picturesque *fiasco* covered in *raffia*. In terms of flavour, Orvieto

RECOMMENDED PRODUCERS
Barberani-Vallesanta
Bigi
Cantina Co-operative
Vitivinicola Orvieto
La Carraia
Castello della Sala
Decugnano dei Barbi
Fattoria dei Barbi
Palazzone
Salviano
Luciano Sassara
Tenuuta Le Velette

is yet another testimony to the banality of the Trebbiano grape, which makes up 40 to 65 per cent of the wine. It comes in *seco* (dry), *abbocato* (medium-dry), *amabile* (medium-sweet) and *dolce* (sweet) versions. Conscientious growers in the Classico zone can make a wine of substance, especially if they use the 20 per cent Malvasia they are allowed, but only with the presence of noble rot do any of the wines arise above the merely good level. The best whites of the region are not Orvieto at all, but IGT (*see* **Italy**).

The Orvieto taste Typical Orvieto is pale in colour, clean and crisp, but lacking distinctive character. The better versions have riper, more fleshy fruit, and don't mind a touch of oak. The flavour of the sweeter wines depends on how much botrytis is present, with the best versions being heady and delicious.

Where next? **Frascati** and **Soave**; plus **Gavi** and Lugana.

NOBLE ROT

Out of the strange came forth sweet

No, not an oxymoron, but the driving force behind most of the world's finest sweet wines. Noble rot, otherwise known as botrytis, *Edelfäule* or *pourriture noble*, occurs when a fungal infection called botrytis cinerea attacks ripe, healthy grapes, feeding on their acids and sugars. The grapes shrivel on the vine, their surfaces covered with a grey bloom, and the results look truly dreadful. But there has been a transformation in the grape's make-up: water has evaporated so the flavours are more concentrated, and compounds in the skins such as tannins are released into the grape's flesh. The amount of sugar in each grape actually falls, but the acid level falls even more, and with the evaporation of the water, the result is an ugly but very sweet grape with a complex flavour.

Beneficial noble rot usually appears as a result of humidity. The great sweet wines of Germany, the Loire and Sauternes occur when mists off nearby rivers settle on the vineyards in the morning, and then are blown off in the warm afternoons. It does not spread evenly throughout the vineyard, and skilled pickers often have to make several trips, or *tries*, through the vineyard to pick out the infected grapes. This is an expensive and labour-intensive business, reflected in the price of the wine.

Making wine from nobly rotten grapes isn't easy, either. Pressing these dusty raisins is a painstaking process, as many are reluctant to yield any juice until extensive pressure has been applied. Fermenting the sweet juice also presents its own problems, as yeasts can be reluctant to work in such conditions. (Nothing prevents a winemaker from using nobly rotten grapes in a dry wine. For example, many Australian Rieslings contain some botrytis-affected grapes, as do certain wines made in the Mâconnais.)

The botrytis influence in a sweet wine gives extra texture and richness, as well as often contributing a flavour of apricot kernels. Sauternes, the Loire, Tokáji and Germany are the European regions best known for their nobly rotten wines, all of which are capable of lengthy ageing. Sweet New World versions come from Australia, South Africa, California and New Zealand – although EU regulations mean that at the time of writing, only Australia can export them to Europe.

Where next? The other method of making sweet wine is the *passito* method, which uses grapes that have dried either on the vine before picking or in special sheds afterwards. Italy is the specialist country for such wines, *vin santo* being the best and most famous.

Paarl

More than just an understudy to Stellenbosch
Grape varieties Chardonnay, Sauvignon Blanc,
Chenin Blanc, Riesling
Style From simple to complex, dry to sweet, still to fizzy
Quality/Price *····⟩****/£····⟩££££

RECOMMENDED PRODUCERS
Backsberg
Bellingham
Boschendal
Cabrière
Claridge
Fairview
Fredericksburg
Glen Carlou
Haute Provence/Agusta
KWV
La Motte
Nederburg
Plaisir de Merle
Villiera

Stellenbosch has more famous wineries, but Paarl is considered by many South Africans to be the home of their country's wine industry. This is largely because Paarl is also home to the KWV (see **South Africa**), but there are extensive further vineyard plantings in the region – more, in fact, than in Stellenbosch.

Paarl is often thought of as having a warm climate, suitable only for simple commercial wines. This is partially true, but get away from the central plain and there are cooler spots with better soils and aspects. The sub-region of Franschhoek has attracted many producers looking to make high-quality whites, and it is also home to one of South Africa's finest sparkling wine producers, Cabrière Estate.

As in many of South Africa's traditional wine regions, the plantings in Paarl of fashionable varieties such as Chardonnay and Sauvignon Blanc are still small, and there is plenty of Chenin Blanc and Colombard varieties traditionally used for brandy production. Where grown, Riesling can be excellent, and a few go-ahead producers (most notably Fairview) have experimented with other varieties such as Sémillon and Viognier.

The Paarl taste Given the diversity of *terroirs* and ambitions of the producers in the region, there is no such thing as a Paarl style. The wines fall broadly into two camps. There are those which are mass-produced from vines grown on the flat plain, and in which there is very little flavour to speak of, whatever the variety. Then there are those from much smaller wineries in cooler spots, made by people who have quality at the front of their minds. Chardonnay from such producers can be excellent – although, again, there is a variation in style, from crisp and unwooded to rich, buttery, oaky wines.

The lack of successful Sauvignon Blancs from the region suggests that either growers are picking too early, before the flavours have developed, or the region is simply too warm for the variety. There are a few producers making superior Chenin Blanc, with or without oak, and these can be very good, with lemony fruit to the fore.

Where next? Compare the top Paarl wines with those from other South African regions, especially neighbouring **Stellenbosch**.

Pessac-Léognan

So *that's* how dry white Bordeaux should taste

Region Bordeaux

Grape varieties Sémillon, Sauvignon Blanc, Muscadelle

Style Opulent yet restrained, with a smoky-oak influence

Quality/Price ***····⟩*****/£££····⟩£££££

Pessac-Léognan is a comparatively recent appellation. It was created in 1987, when the authorities lumped the ten best communes of the Graves region together under their own appellation. These all lie in the north of the region, clustered around the city of Bordeaux. This is where most of the gravelly soil from which the Graves region takes its name is found. Travel south from Bordeaux and the gravel gives way to rather heavier clay soils. At the time of the designation, the best Graves châteaux, whether inside the new region or not, were beginning to move away from the dull and dreary whites that had characterised the region for so many years and starting to make wines of genuine class.

The creation of Pessac-Léognan seems to have been the catalyst needed to spur many other producers – again, both inside and outside the new region – on to better things. Today's dry white Bordeaux, with the wines of Pessac-Léognan at its head, presents a very attractive alternative to burgundy.

Most producers eschew the use of Muscadelle in their blends and concentrate on Sémillon and Sauvignon Blanc, usually with a higher proportion of the latter. Barrel-fermentation and ageing is now widespread, and the wines are all the better for it.

The Pessac-Léognan taste These are the French wines which, at their height, can match *grand cru* burgundy for weight, depth of flavour, use of oak and longevity. Yet they need time to show their class, and drinking them in their youth can lead you to dismiss them as tinned pear juice smothered with oak.

With age, they develop richer, rounder flavours, still with that touch of pear, but with more of an earthy character appearing. If Sauvignon Blanc dominates, they can often be quite pungent. Those with a high proportion of Sémillon have a fat, wax-and-lanolin character, and usually have the most structure and depth.

Where next? First of all, see whether these wines stand out above those labelled plain "**Graves**". Then have a look at what the **California** and **New Zealand** (especially **Hawke's Bay**) winemakers are doing with **Sauvignon Blanc** and **Sémillon**.

Pfalz

Germany's dynamic side
Grape varieties Riesling, Müller-Thurgau, Kerner,
Silvaner, Scheurebe
Style Fairly full-bodied in German terms, with fleshy Rieslings
Quality/Price *⋯⟩*****/£⋯⟩£££££

RECOMMENDED PRODUCERS
Bassermann-Jordan
Josef Biffar
Bürklin-Wolf
Kurt Darting
Köhler-Ruprecht
Karl & Hermann Lingenfelder
Herbert Messmer
Georg Mosbacher
Müller-Catoir
Reichsrat von Buhl
Karl Schaefer
Wegeler-Deinhard
JL Wolf

This place should be promoted like mad, as its wines offer the ideal introduction to German Riesling. The climate here isn't knife-edge marginal, and the region's Riesling, while still stamped with the German hallmark of acidity, has a plumpness that will strike chords with many who have cut their teeth on New World wine.

The Pfalz is split into two *Bereiche* (districts), with Riesling performing better in the northern *Bereiche* Mittelhaardt/Deutsche Weinstrasse. The finest vineyards are in the *Grosslagen* of Wachenheim, Forst, Deidesheim and Bad Dürkheim. Quality is not as high in the other *Bereiche*, the Südliche Weinstrasse, with the widely planted Müller-Thurgau being used for Liebfraumilch. However, there are a few growers, such as Herbert Messmer, whose wines are worth looking out for.

Messmer is just one of a growing band of enlightened producers who have taken it upon themselves to show that the Pfalz can match the best of the Rheingau and Mosel-Saar-Ruwer. Some of these are relative newcomers, but the most encouraging sight is the way in which, after years in the doldrums, more established estates (especially the Reichsrat von Buhl) have turned themselves around and are now putting quality very much to the fore. Riesling is the grape behind many of the best wines, but Scheurebe, Rieslaner and Gewürztraminer are also being used to good effect.

The Pfalz taste While Pfalz Rieslings may lack the racy grandeur of Rheingau wines, they share their fullness of flavour. The best have a lovely balance between full, ripe fruit flavours and acidity, although there is seldom the rapier-like acidity of other regions. Scheurebe's tell-tale sign is grapefruit, usually ripe but still with a slightly bitter, pithy edge, while Gewürztraminer errs on the plump side. The sweet wines can be marvellous, heady and honeyed, sumptuously fruity, yet with just enough acidity to stop them wobbling over.

Where next? Begin with the **Rheingau** and **Alsace**, as the Pfalz seems to sit between the two in style – the flavour of the Rheingau style, with the flesh of the Alsace wines. Austrian white wines will also make interesting comparisons.

Piedmont

You can't drink Barolo all the time

Best-known wines Asti, Moscato d'Asti

Grape varieties Moscato, Cortese, Arneis, Favorita, Erbaluce, Chardonnay, Sauvignon Blanc, Gewürztraminer

Style From crisp and dry to sweet and frothy

Quality/Price **·····>****/££·····>£££££

It's a mistake to think that Asti, its finer and less fizzy relative Moscato d'Asti, and Gavi are the only white wines made in Piedmont. While reds dominate, the region is dotted with several whites – some DOC, some not. Perhaps their most refreshing aspect is that they don't rely on Trebbiano. Cortese is the driving force behind Gavi, while Arneis, for many a superior grape, is used in Roero and Langhe.

Langhe wines can also use another interesting variety, Favorita, as well as Chardonnay, which appears in many vineyards throughout the region. The other indigenous variety of note is Erbaluce, which makes simple dry whites, but some excellent *passito* wines.

The stunning hill of Calamandrana in Piedmont's Asti region

The Piedmont taste The Arneis grape makes a delightful wine for drinking young: medium- to full-bodied, rich in texture, gently smoky, with flavours in the spectrum inhabited by ripe apples, pears, quince and lightly roasted nuts, and good, crisp acidity. Favorita makes a pale, lightweight, delicate,

but beautifully perfumed wine – more reminiscent of Germany than Italy. Erbaluce is unremarkable as a dry wine, but sweet versions are fragrant and full of flavour.

Where next? See how Piedmont's whites compare with those of **Friuli-Venezia Giulia** and **Trentino-Alto Adige**.

Pinot Blanc

All-purpose variety
Style Not very fruity; can vary from steely to full and biscuity
Grown in Alsace, Italy, Germany, Austria, California and Oregon

Pinot Blanc wine seems to have two roles in life: as a sound (if modest) food wine, and as a base for sparkling wine, particularly in Italy. It is usually made into a dry wine, though it is occasionally found in sweet blends. Like Pinot Gris, it is a mutation of the red grape variety Pinot Noir, although neither Pinot Blanc nor Pinot Gris challenges the imagination of winemakers or drinkers in the way their red cousin does. Pinot Blanc is not related to Chardonnay, although there has been, and sometimes remains, confusion between the two. Walking through vineyards in northern Italy, it is often impossible to tell which variety is which; even the owner doesn't always know. The Italian regions that grow Pinot Blanc most successfully are Friuli-Venezia Giulia, Trentino-Alto Adige, Veneto, and Lombardy for the sparkling wines of Franciacorta.

Pinot Blanc's other main outpost is Alsace, where, again, it is used to make both still and fizzy wines. Here it is less highly regarded than Pinot Gris – despite being more food-friendly. Elsewhere in France it remains a permitted variety in many white burgundies, although its use is very small. In Germany, as Weissburgunder, it is dry, medium-bodied and low in acidity – a marked contrast to Germany's predominantly light, floral, sweet styles. Pinot Blanc spreads eastwards through Austria, where it can make quite rich wines, and into Eastern Europe, where, as yet, nothing of any note has been made.

The Californians try to spruce it up with barrel-fermentation and ageing, and some of the resulting wines can be slightly buttery and very good. However, there is some debate as to whether the grape they have is true Pinot Blanc and not the Melon de Bourgogne of Muscadet. Further north, the variety is catching on in Oregon, with one grower going so far as to graft all his Chardonnay vines over to Pinot Blanc. Canada's vintners have also begun to experiment with it.

The Pinot Blanc taste It is somehow easier to understand Pinot Blanc by describing what it isn't. It is not an aromatic variety: a certain neutrality is common to most examples. The taste, like a featureless rock face, does not offer many hand-holds. It does not, for example, shout nettles and blackcurrant leaves like Sauvignon Blanc, nor nuts and oak like mature Chardonnay.

Pinot Blanc is quite content to turn out modest, unassuming, predominantly dry wines, of light to medium body and moderate acidity. Some, from cooler regions, are appley, maybe a little steely; others are more buttery or biscuity. Some are lightly spicy and many have a gently creamy feel to them. In this respect, some of the better Pinot Blancs may stand in for some of the less ambitious Chardonnays, but on the whole, Pinot Blanc is simpler and less distinctively flavoursome. It is a wine to drink young, generally within a year or two of the vintage.

Where next? The other white Pinot grape, **Pinot Gris**, is an interesting next step, and more unusual; or try **Chardonnay** to see why it is supposed to be better.

Pinot Gris

The spicy Pinot
Style From light and fresh to rich and oily, but (hopefully) always with a spicy bite
Grown in Alsace, Italy, Germany, Austria, Romania, Hungary and Oregon

The diversity of dry white wines made with Pinot Gris is alarming. As Pinot Grigio in northeastern Italy, it is often watery-pale, light in aroma and weight, and in some cases, very light in flavour. By contrast, top Alsace Tokay-Pinot Gris can be golden in colour, occasionally with a pink tinge, with a heady, spicy bouquet, a rich, oily texture and plump citrus-fruit and ginger flavours. It is hard to believe it's the same grape – but it is.

Most other regions steer a path somewhere between the two styles. In Germany, where it is also called Ruländer or Grauburgunder, it produces soft but unusually full-bodied wines by German standards, with the best coming from Baden. Austria, Switzerland (Malvoisie de Valais), Romania and Hungary (where it is known as Szürkebarát) also have plantings. Alsace is not the only French region with Pinot Gris. In the VDQS of Coteaux d'Ancenis, close to the mouth of the Loire, it appears as Malvoisie. In Burgundy, as with Pinot Blanc, it is a permitted variety in many white wines and in all red ones; however, there are probably few Chambertins that are 100 per cent Pinot Beurot, as it is called locally.

The popularity of Italian varieties has caused many New World producers to plant Pinot Grigio, although some have had to change their labels to read Pinot Gris. Australia, California and New Zealand all make increasingly successful versions, but Oregon is the place that has embraced it most emphatically.

The Pinot Gris taste As mentioned earlier, there is a large diversity in styles of Pinot Gris. The best Italian versions from Friuli-Venezia Giulia are crisp and fresh, with a rich, waxy texture and nutty, spicy, appley fruit.

In Alsace, even the humble versions have body and spice, while better wines can have hints of smoke, honey and butter, allied to flavours of peaches, crystallised fruit and minerals. It usually seems that there is insufficient acidity for them to age, but they do so remarkably, especially the sweeter wines.

New World Pinot Gris has the crispness of Italy and the spicy fruit of Alsace, plus a creamy, oaky veneer when barrel-fermented and aged. As yet, the wines do not achieve the complexity of the finest Alsace Pinot Gris, but examples such as New Zealand's Dry River show that they may very well do so one day.

Where next? Pinot Grigio from **Trentino-Alto Adige** and **Friuli-Venezia Giulia** can be followed up by virtually any other local varietal. If you develop a taste for the big, spicy **Alsace** style, move downwards in spiciness to **Pinot Blanc** or upwards to **Gewürztraminer**.

Port (White)

The first duty of port is to be red

Region Douro
Grape varieties Malvasia Fina and Malvasia Grossa
Style Nutty and full-bodied, but often rather clumsy
Quality/Price *·····⟩***/£££

RECOMMENDED PRODUCERS
Churchill Graham
Ferreira
Niepoort
Fladgate and Yeatman (Taylor's)

White port is a curious drink – made, one suspects, just to show that it can be done. It comes in various sweetnesses and is made in the same way as the red stuff. Sitting on a verandah peering out over the Douro after a hard day of tasting your way through several stout vintages, a chilled white port and tonic with ice and lemon hits the spot perfectly, cleaning out the system in preparation for dinner. Remove the situation and the spell is broken.

The Port (White) taste White port has a nutty character, perhaps with a vague hint of citrus fruit and resin. Good versions of whatever sweetness have

Vila Nova de Gaia, opposite Oporto, is home to the port lodges

a fresh, clean finish, but too many are coarse and flabby. If you have to add tonic, lemon and ice in order to make it palatable, something is wrong.

Where next? Move up to **Sherry** for more character, or try a chilled tawny port instead.

Pouilly-Fuissé

The Pouilly that isn't made from Sauvignon
Region Mâconnais, southern Burgundy
Grape varieties Chardonnay
Style Fleshy and rich, often with hints of cooked apple
Quality/Price ***⋯⟩****/£££⋯⟩£££££

RECOMMENDED PRODUCERS
Daniel Barraud
Roger Cordier
Domaine Corsin
Jean-Paul Drouin
Jeanne Ferret
Michel Forest
Guffens-Heynen
Manciat-Poncet
Gérard Martin
Roger Saumaize
De la Soufrandise
Verget
Vincent

The star appellation of the Mâconnais has nothing to do with the Sauvignon-based wines of Pouilly-Fumé in the Loire Valley. Pouilly-Fuissé is a hilly region with a variety of soils and aspects, so the wines can differ widely in style and quality. The famous name is still much abused, used by some rather insipid wines that are little better than Mâcon Blanc. However, there are fewer of these now, although the prices are no more sensible.

The Pouilly-Fuissé taste On a good day, Pouilly-Fuissé can be a dead ringer for a Côte de Beaune wine, quite tight and minerally but with a richness of flavour and plenty of appley fruit. Oak is usually used with sensitivity, with many producers making great wines without recourse to barrels.

It is quite a way further south here than in the Côte de Beaune, and in warm vintages some of the wines can lack acidity and be too fat. Conversely, in cooler years, when other parts of Burgundy make rather pinched wines, Pouilly-Fuissé can be as well balanced as anything in the region.

Where next? Good **Mâcon**-Villages and St-Véran are similar in style, and cheaper. **Meursault** is the **Côte de Beaune** wine which Pouilly-Fuissé resembles most closely.

Provence

It's so much nicer in Nice
Best-known wines Rosé in funny bottles
Grape varieties Ugni Blanc, Grenache Blanc, Clairette and Rolle
Style From insipid rosé to powerful, rich whites of real character
Quality/Price **⋯⟩****/£££⋯⟩£££££

RECOMMENDED PRODUCERS
Bunan
De la Courtade
De Calisanne
De Fonscolombe
Ott
Pibarnon
Routas
François Sack
(Clos Ste-Magdelaine)
De Seuil
Simone
De Trevallon
De Triennes

It's understandable, really. With a captive market of well-heeled tourists on the Côte d'Azur who aren't too concerned about what they drink or how much they pay for it, it's no surprise that few producers in Provence can be bothered to make much of an effort with their wines. The region's rosé, often in bizarre, wine-rack-unfriendly bottles, is the prime source of overpriced mediocrity.

However, most of Provence's whites, based on second-rate varieties such as Ugni Blanc, Grenache Blanc, Clairette and Rolle, aren't a lot better. So although the ACs of Coteaux d'Aix en Provence, Côtes de Provence and Coteaux Varois cover thousands of hectares, only a few of those hectares produce wine worth seeking out. There are some smaller appellations of note, such as Palette, home of Château Simone, and the small fishing village of Cassis, between Toulon and Marseille, where François Sack makes the fine Clos Ste-Magdelaine. The wines of Bellet and Bandol can be good but, like many in Provence, they are pricey.

The *vin de pays* concept has never caught on in Provence as it has in Languedoc-Roussillon region to its west, but there are some good wines made outside the appellation laws. Domaine de Trevallon makes a blend of Marsanne and Roussanne which can match all but the finest white

Hermitage, while Château Routas' Coquelicot (Chardonnay with Viognier) is also admirable.

Where next? Have a look at the speedily improving whites being made along the coast in **Languedoc-Roussillon**.

RECOMMENDED PRODUCERS

Louis Carillon
Jean Chartron
Gérard Chave
Leflaive
Marquis de Laguiche
(Drouhin)
Paul Pernot
De Puligny-Montrachet
De la Romanée-Conti
Etienne Sauzet
Thénard

Puligny-Montrachet

It doesn't get better than this
Region Burgundy
Grape varieties Chardonnay
Style Dry, firm, steely yet opulent
Quality/Price ***·····⟩*****/££££·····⟩£££££

Imagine a victor's rostrum. On the outside are the second and third places, in the centre is the winner. So it is with Puligny-Montrachet, flanked by Meursault and Chassagne, but rising above both. Textbook Puligny is elegant yet concentrated, fruity yet refined, full-bodied yet with steeliness.

Indeed, apart from an enticing flush of youth, drinking such a wine when it is too young will leave you wondering why it cost so much. But from five years old at *village* level, eight years for *premier cru* and ten years-plus for *grand cru*, the experience is a revelation. Puligny has four *grands crus*: Bâtard-Montrachet and Le Montrachet are shared with neighbouring appellation

Chassagne-Montrachet, while Chevalier-Montrachet and Bienvenues-Bâtard-Montrachet are exclusive to Puligny. In addition, there are 11 *premiers crus*, the best of which are Caillerets, Clavoillon, Folatières and Pucelles.

The Puligny-Montrachet taste Normally sane wine experts turn gooey when presented with a Puligny *grand cru* at the peak of its development. Writing tasting notes becomes pointless. You wonder how a wine can be so incredibly dry and firm, yet impossibly rich and opulent at the same time. You wonder where the extra flavour comes from, and try to separate the toasty, smoky, roasted-coffee tone from the nuts and spice, and the nuts and spice from the honey and cream. But you can't – it is all one, integrated, complete – so you give up and enjoy it. You might as well; you've paid enough for the privilege. These are among the very best white wines in the world.

You cannot expect the same intensity from the *premiers crus* and village wines, but they still make for a very pleasant experience.

Where next? Dry white wine doesn't get much better than this, although you may find equal quality from growers in **Chassagne-Montrachet** and **Meursault**. Only **California** has approached such intensity in its **Chardonnay**s, but without such subtlety. Why not try **Riesling** to see if the finest thrill your taste buds in the same way?

Rheingau

Home of hock
Best-known wines Schloss Johannisberger
Grape varieties Riesling
Style Spicy, rich, citrus fruit with minerally overtones
Quality/Price **⸱⸱⸱⸱⸳*****/££⸱⸱⸱⸱⸳£££££

RECOMMENDED PRODUCERS
JB Becker
Georg Breuer
Franz Künstler
Josef Leitz
Balthasar Ress
Schloss Johannisberg
Schloss Rheinhartshausen
Schloss Schönborn
Langwerth von Simmern
Wegeler-Deinhard
Robert Weil
Domdechant Werner

For many drinkers, the greatest German wines come from the southwestward flowing stretch of the River Rhine. The slope of the Rheingau vineyards, facing due south, is broader and gentler than the best sites in the Mosel. Yet the ripeness of the grapes in very good years is remarkable, helped by the reflection of the sun off the river straight onto the vines.

Bereich Johannisberg covers the whole Rheingau, and by *Bereich* (district) standards, these wines can be reasonably good. It is better to enjoy the best wines for their style and individuality – head for the wines from the towns of Hochheim (hence the English term "hock" for nearly anything from the Rhine), Rauenthal, Eltville, Erbach, Hattenheim, Oestrich, Johannisberg and Rüdesheim.

Most of the Rheingau's finest producers belong to the Charta association, whose aim is to preserve the purity and reputation of Rheingau Riesling. In order to attain Charta status, a wine must be made from 100 per cent estate-grown Riesling with a potential alcohol level 0.5 per cent higher than the minimum for the relevant Qualitätswein mit Prädikat level (*see* **Germany**). It must also have a sweetness level of 9 to 13 grams per litre of residual sugar, which corresponds to just off-dry. Charta has taken an additional (and, as yet, unofficial) step in designating which vineyards in the Rheingau are *Erstes Gewächs*, or first growths. For a wine to qualify for this level, it must have a minimum alcohol level of 12 per cent and be deemed of sufficient quality by a special panel. Charta has its critics, but its efforts to increase the standard of Rheingau wines are being rewarded – and should be applauded.

The Rheingau taste These are wines flowing with fruit and honey, but the best, while intense and concentrated, are never too obvious or generous; they tease with the spicy promise of something more. Riesling's minerally acidity is the engine-room, the power-house that drives them forward, kicking them into life; the spirit that animates the body. No German wine is really big enough to qualify as a meal in itself, but Rheingau Rieslings are laid out like an elegant buffet that provides a complete and balanced diet. Only when we get to the *Beerenauslesen* and *Trockenbeerenauslesen* (*see* **Germany**) do the peaches and cream pile on such luxury and opulence that we wonder guiltily if we are having too much of a good thing.

Where next? Cross to **Rheinhessen** and beyond to the **Nahe** for earthier, more robust versions of the **Rheingau** taste. Better still, compare Rheingau **Riesling**s with Mosels (*see* **Mosel-Saar-Ruwer**) – lighter, less intense, more floral – and then with **Alsace** Riesling – heavier and stronger, but drier on the whole.

RECOMMENDED PRODUCERS
Heyl zu Herrnsheim
Gunderloch
Louis Guntrum
Kühling-Gillot
Villa Sachsen
Schales

Rheinhessen

Lieb land
Best-known wines Liebfraumilch
Grape varieties Müller-Thurgau, Silvaner, Riesling
Style Mostly bland, but a few ripe, soft Rieslings
Quality/Price *····}****/£····}£££££

Some of Germany's most famous (and infamous) wine is produced in this rather amorphous region south of the Rheingau. Along with its soft, flowery Rieslings, Rheinhessen makes some 55 per cent of Germany's Liebfraumilch. It is also the home of Nierstein – a Rhineside village in whose name wines as diverse as Niersteiner Hölle and Niersteiner Gutes Domtal are produced; the first is a small vineyard of some 5.5 hectares (14 acres), the latter applies to the production of no fewer than 15 villages scattered to the west. So much for Teutonic precision.

Furthermore, the *Bereich* Nierstein covers about a third of the output of the whole of Rheinhessen. Too much Niersteiner is called Niersteiner for the producer's benefit – for marketing reasons, rather than on grounds of style or quality. The trouble is that the junk obscures our view of the good stuff. For the good stuff, head for the Rieslings of the nine villages on what is known as the Rhine Terrace: Nierstein, Bodenheim, Oppenheim, Guntersblum, Ludwigshöhe, Dienheim, Alsheim, Mattenheim and Nackenheim. Wines from Bingen can also be good.

The Rheinhessen taste When Rheinhessen wines are made from Müller-Thurgau or Silvaner, they will very likely appear as bland *Bereich* Nierstein or Liebfraumilch. However, when they are made from Riesling, and from a specific vineyard on the Rhine Terrace, they can have a flower-like fragrance and a beguiling, sunny softness denied their nearest cousins in the Rheingau, and be on a par with some of these cousins for quality. Many Rheinhessen wines can reach a refined and classy maturity. There is nothing brash or breezy about Rheinhessen Rieslings; mildness and softness are the keynotes.

Where next? See the **Rheingau** or **Pfalz** for variations in the Rhine style, **Franken** for a drier style, or **Austria** for more depth and less sugar.

Rhône

Take a well-earned break from Chardonnay
Best-known wines Condrieu, Tavel Rosé
Grape varieties Marsanne, Roussanne, Viognier, Clairette, Grenache Blanc, Bourboulenc
Style From fat and peachy to Asti-like sparklers
Quality/Price **⋯⟩****/££⋯⟩£££££

The styles made in the northern and southern Rhône are quite different. The northern sector has the Viognier wines of Condrieu and Château Grillet and the remarkable, long-ageing Marsanne/Roussanne wines of Hermitage; plus those of St-Joseph, Crozes-Hermitage and St-Péray (which also makes sparklers). Out on a limb between north and south are the Diois vineyards – Clairette de Die is made here from Clairette

RECOMMENDED PRODUCERS

Achard-Vincent
D' Aquéria
De Beaucastel
Clairette de Die Co-op
Auguste Clape
Gerard Chave
Clos des Papes
Jean-Luc Colombo
Des Entrefaux
Font de Michelle
Jean-Louis Grippat
Etienne Pochon
Rayas
St-Estève
Ste-Anne
Du Vieux-Télégraphe

and Muscat Blanc, and produced in the *méthode ancestrale*, which involves just one fermentation. Any *méthode champenoise* sparkling wines made here using 100 per cent Clairette must now be called Crémant de Die. There is also some Chardonnay and Aligoté grown for the Châtillon-en-Diois AC.

The southern Rhône's best-known white wine is the luscious, syrupy, *vin doux naturel*, known as Muscat de Beaumes-de-Venise. A typical southern white wine is a blend of Clairette, Grenache Blanc, Bourboulenc and Roussanne. Improved winemaking has brought freshness where there once was stolidity, but flavour is not a strong point of many of the wines. However, some Châteauneuf-du-Pape and the occasional Lirac and Côtes du Rhône-Villages can rise above the mundane. Lirac also makes some decent rosé based on Grenache, although neighbouring Tavel is better known for its pinks.

The Rhône taste With the northern whites, Marsanne brings the fat, peachy fruit while Roussanne provides the finesse and perfume. Hermitage is the best of these, but occasional wines from St-Joseph and Crozes-Hermitage can approach Hermitage in style, if not in absolute quality and longevity. For wines based on Viognier, *see* **Viognier** and **Condrieu**. Clairette de Die is the Rhône's answer to Asti: lovely grapey fizz that is hard to resist.

It can be difficult to find huge amounts of flavour in many of the whites from the south, even when cold fermentation has brought freshness. The finest have flavours varying from apple and quince to pineapple and peach (including the nutty kernel), and are best drunk young.

Where next? **California** has embraced certain Rhône white varieties with passion and success, and **Australia** has a couple of outposts of Marsanne. Closer to home, look at what producers in **Languedoc-Roussillon** are doing with the same grapes. See also specific entries for **Condrieu/Château Grillet** and **Muscat de Beaumes-de-Venise**.

Rías Baixas

Spain's finest white?
Region Galicia, northwest Spain
Grape varieties Albariño
Style Delicately aromatic, with peach and apricot flavours
Quality/Price **⋯⟩****/£££⋯⟩££££

In a country curiously devoid of interesting white wines, Rías Baixas stands out as a shining exception. The grape behind these aromatic, exotic wines is Albariño, and the Spanish enjoy its flavours so much that *bodegas* in Rías Baixas

Galicia in northwest Spain produces excellent, racy, zesty white wines

have no problem demanding fairly steep prices for their cherished products. The best are very good, and go brilliantly with seafood, spicy Asian dishes and many other foods. Even the hangers-on usually pass muster, so it is surprising that no enterprising souls in another Spanish region have planted Albariño in their vineyards.

The Rías Baixas taste Rías Baixas presents quite a contrast from other Spanish whites, as it is light and delicately aromatic, with lightly spicy, peachy fruit and the occasional hints of cream and nuts. A few producers use a small amount of oak, but the wines are generally best unsullied by wood.

Where next? Just south of the border in **Portugal**, some **Vinho Verde** is made from Alvarinho, as it is known locally. No other Spanish wine comes near Rías Baixas in style, although the best of **Rueda** and **Rioja** are of a similar quality.

Riesling

Move over Chardonnay
Style From simple and citric to steely and slatey, dry to
syrupy-sweet, and still to sparkling
Grown in Germany, Austria, Alsace, Australia, New Zealand,
the US, South Africa and Canada

For many years, there have been rumours of a Riesling revival, most of them greatly exaggerated. But today – ah, how many optimistic wine writers with rose-tinted computer screens have begun articles with these words? However, it genuinely does seem that a "But today..." is now justified. A generation brought up on Chardonnay is looking for something else to drink. Liebfraumilch consumption is declining (many Liebs contain no Riesling), while sales of finer German wines are on the increase. Producers in places as far apart as Washington State in the US and the Clare Valley in South Australia are finding that they don't have enough Riesling to meet their projected requirements.

What we say is "about bloody time, too". It may seem surprising, but many people consider Riesling to be the world's most aristocratic white grape variety. Yes, they even put it above Chardonnay, the grape behind such noble Burgundian wines as Puligny-Montrachet and Corton-Charlemagne. There is nothing strange, though, about wanting to put Riesling at the top of the tree. It makes magnificent wines in Germany along the Rhine and Mosel rivers, culminating in rich, sweet, yet sometimes ethereally light wines with very, very long names. It has travelled the world with great success, making wines that vary from very dry to very sweet. Germany may produce the largest number of fine Rieslings, but the best from New Zealand, Australia, Austria and Alsace are of comparable quality, with South Africa, the US and Canada not far behind.

Wherever it is grown, Riesling is adept at picking up the character of the local *terroir*, even at yields that would be considered high for other varieties. It has two other notable attributes. Firstly, it's a very hardy vine, able to survive cold winters – hence its popularity in cooler regions. Secondly, a more important characteristic is its acidity. When grapes of most varieties approach maturity, their natural sugar level rises and acidity decreases. Riesling grapes, however, are capable of maturing further, with the sweetness increasing and the acidity remaining more or less stable. This means that the wines made from late-picked or nobly-rotten grapes are seldom cloying. It is this acidity that helps Riesling mature beautifully in bottle, developing intriguing scents and flavours over a decade or two.

A word of warning, however. There are many wines labelled "Riesling" which are made from lesser grapes such as the unrelated Welschriesling. Eastern Europe is the main culprit here, although Italy's Riesling Italico is also Welschriesling, while some Germans and Swiss use the rather misleading term Riesling-Sylvaner for Müller-Thurgau. Such practices only serve to give the real thing a poor reputation. Names for authentic Riesling around the world include Rhine Riesling, Rheinriesling, Weisser Riesling, White Riesling, Johannisberg Riesling and Riesling Renano.

The Riesling taste While Riesling is rarely as pungent as Muscat or Gewürztraminer, it is still an aromatic grape. The wines made from it are generally light- to medium-bodied, with fruit in the apple-and-citrus spectrum accompanied by floral hints. Occasionally there is a grassy, herby smell, while some wines are reminiscent of apricots, honey and nuts. Even sweeter versions, made either from ultra-ripe grapes or those that have been affected by botrytis (*see* **Noble Rot**), can retain a feeling of lightness and freshness, thanks to the acidity. As the wines age, they often acquire a petrol or kerosene smell, which may sound disgusting but is surprisingly attractive. The sweet wines can be among the longest-lived wines in the world.

Unlike Chardonnay, there is really not too much winemakers can do to add interest to Riesling. A few producers have experimented with malolactic fermentation and barrel-ageing, but the results have been generally unimpressive – which means that all you are tasting is what was in the grapes. Cheap Riesling tastes of far more than cheap Chardonnay, but move up the scale and the vineyards themselves start to put their oar in. You can taste the minerals, the slate, the clay in the soils in certain wines – usually those from Alsace, Austria and Germany.

That acidity again comes in handy for sparkling Rieslings, the best of which come from Germany (*see* **Sekt**). The best examples, made by the *méthode champenoise*, need time to settle down, but develop an intriguing mix of floral, petrolly Riesling aromas and the toasty character of bottle-aged fizz.

Where next? **Chenin Blanc** is the other grape with high acidity capable of making a wide variety of styles, especially in the **Loire**.

Rioja

Identity crisis
Region Northern Spain
Grape varieties Viura, Malvasia, Garnacha Blanca
Style From rich and oaky to quite neutral, but should have a hint of lemon
Quality/Price ****····\}****/££····\}£££££**

RECOMMENDED PRODUCERS
Artadi
Bodegas Beronia
Campo Viejo
CVNE (Compañia Vinícola del Norte de España)
López de Heredia
Marqués de Cáceres
Marqués de Murrieta
Martínez Bujanda
Montecillo
Bodegas Riojanas

In the beginning, there was white Rioja (golden-yellow Rioja would perhaps be a more accurate description). It was made from Malvasia, and aged for ages in oak barrels. Sometimes it emerged like a rich and complex white burgundy, but more often it emerged flabby, over-oaked and badly oxidised.

"Chapter two" was the backlash against these wines. The low-yielding and oxidation-prone Malvasia began to be displaced in favour of the easier to cultivate but undistinguished Viura. Out went the oak, or at least most of it; in came the stainless-steel tanks. The resulting wines were crisp and sprightly.

They were also devoid of character and struggled to last a year in bottle. We are now in "Chapter three", with producers trying to find a halfway house between the two styles. Viura still dominates, although a few traditional houses maintain a high percentage of Malvasia. In an attempt to add interest to the wines barrel-fermentation is becoming popular, and the wines have improved as a result. But we are still not talking about a world-beating style. The best white Riojas remain the old-fashioned ones, such as Marqués de Murrieta's Castillo Ygay and López de Heredia's Viña Tondonia, but these are rare. Perhaps the producers should concentrate on reds and leave the whites to Rueda, Somontano, Penedès and Rías Baixas.

The Rioja taste The clean, unoaked style is crisp and fairly neutral, although some examples have lemon and grapefruit flavours. The traditional wines have something of that lemon, too, but here it is rich, buttery lemon curd, with a hint of pine and plenty of body to stand up to the new-oak flavours. Halfway between are wines with more of that lemon, together with a light, creamy, vanilla quality and a hint of spice from the use of oak.

Where next? The Spanish regions making the most interesting wines are Somontano, Penedès (*see* **Catalonia**), **Rueda** and **Rías Baixas**. Try the whites of **Bordeaux** to see how they have progressed in recent years. For rich, oaky wines try a top **Burgundy** or New World **Chardonnay**.

Rosé

Forget the image and chill out on a summer's day

Pink wine is unusual in that our decision to drink it often depends as much on the weather as on the quality of the wine. Grill anybody on a beach for half a day, and plunge them into a salty sea; then shower them, seat them in a restaurant, and what is the first thing they ask for? "Ooh, a lovely bottle of chilled rosé, please."

And they are absolutely right. Nothing is nicer than that first glass; it quenches the thirst wonderfully, and it almost feels like you're not drinking. Provençal winemakers have been wise to this phenomenon for a long time, and have produced lots of rosé. It is so impressive at the time that we take a bottle home with us to a cool, damp, foggy climate – with predictably disastrous consequences.

Yet with the right kind of sales talk we can be induced to have another go. Those who remember Mateus Rosé with fondness do so not for its simple, slightly sweet flavour and spritzy prickle, but for the memories of first loves and table lamps. California's success with pink wines owes nothing to their bland sweetness and plenty to the marketing men who decided to label them "Blush" or even in the case of Zinfandel, "White" (*see* **Zinfandel**).

Of course, real macho drinkers shudder at such images, and continue to eschew rosé. This is a pity, as there are a growing number of extremely pleasant wines from all around the world for which sun, sea and swordfish – and a clever marketing campaign – are not prerequisites. Bung a bit of food-colouring in them, and the steak eaters won't utter a word.

How rosé is made Most pink wine is made from red grapes. They are crushed, and the juice and skins are left in contact for a day or two while the must begins to ferment. This is just long enough for the juice to take some colour from the skins, but not long enough to make it red. The juice is then run off and continues fermenting on its own, just like most white wine. Honourable exceptions include pink Champagne, which can be a blend of red and white wines.

While in France at least it is usually the lighter red grape varieties such as Cabernet Franc, Pinot Noir and Gamay that are used to make rosé, in theory any red grape variety may be used. Many producers anxious to improve the colour and flavour of their red wines will bleed some light-coloured juice out of their fermenting vats after a short time and produce a rosé from it; *saignée* is the French word for such a wine.

The Rosé taste The varietal flavour should show through in the wine, but the essence of rosé is its fresh-faced pinkness and bright, breezy, snappy, thirst-quenching appeal. As soon as rosé begins to take itself seriously, it is done for. Oak is a definite no-no. Although certain rosés can age – a 1961 Cabernet d'Anjou aged 35 was a revelation – the general rule is to drink the youngest available. Those with a red tinge tend to be fresher and fruitier than those with an orange colour, which often indicates a touch of oxidation.

Where next? Light reds such as **Alsace** Pinot Noir, Beaujolais Nouveau (or Primeur) and Italian reds such as Bardolino and the lighter style of Valpolicella. See also the entries for **Australia, Bordeaux, Burgundy, Champagne, Chile, Languedoc-Roussillon, the Loire, Navarra, New Zealand, Provence, Rhône, Rioja, South Africa, Trentino-Alto Adige, Veneto** and **Zinfandel**.

Rueda

RECOMMENDED PRODUCERS

Bellondrade y Lurton
Castilla la Vieja
Hermanos Lurton
Marqués de Griñon
Marqués de Riscal

Potentially very interesting
Region Northwest Spain
Grape varieties Verdejo, Sauvignon Blanc, Viura, Palomino
Style Fresh and fragrant with peachy fruit; can be quite classy
Quality/Price **·····⟩****/£·····⟩£££

Although not well known, the white wines of Rueda in northwest Spain show considerable promise and are well worth seeking out. They owe their extra bit of class to the local Verdejo grape (which must make up 25 per cent of basic Rueda and at least 60 per cent of Rueda Superior) and to modern winemaking by the few good producers.

In the 1970s, Marqués de Riscal was the first to show the potential of the region, while the star of the 1990s is the barrel-fermented Bellondrade y Lurton, made by a member of the famous Bordeaux Lurton family.

The Rueda taste Basic Rueda is fresh, clean and lightly aromatic, with a soft, herbaceous and slightly nutty flavour, and it should be drunk young. The best wines have the class, structure and texture of a great dry white Bordeaux. Such wines have little track record for ageing, but they are built to withstand at least five years in bottle. Palomino grapes produce light, sherry-style *finos* and *amontillados* which undergo *flor* treatment but not the *solera* system.

Where next? See how the best of **Rueda** stacks up against wines from Somontano, **Catalonia** and **Rías Baixas**.

Sancerre and Pouilly-Fumé

Home of Sauvignon Blanc
Region Central Loire Valley
Grape varieties Sauvignon Blanc, Pinot Noir
Style Nettles, flint, gooseberry, elderflower, blackcurrant leaf
Quality/Price **····}****/£££····}£££££

RECOMMENDED PRODUCERS

Franck & Jean-François Bailly
Henri Bourgeois
Cailbourdin
Jean-Claude Chatelain
Cotat
Lucien Crochet
Didier Dagueneau
Pascal Jolivet
De Ladoucette
Alphonse Mellot
Henry Pellé
Vincent Pinard
De Tracy
Vacheron
André Vatan

Sauvignon Blanc thrives on chalky slopes cut by the river Loire 320 km (200 miles) inland from the Atlantic. Until New Zealand came on the scene, Sancerre and Pouilly-Fumé virtually had the crisp, nettley, grassy Sauvignon market sewn up. Indeed, the way in which many Sancerre and Pouilly-Fumé producers have failed to improve their wines and the prices they charge leads you to believe that they still think they're invincible. But others have moved with the times. Grapes are being picked riper, yields are being reduced voluntarily, oak barrels are appearing in some cellars, and the wines are improving without losing their identity. As in much of France, the best are getting still better, while the rest are being left behind.

The Sancerre and Pouilly-Fumé taste Sancerre at its tangy best is as clean as a whistle, with a whiff of nettles, gooseberries, grapefruit, blackcurrant leaves and asparagus. It has a steely, flinty quality about it that nowhere else quite seems to manage. This is especially true of wines from the villages of Bué and Chavignol, where the soil is similar to that of Champagne and Chablis. The soils of Pouilly-Fumé are generally heavier, so while the wines are usually very similar in style, they sometimes have a little more body and roundness, slightly riper fruit, perhaps, as well as a pronounced smokiness – hence the Fumé.

Even with the riper style of wine being made today, both Sancerre and Pouilly-Fumé can be quite severe in their youth, often needing a year or two from vintage to settle down, and in some cases perhaps four years or more. Where oak is used, its impact on the wines depends on the quality of the fruit. The best are rich and creamy and have more in common with top Pessac-Léognan wines and even burgundies.

Sancerre also makes small amounts of rosé from Pinot Noir, which in good years can have the raspberry flavours of the grape allied to a wonderful floral freshness.

Where next? Other **Sauvignon**s from the **Loire** include Menetou-Salon, Reuilly and Quincy. **New Zealand** is the competition.

Sardinia

Nice place; shame about the whites
Best-known wines Nuragus di Cagliari
Grape varieties Malvasia, Vernaccia di Oristano, Nuragus, Vermentino, Torbato, Trebbiano
Style Most whites are simple thirst-quenchers
Quality/Price *⋯⟩***/£⋯⟩£££

The generous would say that no one has yet fully exploited Sardinia's potential for white wines. The pragmatic would ask, *"What* potential?". Ruggedly beautiful as the island is, there are few white wines of interest, a fact not helped by the grape varieties grown here, which veer towards the neutral. Malvasia di Bosa from near Alghero is one of the more interesting wines: sherry-like, and made either dry or, more commonly, rich and sweet, with a bitter note like Spanish *oloroso*. Vernaccia di Oristano (no relation of the Tuscan Vernaccia) is similar in style. There are also some rosés made from Cannonau (Grenache) and Carignano (Carignan).

The Sardinian taste Sardinia's efficient co-ops turn out Nuragus di Cagliari in some quantity. It is sometimes slightly salty, but never rises beyond the thirst-quenching level. Vermentino di Gallura has an assertive, earthy, aromatic style, but again is seldom exciting. Sella & Mosca's range includes a decent Sauvignon and a fine dessert wine made from a local variety called Nasco.

Where next? Mainland **Italy** offers many crisp but often dull whites, so why not see what **Sicily** has to offer?

Sauternes and Barsac

The world's greatest sweet wine
Region Bordeaux
Grape varieties Sémillon, Sauvignon Blanc, Muscadelle
Style Honeyed, syrupy, toasty and creamy, with nuts, apricots and many other flavours
Quality/Price **⋯⟩*****/£££⋯⟩£££££

This is one of the classic wine styles, much copied around the world, but rarely equalled. Sauternes is an appellation within Graves, at the southern end, near Langon. Next door, across the River Ciron, is Barsac, making similar wines that can call themselves either Barsac or Sauternes. Between them, the two ACs cover five communes: Barsac, Preignac, Bommes, Fargues and Sauternes, which constitute the First Division. The region was classified, with the red wines of the Médoc, in 1855. Its only *premier grand cru* ("first great growth") is Château d'Yquem, and there are 11 first growths, 14 second growths and several *crus bourgeois*.

RECOMMENDED PRODUCERS
CONTINUED

Nairac
Rabaud-Promis
De Rayne Vigneau
Rieussec
St-Amand
Suduiraut
La Tour Blanche
D'Yquem

The conditions of warmth and humidity that help to make these wines special are not quite matched in the neighbouring appellations of Cérons, (*see* **Graves**), Ste-Croix-du-Mont, Cadillac or Loupiac (*see* **Bordeaux**). These appellations can make good wines, but they rarely have the intense lusciousness of Sauternes.

Sauternes and Barsac are special for several reasons. Autumn mists rise from the rivers Garonne and Ciron, and are shooed away by the sun as the day wears on, making this an ideal breeding ground for botrytis (*see* **Noble Rot**). The pickers have to traipse through the vines several times over a few weeks, harvesting stickily and virtually berry by berry. Because of the concentration, each vine yields as little as a glass of wine, rather than the bottle or two some growers elsewhere might expect to harvest. Once this process is understood, the prices asked begin to seem more reasonable.

Sémillon is the mainstay, valued for its richness, body and prime susceptibility to botrytis, while Sauvignon Blanc supports with balancing acidity. The third grape, Muscadelle, can be pleasantly perfumed but is less distinctive than the other two, and seldom exceeds ten per cent of a vineyard's plantings.

Great Sauternes cannot be made every year. It is quite possible for prolonged autumn rain to ruin a crop that looked to be progressing well. By then, it is too late for the producer to do anything about it so, in anticipation of this, he would probably not gamble the whole crop. He would pick some grapes under normal conditions and make a dry, bread-and-butter wine to keep his accountant happy, hoping that, if conditions turn out right and botrytis occurs, he will have jam with it.

Alternatively, if the vineyard were only partially affected by botrytis, and the producer had neither the money nor the skilled labour to collect grapes individually, he might harvest the whole lot, ripe and rotten together, and make a neither-this-nor-that sort of wine. These partially botrytised wines are rarely successful, and make the least exciting Sauternes – sorry, *second* least exciting; some producers just *chaptalise* (add sugar to) their wines before fermentation.

The Sauternes taste The appeal of these wines is their honeyed, sweet, glycerine-smooth, concentrated richness. The fruits they evoke are peaches and apricots; sometimes raisins in a very mature wine. Sauternes is, if anything, bigger, richer and more luscious than Barsac. Alcohol is high in both (around

13 to 14 per cent), but despite the sweetness, the just-balancing acidity keeps them animated. With oak age, Sauternes develops spicy, toasty flavours, and a remarkable change in colour takes place, from golden-yellow through russet and coppery-bronze to deep tawny. They are wines that definitely need maturing to allow the depth and spectrum of flavours to emerge: 10 to 20 years is normal; the lighter vintages can be enjoyed at 6 to 8 years. Some top wines from better years soldier on for longer than the patience of most drinkers.

Where next? **Bordeaux** has the cheaper, but less interesting sweet wines of **Graves** Supérieures, Cérons, Loupiac, Ste-Croix-du-Mont and Cadillac. With the exception of a few German and Austrian wines, European sweeties in a similar vein are few and far between. The closest the New World comes is with the **Semillon**-based wines of **New South Wales**.

Sauvignon Blanc

The smelly one
Style Gooseberry, asparagus, nettles, blackcurrant leaf – and cat's pee
Grown in The Loire, Bordeaux, Languedoc-Roussillon, Austria, Italy, Spain, New Zealand, Chile, Australia, California, South Africa...

In the white-grape firmament, Sauvignon Blanc definitely comes in the top ten, but it will never hit number one because Riesling and Chardonnay won't let it. It makes direct, in-your-face wines that have a crunchy, green freshness –

rather like biting on a just-picked pea-pod. Such flavours are easy to understand, but that doesn't make them easy to love, so many producers look to tone down Sauvignon. One of the easiest of these is to leave a little residual sugar in the wines, not so much as to make them appear sweet, but just enough to make them seem richer. A solution used by producers in Bordeaux is to use the fatter Sémillon to tame Sauvignon, while another is to ferment and age the wines in barrel, which again knocks off the gawky edges. However, decent Sauvignon should always have a tautness to it, and if you don't like it, take your glass elsewhere.

Many winemaking regions have Sauvignon in their vineyards, although few have fully mastered the variety. The Central Loire Valley in France was the first place to get it right with the wines of Sancerre and Pouilly-Fumé. For some, these are still the finest expressions of the grape, although success has made many of the growers complacent. The region that has stepped in to take over the Sauvignon crown is Marlborough, on New Zealand's South Island. The first vines were only planted in 1973 – but there are already several wineries making first-class versions, led by the famous Cloudy Bay. Other parts of the country have followed suit and planted Sauvignon, with Nelson, Martinborough and Hawke's Bay enjoying particular success.

Californians aren't too keen on the grassy, vegetal style of Sauvignon as typified by the Loire and then caricatured by New Zealand. They make much riper versions and often follow the Bordeaux path of using oak and some Sémillon to iron out the creases in their Fumé Blanc, as it is sometimes labelled. In a high-class Bordeaux dry white, Sauvignon usually constitutes slightly more than half the blend, with Sémillon making up the balance.

Australia has struggled to find regions cool enough for Sauvignon, and many wines have been too flabby and ungainly, like unset jelly. However, regions such as Adelaide Hills, Margaret River, Coonawarra and the Pyrenees in Central Victoria are now making some excellent versions that stand comparison with New Zealand's best. Much of South Africa is too warm for Sauvignon, but that doesn't stop it from being planted in many vineyards. Taste the wines, and it is often obvious where producers have had to pick too early while the grapes still have some acidity but before the flavours have had a chance to develop fully. However, the quality of wine from Constantia and the cooler parts of Paarl and Stellenbosch improves with each vintage.

Chile's problem with Sauvignon is that much of what they call Sauvignon Blanc is actually Sauvignonasse, a different and inferior grape. Producers who have gone out of their way to obtain the true Sauvignon can make some impressive wines, especially in the Casablanca Valley.

The Loire and Bordeaux aren't France's only sources of Sauvignon. Sauvignon de St Bris is a Burgundian outpost of the variety, while the Languedoc has several *vins de pays* whose quality belies the often warm conditions in which they are produced – perhaps the South Africans should go and see how they manage it. Spain (Rueda) and Italy (Tuscany, Friuli-Venezia Giulia) are showing that they can make fine Sauvignon, but Europe's surprise success story is Styria, in southern Austria. While some of the wines from here can be just too tartly acidic, a small but increasing number are of world class. Eastern Europe has plenty of Sauvignon, but with the exception of a few Hungarian examples, there is little of note.

The Sauvignon taste Next to Gewürztraminer, Sauvignon Blanc is perhaps the most easily recognisable of grape varieties. It doesn't just smell, it pongs – of nettles, gooseberries, crushed blackcurrant leaves, asparagus, tropical fruit... yes, even cat's pee. Serious versions can have earthy, minerally notes, and occasionally gun-flint or slate.

The aromatic assault continues on the palate. Young wines that don't have something to round out the flavours (like a touch of oak, some sweetness or Sémillon) can be forbidding. Too much oak is a mistake, as by the time the oak flavours have integrated, the freshness of Sauvignon has subsided. With few exceptions – the occasional white Bordeaux or Sancerre, for example – Sauvignon does not improve with age; it changes, getting fatter and acquiring an almost Gewürztraminer-like spiciness, but it loses its youthful exuberance.

Where next? The next logical step is **Sémillon**, which in cool regions can develop a grassy, herbaceous smell. A slight change of tack would be Grüner Veltliner in **Austria**.

Sekt

In search of Sekt's appeal
Region Germany
Grape varieties The best are based on Riesling
Style Floral and peachy, with petrolly overtones in the good wines
Quality/Price *···⟩***/££···⟩££££

RECOMMENDED PRODUCERS
Fürst von Metternich
Fürstlich Castell'sches D
Kessler
Köhler-Ruprecht
Max Ferd Richter
Schloss Reinhartshausen
Wegeler-Deinhard

Germany produces a lot of sparkling wine, but nearly all of it is consumed by Germans. This is no great loss to the rest of us, however, as much of it is ordinary in the extreme. Almost all Sekt, as it is called, is made by the *cuve close* method and has precious little character since much of it is made from imported base wine trucked in from other parts of Europe.

Since 1994, wines labelled *Deutscher Sekt* must be made entirely from German grapes. Those from a named German region go under the snappy name of *Deutscher Qualitätsschaumwein Bestimmter Anbaugebiete (Deutscher Qualitätsschaumwein BA* for short). The best wines are usually those made by the *méthode champenoise* from 100 per cent Riesling, although some impressive Pinot Noir rosés have been produced in recent years.

The Sekt taste Most Sekt is made in industrial quantities and has a taste to match. The best 100 per cent Riesling *méthode champenoise* examples can have fruit flavours ranging from ripe and peachy to subtle and floral. The Riesling flavours usually overwhelm any brought to the wine by the *méthode champenoise*, but yeasty hints occasionally poke their way through.

Where next? Many New World sparkling wines equal the quality of good all-**Riesling** Sekt: a little sweetness, lots of fresh fruit. Most other sparkling wines, such as **Saumur** and **Cava**, are better value.

Sémillon

Underrated and potentially aristocratic
Style Waxy, lemony fruit; developing toasty characters with age
Grown in Bordeaux, Australia, the US, New Zealand, South Africa

Sémillon is a grape it pays to have as a friend. It is more than the poor man's Chardonnay – which is the way some New World regions treat it. It is more than a buffer for the more boisterous Sauvignon Blanc in the wines of Bordeaux. Yet because it can be muted as a young wine, many people pass it by in favour of something more obvious.

Sémillon's greatest role is in the sweet wines of Bordeaux, where its ripe fatness and proneness to noble rot make it the favoured variety, forming 80 per cent of a typical blend. In the region's dry wines, it is the "fat one" of the Laurel and Hardy duo, lending weight to the partnership and, by dint of its ability to age gracefully, preventing many a thin Sauvignon Blanc from falling embarrassingly flat on its face before the end of the first reel. Sémillon also appears in many other dry and sweet wines from Southwest France.

The other region in which it is highly regarded is the Hunter Valley in New South Wales, where it was, until recently, labelled Hunter River Riesling. As Semillon (you don't expect Aussie wine to have a French accent, do you?), the wines it produces here are unique, developing a distinctive, rich, toasty style after long ageing in bottle. The grape's popularity has spread to other Australian wine-growing regions, with parts of South Australia and Western Australia making wines – often with oak influence – that are every bit as good as those from the Hunter. The finest sweet versions, especially from Griffith in New South Wales, can be a match for Sauternes. That Australian creation, the Semillon/Chardonnay blend, can be very attractive, with the fat of the former and the fruit of the latter.

In New Zealand, California and Washington State, Sémillon is used mainly in Bordeaux fashion: in blends with Sauvignon Blanc. Barrel-fermentation and ageing is usually a factor in the American wines and in some New Zealand versions. South Africa is still coming to terms with the grape, but results have been promising, with the growers of Constantia making some of the best wines. Sémillon used to be widely grown in Chile, mainly for wines sold on the domestic market, but it is now disappearing from many vineyards.

The Sémillon taste Sometimes young Sémillon, especially that of New Zealand, can display an aromatic, herbaceous, grassy smell, highly reminiscent of Sauvignon Blanc. It is difficult to believe that it will ever progress to anything more substantial. The difference is on the palate: Sémillon has noticeably more weight and body than Sauvignon. While the latter will peak relatively early and rarely improve after a couple of years, Sémillon goes from strength to strength.

This is why the two varieties are often blended together. Sauvignon seduces with its aromatic power and masks its partner's initial shyness. Sémillon makes up for Sauvignon's lack of body and fills out the wine when Sauvignon retreats. When mature, the wines have a weight, a roundness and a butteriness reminiscent of Chardonnay. The amazing thing is that Sémillon can do this without any oak-ageing. The citric tang of youth is not wasted, either. That is what keeps it lively, holding flabby, middle-aged spread at bay.

Few people can be bothered to mature high-class Sémillon from Bordeaux or the Hunter Valley for the decade or more it needs. There is a short-cut, however, in the shape of oak-ageing, which creates a rich, mellow, rounded style in a fraction of the time. It is by no means as classy as the real thing, but for most purposes, and most pockets, it will do nicely, thank you.

Where next? Sémillon provides a logical step on the way to **Chardonnay**. It does not always have the full, flavoursome, stylish completeness of Chardonnay, but it is the grape variety that comes closest to it. The different Sémillon styles – young and lemony, young and oaky, or mature and buttery – easily find an equivalent among the various styles of Chardonnay, but generally this will involve moving upwards in price.

Sherry

Looking for a bargain?
Region Andalucía, southwest Spain
Grape varieties Palomino, Pedro Ximénez, Moscatel
Style Tangy, sometimes even salty, yeasty, dry and nutty
Quality/Price **⋯⟩*****/£⋯⟩£££££

Psst! Do you want to know a secret? Never mind: I'll tell you anyway. For the price of a thimbleful of Montrachet, you can have a whole bottle of wine that is every bit as intense, every bit as venerable, every bit as exciting. That's right, sherry. Real sherry – from tangy dry *fino* through nutty dry *amontillado* to rich dry *oloroso* – is fabulous to drink, unbelievably underrated and is almost given away when you consider the time and effort that goes into making it.

What all these sherry styles have in common, you notice, is dryness. The sweet or cream sherries – which still, sadly, make up a huge proportion of the wines sold outside Spain – get their sweetness from a variety of sweetening agents, some of which have nothing to do with grapes at all. There are some great sweet sherries, but they are few in number, and as a rule of thumb, all good sherry is dry. It comes from the southwest corner of Spain, around the town of Jerez de la Frontera.

The actions of the sherry *bodegas* in getting the rest of the world's producers to remove the word "sherry" from their similarly styled wines must be applauded. At the same time, preventing them from using the terms *fino*, *amontillado* and *oloroso* to describe their wines was a less constructive initiative. Growers in Montilla, for example, are now forbidden to label their wines *amontillado*, which means literally "in the style of Montilla".

Palomino is the main grape used to make sherry. Moscatel (Muscat of Alexandria) and Pedro Ximénez (PX for short) are the other permitted varieties, although they take up less than five per cent of the vineyards, and are used almost exclusively for sweetening purposes.

It may seem that there are several categories of sherry, but all begin their lives as either a *fino* or an *oloroso*. Grapes for the elegant *finos* are grown on the dazzlingly white *albariza* soils reminiscent of Champagne country, while those for *olorosos* come from heavier soils. Whatever the intended style, the newly fermented wine, poured into a cask (at around 11 per cent alcohol), is unremarkable, but it is from here onwards that the magic begins.

The winemaker will assess all the barrels of wines and separate those intended for *finos*. These are then fortified to around 15.5 per cent. *Fino* derives its unique yeasty character from a pale, wrinkly, yellowish mould called

flor which occurs naturally in the region and grows on the surface of the wine. The *flor* ensures that the wine undergoes a partial and very slow oxidation process, increasing esters and aldehydes along the way and giving *fino* its fresh tang. It thrives at an alcohol level of 15 to 16 per cent – hence the degree of fortification.

All sherry is produced by fractional blending in what is known as a *solera* system, which uses a three-row pyramid of barrels of variously aged wines. A quarter to a third of the wine is drawn off from the barrels in the bottom row (the *solera*) and is replenished with younger wine from the barrels above it; this in turn is replenished with even younger wine from the barrels above them, and so on. Each row above the *solera* is called a *criadera* (the word means "nursery") and there can be as many as 14 barrels, or *botas*, in them. The *botas* in the *solera* are those from which wine is eventually drawn off for bottling.

A typical *fino* emerging from the *solera* system is five to ten years old. Away from the influence of *flor*, it quickly deteriorates, so the youngest, freshest wines are the best; a bottle of *fino* should ideally be consumed at one sitting. *Manzanilla* is *fino* produced in the area of Sanlúcar de Barrameda, where the nearby sea has an influence on the *flor* and creates wines with a noticeably salty tang.

The *flor* can linger for longer than eight years, especially if the casks are regularly topped up with small amounts of younger wines (although very old *fino* is rare). However, the *flor* eventually dies, and in its absence, the wines continue to develop in cask, but now without their special blanket of mould.

With further cask age, a wine becomes a *fino-amontillado* (*manzanilla pasada* in Sanlúcar) and finally a true *amontillado*. Wine not intended for *fino* production is fortified to around 17.5 to 18 per cent, at which level *flor* cannot survive. This will become *oloroso* sherry; as it develops in barrel, it gains more concentrated flavours, and thanks to evaporation, it also becomes slightly more alcoholic with age. The best sweet *olorosos* are made by adding wines made from sun-dried PX grapes, and there are occasionally wines that are 100 per cent PX.

Some of the finest sherries are matured in small quantities by doctors, lawyers and others with spare cash and time on their hands – more as a hobby than a business. Unlike the blends from big *bodegas*, with numerous *botas* in each *criadera*, these small producers may have no more than half a dozen. The wines from such small producers are called *almacenista* sherries. Originally they were sold to the large *bodegas* to give depth and character to some of their commercial blends, but in the last few years, firms such as Emilio Lustau have done a great service by bottling some of them unblended, straight from a single cask. Most of these are uncompromisingly dry, and each is made in a different and unrepeatable style.

There is another style of sherry called *palo cortado*. Definitions of exactly what this is vary from producer to producer, with vague mutterings along the lines of it being a wine which began life as a *fino* and then the *flor* died, causing the sherry to take on the characteristics of an *oloroso*.

The Sherry taste *Fino* sherry should be light, with a delicately yeasty smell, a slightly austere bite and a fresh, tangy flavour. *Manzanilla* is much the same, but with a zesty, salty, sea-air character. *Amontillado* may have something of the tang, but is nuttier and far more concentrated in flavour. Richer still is *oloroso*, with its deeper, more sultry, nutty fragrance and raisiny maturity, sometimes with the bitter-sweet flavour of burnt caramel. It is usually dry, though sometimes the bitter edge becomes so shockingly brutal that a little sweetening wine is added to the *oloroso* for balance – not enough to obscure the flavours of the sherry, just enough to harmonise them. Sweeter versions maintain the intensity but have more treacly lusciousness. The sweetest wines of all, the 100 per cent PX wines, are like Liqueur Muscat: full of intensely treacly rum 'n' raisin flavours and ideal for drinking with Christmas pudding or for pouring over good vanilla ice-cream.

Where next? The wines of **Montilla** are similar in style but never reach the same heights. The occasional wine from **South Africa** and **Australia** can impress, but there is nothing in the world quite like sherry. Try other fortified wines, including **Málaga**, **Madeira**, **Marsala**, Australian **Liqueur Muscat and Tokay** or the **Jura**'s *vin jaune*.

RECOMMENDED PRODUCERS
Alcamo
Marco de Bartoli
Benanti
COS
Donnafugata
Duca di Salaparuta (Corvo)
Florio
Carlo Hauner
Salvatore Murana
Planeta
Rapitalà
Scammacca del Murgo
Tasca d'Almerita (Regaleali)
Terre di Ginestra

Sicily

Move over Marsala

Best-known wines Corvo, Marsala

Grape varieties Grillo, Inzolia, Catarratto, Malvasia, Chardonnay, Moscato

Style Luscious Moscato; crisp, nutty, dry whites

Quality/Price *······⟩****/£······⟩££££

It would be inaccurate to say that Sicily's wine industry is booming, but there is now rather more of interest on the island than was the case not so long ago. The decline in popularity of Marsala has left growers with rather a lot of grapes they need to use for something. Grillo, Inzolia and Catarratto, the main Marsala grapes, are never going to challenge Chardonnay's world dominance, but cool fermentation can transform them into very pleasant, everyday wines, especially the rich and slightly spicy Grillo. These and other local varieties are used in the improving DOCs of Alcamo and

Traditional winemaking facilities and rugged landscapes are an inspiring feature of Sicily

Etna. However, many of the best dry wines, such as Regaleali's Nozze d'Oro and Planeta's Chardonnay, are non-DOC.

The finest DOCs are those for sweet wines. Malvasia delle Lipari comes from a group of tiny islands to the north of Sicily, and there are several wines based on Moscato here, including the Muscat of Alexandria, sometimes known as Zibibbo. The best of these are Moscato di Pantelleria and Passito di Pantelleria from the island of – you guessed it – Pantelleria, which lies closer to Tunisia than to mainland Italy.

The Sicilian taste Sicilian dry whites are nutty and fresh, usually quite simple; sometimes with spicy, pine-like aromas and a slightly oily texture. Malvasia delle Lipari is a rich, honey-and-apricots wine, while Moscato di Pantelleria has flavours of orange and – in the case of *passito* styles – raisins, with the acidity to keep it in balance and help it age for around five years.

Where next? Sardinian dry white wines provide contrasts, and some similarly interesting sweet wines. Compare the sweeter Sicilian wines with Tuscan **Vin Santo**.

Soave

Soave, and occasionally sophisticated
Region Veneto
Grape varieties Garganega, Trebbiano, Chardonnay
Style Dry and nutty, with a creamy texture
Quality/Price *--->****/££--->££££

RECOMMENDED PRODUCERS

Anselmi
Boscaini
La Cappuccina
Ca' Rugate
Gini
Lamberti
Stefano Inama
Pieropan
Pra
Suavia
Zenato

Soave comes from the Veneto region, a sister to the red wines of Valpolicella and Bardolino. Originally the hills around the walled and castle-crested town of Soave produced good, everyday drinking wine for nearby Verona. These hills now constitute the central Soave Classico zone, but the flat, surrounding plains, where, year after year, characterless wine is produced on an industrial scale, have diluted both the wine and its reputation.

Things are looking up for Soave. Producers Pieropan and Anselmi have been largely alone in promoting serious Soave for many years, but now they have a growing band of young allies, as exemplified by Stefano Inama. Under new laws, the wines can now include up to 30 per cent Chardonnay to supplement Trebbiano and Garganega – and they have improved as a result. *Recioto* di Soave, a traditional but neglected style of Soave, is coming back into favour. Bunches of grapes are laid out to dry on racks in a shed. Early

Lofts are used to dry grapes for *recioto*, a northeast Italian white dessert wine

picking ensures good acidity; drying and shrivelling concentrate the sugar. Like *recioto* from Valpolicella, the end product is so concentrated that you can barely believe it has any connection with the standard stuff.

The Soave taste Straight Soave is as often as not bland and anonymous, but Soave Classico from the best producers derives its medium weight from the greater concentration produced by lower yields. It is very lightly perfumed, almondy and dry, with a texture variously described as creamy, oily or even silky. The arrival of Chardonnay has added more peachiness to the fruit. Although Soave is meant to be drunk young, some of the best single-vineyard wines can still taste surprisingly good seven to eight years after the vintage. *Recioto* di Soave is a rich, golden, honeyed wine, rarely as luscious as Sauternes, but with creamy, ripe fruit to the fore.

Where next? See how top Soave measures up against other northern Italian whites from **Piedmont**, **Trentino-Alto Adige** and **Friuli-Venezia Giulia**.

RECOMMENDED PRODUCERS

Arrowood
Benziger
Carmenet
Chalk Hill
Château St Jean
Clos du Bois
De Loach
Dry Creek

Sonoma

Napa without the hype

Grape varieties Chardonnay, Sauvignon Blanc
Style Fine, fruity Chardonnays; dry and minerally Sauvignons
Quality/Price ***⋯⋯⟩*****/£££⋯⋯⟩£££££

After a tour around neighbouring Napa, a visit to Sonoma is a welcome relief. Carefully pressed jeans and shoulder pads are refreshingly absent. The folk here look relaxed and talk relaxed, and sometimes even forget to say, "Have a nice day". The wines, however, are just as serious as Napa's.

Sonoma is rather more higgledy-piggledy than Napa. The Carneros region, at the southern end of the valley, extends into Napa, and the breezes coming off the San Francisco Bay produce a cool climate that is ideal for Chardonnay vines. Travelling north into Sonoma Valley, red wines begin to dominate, although Matanzas Creek on the southeastern outskirts of Santa Rosa makes fine Chardonnay and Sauvignon Blanc.

The Russian River Valley extends west and north of Santa Rosa. The Russian River itself flows eastwards to the sea, and the fogs it sends up the valley make this excellent Chardonnay country. The Dry Creek, Alexander and Knights valleys lie to the north and tend to be red territory, although pockets of Sauvignon Blanc and Chardonnay can be found.

Yes, with the exception of a fair amount of Sauvignon Blanc, white wine in Sonoma means Chardonnay – which is a pity, as the few Rieslings and Gewürztraminers that can be found in this region are superb, as is Arrowood's Viognier. The sparkling wines, especially those of Iron Horse, are also worth looking out for.

RECOMMENDED PRODUCERS CONTINUED

Gallo Sonoma
Geyser Peak
Hanzell
Iron Horse
Jordan
Kenwood
Kistler
Matanzas Creek
Peter Michael
Quivira
Rochioli
Simi
Sonoma Cutrer
Marimar Torres

Climatic conditions such as fog, influence winemaking decisions in Sonoma

The Sonoma taste The best Sonoma Chardonnay is complete and complex wine, with various fruits (apples, peaches, mangoes, pears) flitting into the picture, backed up with biscuity characters and hints of butter. There is sometimes a rather heavy hand with the oak, but most wines calm down with time in bottle. Sauvignons vary from dry, pithy and minerally to big, rich quasi-Chardonnays, encased in smoky oak.

Where next? See how the best **Chardonnays** of the Russian River Valley compare with those of **Carneros** or of the regions south of San Francisco; plus try the Central Coast wines (*see* **Monterey and San Francisco Bay**).

South Australia

The engine room of Australian wine
Best-known wines Eden and Clare Valley Riesling
Grape varieties Riesling, Chardonnay, Semillon, Sauvignon Blanc
Style Err, Australian
Quality/Price ** ⸱⸱⸱⸱⸳> **** / £ ⸱⸱⸱⸱⸳> £££££

Vines are planted to follow every contour of the landscape in South Australia

South Australia is far and away the largest wine-producing state in Australia, churning out some 60 per cent of the country's wines. The Riverland region alone, sprawling along the banks of the Murray River towards the state borders

with Victoria and New South Wales, is responsible for over a quarter of all Australian wine. But, if this sounds to you like an emphasis on quantity rather than quality, think again, for the beauty of South Australian wine is that it meets the needs of every section of the market, whatever the price range.

Some of Australia's finest Rieslings, Semillons, Sauvignon Blancs and Chardonnays are produced here. Adelaide Hills is the trendy region, while the Barossa, Clare and McLaren Vale are prime sources of brilliant-value, full-flavoured wines with a few stars into the bargain. South of Adelaide, on what has become known as the Limestone Coast, red grapes rule in Coonawarra, but nearby districts such as Padthaway, Robe, Mount Benson and Wrattonbully are showing great promise.

And then there is the Riverland. Production here is vast. The region is basically a desert through which the wide, sluggish Murray River ambles like a wandering strand of rogue spaghetti. If it rains, it makes national headlines. Irrigation is everything, and quality is typically basic – by Australian standards. (If only cheap Californian, Italian and Spanish wines were so reliable and had so much flavour.) There are even some finer wines from companies such as Angove's, Berri Renmano and Kingston Estate: rich, full-flavoured Chardonnays that are not afraid to flex their boomerang-throwing muscles, and Sauvignon Blancs which may lack subtlety but are honest and full of varietal flavour.

Where next? Compare the cheaper wines with those made in similar conditions in **Victoria** (Mildura) and **New South Wales** (Riverina), or in the central valleys of both **California** and **Chile**. See specific entries for **Adelaide Hills**, **Barossa**, **Clare**, **Coonawarra** and **McLaren Vale**.

Southwest France

In search of a corporate identity
Best-known wines Jurançon, Monbazillac and
Vin de Pays des Côtes de Gascogne
Grape varieties Sauvignon, Sémillon, Muscadelle,
Mauzac, Manseng, Len de l'Elh
Style Diverse and fascinating
Quality/Price **⋯⋯⟩****/£⋯⟩££££

RECOMMENDED PRODUCERS
De Bachen
Berticot
Du Bouscassé
Brana
Lafitte-Teston
De Laulan
Montus

This region would be rather better known were it not for the fact that it surrounds a rather more prestigious wine-producing area – Bordeaux. Many of the wines of the southwest pay homage to their famous neighbour, using Sauvignon, Sémillon and Muscadelle to fashion (CONTINUED ON PAGE 136)

Sparkling Wine

Who needs a corkscrew?

Sparkling wines are mood-lifters. A glass or two of fizz not only tantalises the taste buds but makes the world a friendlier place. It is no surprise, then, that in practically every country where wine is made, you'll find some frothy versions: England, Venezuela, Luxembourg... even India. Its sheer ubiquity is testament to the almost magical alliance of wine and carbon dioxide (CO_2).

For CO_2 is what the bubbles are made of. There are several different ways of making sparkling wines. The easiest is simply to pump CO_2 into a wine as happens with lemonade. This method is a bit primitive – the bubbles are usually rather large and they don't hang around too long – but it works. Probably the oldest technique is the *méthode rurale*, where the wine is bottled before it has completed its alcoholic fermentation, which is then finished off in the bottle, thus giving the wine some fizz. This method is not easy to regulate, so is rare; although Blanquette Méthode Ancestrale, the Rhône's Clairette de Die, and Gaillac are still made in this way.

All other ways of creating bubbles in wine involve a second fermentation. The most sophisticated of these techniques is the *méthode champenoise*, which, if not invented in Champagne itself, was certainly perfected there. Wine is made in the normal way and fermented; before bottling, yeast and sugar are stirred in, which produces both carbon dioxide and alcohol. Since the wine is already in bottle, the gas has no way to escape, so it is forced to dissolve in the wine. There is one snag, however. The dead yeast cells and spent nutrients fall to the bottom of the bottle and

The traditional process of *remuage* is a crucial and painstaking part of Champagne-making

form a sediment known as the lees, which will eventually have to be removed. The amount of time a wine spends in bottle on its lees adds a rich creaminess and a depth of flavour to it, and some Champagnes remain there for several years.

Eventually, however, the lees must be removed. To do this, the bottles are gradually shifted from a horizontal position to an upside-down vertical, a process called *remuage*, or riddling, so that the sediment collects in the bottleneck. Traditionally, *remuage* was done by hand, with skilled workers twiddling the bottles daily to slowly shake the sediment downwards.

Today, there are many producers, even in Champagne, using computer-controlled machinery to replicate *remuage* and save time. An even quicker *remuage* is possible with porous capsules, or *billes*, that allow the yeasts access to the liquid but are tight enough to prevent them from escaping into it. A flick of the wrist is all that is needed to get the *billes* to sink to the necks.

Once the sediment has collected on the base of the cork, the neck of the bottle is frozen in cold brine, the bottle turned right-way-up and the cork removed. The plug of sediment and frozen wine shoots out. The wine has been "disgorged", and only a little is lost because low temperature has reduced the pressure. The bottle is topped up straight away with a syrupy liquid known as the *liqueur d'expédition*, which usually contains some sugar, or *dosage*. The customary cylindrical cork is tapped in, which swells to a mushroom shape by the time we remove it.

While all Champagne is made this way, many other sparkling wines around the world are also produced by this method. However, due to EU regulations, they must label their wines using terms such as *méthode traditionelle*, *méthode cap classique* (South Africa) and *"fermented in bottle"*.

The transfer method begins in a fashion similar to *méthode champenoise*, until it is time for the yeasts to be removed. The wine is then emptied into a tank, filtered, and returned to a new bottle. For the tank method (also known as *cuve close* or Charmat), the second fermentation takes place in a sealed tank, after which the wine is filtered and bottled. In theory, these two methods should be able to produce something that tastes every bit as good as the *méthode champenoise* wines, but the base wines of the former tend to be inferior, and the time spent on the lees – whether in tank or bottle – is usually far shorter. The results reflect these factors.

The grape varieties that are best suited to making sparkling wines are those with more neutral flavours, since any aromatic flavours are magnified by the bubbles. Chardonnay, Pinot Noir, Pinot Gris and Pinot Blanc are the most favoured. In additiion, a high level of acidity in the base wines is another must – which is why cooler regions tend to produce the finest wines.

In France, many fizzes are produced (*see* regional entries). Italy is one of the fizziest countries in the world, Germany has its vast Sekt industry, and Spain boasts generally undemanding but good-value Cava.

The US, New Zealand, Australia and South Africa have succeeded in making good commercial sparkling wines, with a few examples showing genuine class. Their potential has been demonstrated by the number of prestigious Champagne firms setting up ventures in these countries.

Where next? Can anything follow fizz?

wines that are every bit as tasty as, and often better than, similarly priced Bordeaux wines. Sadly, however, the dry and sweet wines of Bergerac, Côtes de Duras, Montravel and Monbazillac will never enjoy the same cachet as their neighbour – whatever their quality.

Not all southwest whites are fashioned after Bordeaux. Jurançon uses Gros and Petit Manseng as well as Courbu to make some fascinating wines of various sweetnesses. The same grapes also feature in the blends for Pacherenc du Vic-Bilh (an appellation that covers the same area as the red-only Madiran) Irouléguy along the Spanish border south of Biarritz and the VDQS Tursan. Some wines from these districts, notably Bouscassé's sweet Pacherenc de Vic-Bilh and Château de Bachen's rich, oaky Tursan, can be very classy.

Dry Gaillac is tangy, appley and good value, while the sparkling version, made by the *méthode Gaillaçoise* (*see* **Gaillac**), is fascinating stuff. Also good value are the wines of the VDQS Côtes de St-Mont and the Vin de Pays des Côtes de Gascogne.

Where next? To **Bordeaux** for the **Sauvignon-Sémillon** wines, otherwise eastwards to **Languedoc-Roussillon** to see the closest competitors. See also specific entries for **Bergerac**, **Côtes de Gascogne**, **Gaillac**, **Jurançon** and **Monbazillac**.

Stellenbosch

RECOMMENDED PRODUCERS
L'Avenir
Jordan Vineyards
Longridge Winery
Louisvale
Meerlust
Mulderbosch Vineyards
Neethlingshof
Neil Ellis Wines
Pongrácz
Rustenberg (Brampton)
Saxenburg Wines
Simonsig
Stellenzicht
Thelema
Uitkyk
Vergelegen
Vriesenhof

The Napa Valley of South Africa
Grape varieties Chardonnay, Sauvignon Blanc, Chenin Blanc
Style Crisp, citric Chardonnays, improving Sauvignon Blanc
Quality/Price **⋯⋯****/££⋯⋯££££

The inhabitants of Stellenbosch would never admit it, but it does seem to an outsider that their region is developing along very similar lines to California's Napa Valley, albeit 20 years later. As in Napa, there is a wide diversity of soils with granite, alluvial soils from former river beds, and sandstone often all appearing in a comparatively small area. There is a also wide variation in the climate. The vineyards around and to the north of the town of Stellenbosch are relatively hot, whereas those closer to the coast of False Bay – especially at the higher altitudes around Somerset West – are decidedly cool.

Red wine is the main focus, but nearly all producers are making whites with varying degrees of seriousness. Many are ignoring the variation in climate and simply planting vines in their existing vineyards, often in spots that are too warm for white grapes. Most wineries are extremely well equipped with stainless-steel tanks and French oak barrels, which visitors can examine before visiting the usual tasting room. The vineyards, meanwhile, are not getting quite the same attention. Thus it was in Napa in the 1970s and 1980s.

But just as in Napa, a growing number of people in Stellenbosch are not content simply to bask in the reflected glory of those around them. They are taking more of an interest in the soil and climate and planting their vines accordingly. They are also aware of developments in other parts of the world and are taking those on board that can help them the most. These are the people whose white wines (and usually their reds as well) stand out from the pack. These are the ones who are changing the reputation of Stellenbosch from that of a red-wine region to one where the whites can be just as fine. Let us hope the Napa pricing policy doesn't follow. And let's hope, too, that the rest of Stellenbosch catches them up soon.

The Stellenbosch taste The finest Sauvignons are racy and fresh, not quite as tropically rich as the Marlborough style, but with plenty of crisp, blackcurrant-leaf flavour. The finest Chardonnays have developed beyond the "here's the fruit, here's the oak" stage. They are now richer and fuller, showing more understated fruit flavours and more nutty, creamy notes. Chenin Blanc is the most widely planted grape, and some producers use it to make excellent fleshy, mango and honey-style wines, occasionally with a touch of botrytis. Those who bother to make Riesling and Gewürztraminer usually do a very good job, with the sweet wines from the likes of Neethlingshof ranking among the finest wines of the region.

Where next? Compare the **Chardonnays** and **Sauvignons** with those from **Paarl**, Constantia and Walker Bay, or from further afield regions such as **Marlborough**, **Adelaide Hills**, **Carneros** and Casablanca.

Tokáji

Phoenix from the ashes
Region Northeast Hungary
Grape varieties Furmint, Hárslevelü, Muskotály
Style Raisins, caramel, marmalade, apricots and honey
Quality/Price ***⋯⟩*****/£££⋯⟩£££££

RECOMMENDED PRODUCERS

Disznókö
Megyer
Oremus
Pajzos
Royal Tokáji Wine Company
Tokáji Wine Trust

Anyone who tasted Tokáji from Hungary's communist era would be a trifle baffled as to why it was considered one of the world's great wines. Quality was erratic. The wine undoubtedly had character, but it was debatable as to whether it was actually enjoyable. Today, new brooms have swept through the region, and we are beginning to see greatness reassert itself. For nomenclature's sake, Tokáji is the wine, while Tokáj is the region, in the northeast of Hungary. *Szamarodni*, meaning "as it comes", forms the bulk of all Tokáji produced, and can be dry (*szaraz*) or sweet (*edes*). However good as these can be, the region's reputation rests on the unique and luscious *aszú* wines, made from grapes that have shrivelled, either through noble rot or through exceptionally dry weather.

Aszú grapes are crushed to a paste and then added to an existing *szamarodni* wine of the same vintage. This initiates a second fermentation, and the resulting wine is then aged in barrel for a minimum of three years. The sweetness of the final wine is determined by the number of *puttonyos*, or buckets, of the *aszú* paste added to each *gönc* (cask) of base wine.

Tokájis of three, four and five *puttonyos* are fairly common; six *puttonyos* is only made in exceptional years, while the rare *Aszú* Eszencia is, in effect, an eight-*puttonyos* wine. Rarer still is the nectar called Tokáji Eszencia. As the *aszú* grapes sit around in their containers waiting to be crushed, gravity causes a syrupy, sweet liquid, sometimes up to 60 per cent sugar, to ooze out of them. Tokáji Eszencia is made from this heady fluid.

Among the foreign investors now in the region are insurance companies, Bordeaux châteaux owners and a British-led consortium including Hugh Johnson, and the wines they make are very different from those of the communist era. In the old method of production, the casks were not topped up, allowing a mould similar to *flor* (*see* **Sherry**) to develop on the surface of the wine, also encouraging oxidation. The new winemakers seek to control the effect of both the oxygen and this fungal growth. Some are also pushing for doing away with the barrel-ageing altogether so that the wines can be bottled while they are at their freshest.

The Tokáji taste The dry wines used to be like inferior sherry, but modern production methods have resulted in dry Furmint with good acidity and a tangy-lime flavour. Old-style Tokáji *Aszú* has hints of raisins, caramel and marmalade, with a nutty layer on top. Having done most of its oxidising in the barrel, it is capable of lasting for years – even decades – in bottle, becoming more treacly with age. The new wave of wines have the same sorts of flavours, but are fresher and more concentrated, with hints of apricots and honey from the botrytis. It is too early too say how they will age, but it will be fascinating to watch.

Where next? Old-style Tokáji can be similar to **Vin Santo** or to certain types of **Sherry**. Try a newer version alongside a classed-growth **Sauternes**.

Touraine

Where Chenin meets Sauvignon
Best-known wines Vouvray and Touraine Sauvignon
Grape varieties Chenin Blanc, Sauvignon Blanc
Style Fresh, green, grassy and crisp, with
a few honeyed delights
Quality/Price *>*****/£>£££££

Up the River Loire around Tours, past Anjou and Saumur, Sauvignon Blanc begins to muscle in on Chenin Blanc territory. The climate is among the mildest in France; fruit and vegetables grow so well that the region is known as the "Garden of France", a name adopted by a vast *vin de pays* region. The wines themselves could be said to have a vegetable-garden smell: fresh, green, grassy and crisp.

Touraine Sauvignon never scales the heights of Sancerre, but it's half the price and can be very good. Chenin still has the upper hand in the vineyards, making simple, dry and usually rather acidic wines in appellations such as Coteaux du Loir (no, not a misprint), Touraine-Amboise, Touraine-Mesland and Touraine itself. A step up are Jasnières from the heart of the Coteaux du Loir and Touraine-Azay-le-Rideau, while at the top of the Touraine tree are the wines of Vouvray and the less well-known Montlouis. Both come in various stages of sweetness, and the best wines stand comparison with anything from Anjou-Saumur. There are also sparkling versions, often made in vintages when the Chenin did not ripen sufficiently to make table wines.

There is another white grape in the region called Romorantin, "a wine for those who revel in footnotes", according to Loire authority Jacqueline Friedrich. This grape, which makes wines along Chenin lines, but without as much fruit, is the speciality of vineyards around the village of Cheverny. Cheverny itself is now mainly Sauvignon Blanc, but Cour-Cheverny is 100 per cent Romorantin.

The Touraine taste Touraine Sauvignon has more zip and flair than many a Muscadet or dry Chenin Blanc, with tangy green fruit to boot. The dry Chenins can be dreadful – over-sulphured and under-ripe, with rapier-like acidity masking any fruit that might have been there. However, the best show crisp, appley fruit with hints of wax, honey and nuts.

Thanks to their acidity, these wines develop beautifully, often not reaching their peak for ten years or more. *Demi-sec* wines also range from abysmal to superb, so pick your producer with care. The greatest whites of Touraine are the nobly rotten *moelleux*, or sweet, wines of Vouvray and

Montlouis (and occasionally Jasnières). Splendidly rich and peachy with ripe Granny Smith apple, apricot, nut and honey flavours in their youth, they evolve a richer marmalade character with age, and are capable of lasting for decades (*see* **Vouvray**).

Where next? Upstream to **Sancerre** and **Pouilly-Fumé** for more **Sauvignon**, downstream to **Anjou-Saumur** for more **Chenin**.

Trebbiano

Pale and not very interesting
Style Err..
Grown in Italy, France

One cannot help feeling a little sympathy for this high-yielding grape variety, in spite of the fact that it produces some of the world's most boring wine. In countries where, for centuries, the water has been suspect, Trebbiano has provided a perfectly satisfactory and safe alternative: the wine is colourless, odourless and tasteless, but with a refreshing tang of acidity, and is available in copious quantities. Its freshness, inconsequential lightness and anonymity have been great attractions in societies where wine was regularly drunk at least twice a day. But these qualities in a wine are no longer highly valued outside southern Europe, and it is rather frowned upon these days. In a world where wine is drunk for pleasure rather than necessity and is expected to exhibit a distinctive presence, poor old Trebbiano has few friends.

However much we knock it – and most people do – we cannot hide the fact that it is Italy's most widely planted white variety. Any white Italian wine not called by a varietal name stands a good chance of containing some Trebbiano. In fact, under the name Ugni Blanc, it is France's most widespread, too, but the French have had the sense to turn this thin, acidic little wine into much more palatable Cognac and Armagnac.

Some Trebbiano is also grown in Australia, but even there it has never amounted to more than a blending component or a base for spirits and fortified wines. That, perhaps, is the clincher. If the Australians can't make anything interesting from it, then there really is no hope that some hitherto undiscovered quality will burst out and surprise the world.

The Trebbiano taste This is rather a contradiction in terms. The grape is one of the world's biggest croppers (and tastes like it), which is the reason it is so popular with growers. It has good acidity, which endears it to the spirit producers, but little else of note beyond a sort of vaguely winey feel; it varies from light- to medium-bodied. Occasionally, *very* occasionally in a few Italian dry wines such as Lugana or Trebbiano d'Abruzzo, it can show a little more personality and greater richness. And when used in *vin santo*, it can even be very good, although never as good as when Malvasia is used instead.

Where next? Try Italian wines in which Trebbiano plays a part, but where the dominant variety – **Malvasia**, Grechetto, Garganega, etc – calls the shots (*see* **Italy**).

Trentino-Alto Adige

Crisp and cool
Grape varieties Chardonnay, Gewürztraminer, Goldenmuskateller, Müller-Thurgau, Pinot Bianco, Pinot Grigio, Rosenmuskateller, Sauvignon Blanc, Sylvaner
Style Fresh as a daisy, crisp, light and fruity
Quality/Price **⋯⟩****/££⋯⟩£££££

RECOMMENDED PRODUCERS
Maso Cantanghel
Cantina Viticoltori di Caldaro
Castello Schwanburg
Ca' Vit
CP Colterenzio
Ferrari
Franz Haas
Hirschprunn
J Hofstätter
Aluis Lageder
Mezzacorona
Josef Niedermayr
Pojer & Sandri
CP San Michele Appiano
Cantina Terlano
Tiefenbrunner
Vallarom
Cantina Sociale La Vis

Although the regions of Trentino and Alto Adige are lumped together for administrative purposes, they are in fact very different. Trentino forms the southern half of the region, stretching down from the town of Trento to the northern reaches of Lake Garda. The wines made here are usually varietal, with a huge selection of grapes allowed in the Trentino DOC. If no grape variety appears on the label, the wine will probably be a blend of Chardonnay and Pinot Bianco. Some of the sparkling wines form Trentino can be excellent. Given the climate and the many varieties planted, perhaps there should be some more top-class wines. As they are, they are usually simple and crisp, ideal to sip while admiring the spectacular local scenery, but seldom as heart stopping.

Further north lies Alto Adige. But hang on: why are the road signs printed in German as well as Italian? It all becomes clear when you learn that Alto Adige, or the Südtirol (Southern Tyrol) as German-speakers call it, used to be part of Austria, and was only ceded to Italy in 1921. Many of the region's people still have not fully made the transition. It is just as beautiful here as in Trentino, although slightly cooler, with more of an Alpine landscape.

Alto Adige makes some of Italy's cleanest, brightest, liveliest wines. Ten different white varietals take the Alto Adige DOC (also labelled "Südtirol" or

A castle
nestles in
the Alpine
vineyards of
the Trentino
region

"Süd Tyrol"). Within the DOC, there are five sub-appellations, the best-known of which are Terlano and Santa Maddalena/Sankt Magdalena. (Wines labelled "Valdadige" can come from anywhere in Trentino-Alto Adige, and are usually at the lower end of the quality spectrum.)

Quality here used to be as in Trentino: not as good as it should be. However, in recent years, the producers, including some excellent co-operatives, have been making strides with quality, and the wines are all the better for it. In addition, there are a few small estates whose wines rank as some of Italy's finest; the best known is Lageder.

The Trentino-Alto Adige taste
Trentino wines are generally softer and slightly less acidic than those of Alto Adige, but both are typically fresh, light, crisp, clean and dry. The flavour of the wines depends on the grape variety and the producer. Average yields here are high, a fact that accounts for the lightness of many wines, but the good guys understand that to make decent wines, you need decent grapes, so they tend their vines accordingly.

The Chardonnays are among the lightest anywhere: fresh and sometimes lightly peppery from their hello-goodbye encounter with an oak barrel. The best, such as Lageder's oak-aged Löwengang, smell of sweet cinnamon and nutmeg in their youth, and age gracefully to buttered-toast maturity. Gewürztraminers are delicate, even ethereal, with scents of rose water. The village of Tramin, in Alto Adige, is the supposed source of Traminer, a less "spicy" variant of Gewürztraminer.

Riesling is one of the few wines that does need ageing to bring out its best. In youth, it can be feather-light and undistinguished, but with time (and from a good producer) it deepens in colour and matures into a powerful, honeyed but dry wine of great class. Müller-Thurgau does amazingly well in Alto Adige, too, and on occasions can be piercingly austere, crisp, dry, steely and rather serious. Even plain Sylvaner can be perfumed and attractive here.

Sauvignons are variable, most lacking the incisive fruit that the grape produces elsewhere, while Pinot Grigio and Pinot Bianco (*see* **Pinot Gris** and **Pinot Blanc**) both make generally sound wines, but without the racy, edgy excitement of other varietals. Muscat (called Moscato Giallo or Goldenmuskateller) makes pure and simple wines varying from dry to sweet, which are freshly grapey and easy to enjoy. Sparklers range from Chardonnay with bubbles to some of Italy's finest *méthode champenoise* wines.

Where next? First of all, see what **Friuli-Venezia Giulia** does with the same varieties, then venture northwards to **Austria** and **Switzerland** for wines made in similar conditions.

Tuscany

Proceed with caution
Best-known wines *Vin santo*
Grape varieties Trebbiano, Malvasia, Chardonnay, Sauvignon Blanc
Style From bland to burgundy
Quality/Price *⋯⟩****/£⋯⟩£££££

RECOMMENDED PRODUCERS

Villa Banfi
Baroncini
Caparzo
Castello di Ama
Falchini
Felsina-Berardenga
Frescobaldi
Isole e Olena
Le Macchiole
Manzano
Melini
Ornellaia
Panizzi
Querciabella
Ruffino
Tenuta del Terriccio
Terrabianca
Teruzzi e Puthod

Tuscan reds are great. The whites, however... Well, with the exception of the superb *vin santo*, it's the same story in Tuscany as in much of central Italy, with Trebbiano being the driving force behind a number of DOCs, none of which will ever amount to much. The best that can be said about the wines is that they are inoffensive. Montescudaio and Montecarlo have more personality than most.

The best local grape is Vernaccia, a variety apparently unrelated to others of the same name in Sardinia and other regions. In the environs of San Gimignano, a glorious turreted medieval town, the grape can become a fine and unusual white wine made without the addition of any Trebbiano. It can become a bland and boring one also, so tread carefully.

However, Tuscany's finest dry whites today are almost all made from Chardonnay. Frescobaldi's Pomino Il Benefizio led the way, but now many of the Tuscan producers have some in their vineyards, and the wines can be

Volpaia has
the highest
vineyards
in the Chianti
Classico area
of Tuscany

excellent. Sauvignon Blanc has not caught on as much, although the wines from Ornellaia and Le Macchiole are first rate. Apart from *vin santo*, sweet whites are rare, but a few producers make fine Moscadello di Montalcino.

The Tuscan taste The best Vernaccia is a stylish and elegant, fresh-tasting, slightly creamy wine with a nutty hint and a slightly bitter finish. The Chardonnay is Chardonnay, malleable and ranging from simple, fresh and unoaked to wines that could pass for *premier cru* white burgundy.

Where next? If you really want more **Trebbiano, Italy** has plenty of it. As an alternative to Vernaccia, try **France's Gaillac**. Instead of Tuscan **Chardonnay**, try Chardonnay from **Piedmont, Friuli-Venezia Giulia, Trentino-Alto Adige…**

RECOMMENDED PRODUCERS

Adami
Bortolin Spumante
Canevel Spumante
Carpenè Malvolti
Cavalchina
Col Vetoraz
Desiderio Bisol
Le Vigne de San Pietro
Maculan
Angelo Ruggeri
Vignalta

Veneto

Not just Soave, but not much more
Best-known wines Soave
Grape varieties Trebbiano, Garganega, Tocai, Prosecco
Style Simple, dry whites; light, appley sparklers
Quality/Price *⋯⟩****/£⋯⟩£££££

Trebbiano features in many of the wines, as does Soave's other ingredient, Garganega. Bianco di Custoza is a lively Soave look-alike, while Gambellara, to the east of Soave, must be a minimum of 80 per cent Garganega. Further east still lie the

DOCs of Colli Berici, Colli Euganei and Piave, home of some rather insipid varietal wines and blends, although the occasional Chardonnay and Sauvignon can be pleasant. Breganze is far more interesting, with Maculan's sweet duo Torcolato and Acininobili. Prosecco di Conegliano-Valdobbiadene, or Prosecco (as most people know it), is the sparkling wine Venice drinks. While it never rises to great heights, it can offer a dry and agreeable style, providing it is consumed while young.

The Veneto taste The raw ingredients are mostly uninspiring, so it takes a very good producer to instil character into a wine. With the odd exception such as Maculan, Soave is responsible for the best and the worst of the region, with the other wines falling in style between the two extremes. Prosecco is light and dry, with the best (freshest) wines having a scent of apples and almonds.

Where next? Trentino-Alto Adige and Friuli-Venezia Giulia are both considerably better for white wines. Try **Cava** as an alternative to Prosecco.

Verdicchio

At least it has more character than Trebbiano
Region the Marches
Style Crisp and lemony, with nutty, honeyed hints
Quality/Price *····⟩***/£····⟩£££

This wine, produced in the unfashionable Marches region on the eastern flank of Italy, is made from the fragile, local and eponymous vine, said to date back some 1,500 years. It yields an attractive wine that is light and delicate in style, but it is known worldwide not so much for its taste as for its bottle: a curvaceous *amphora* cleverly promoted by local exporters. Verdicchio dei Castelli di Jesi is the best-known version, but there is also Verdicchio di Matelica, for which the permitted yields are lower – meaning the wine should be better.

The Verdicchio taste Young Verdicchio is lean and lemony, but with an extra year in bottle it develops a more rounded, honeyed, nutty character. Oaked Verdicchios can seem like mini-burgundies, and the sparkling versions can be good, too.

Where next? Cross the Apennines for **Tuscany**'s whites, or go north to **Friuli-Venezia Giulia**.

Victoria

We *are* amused
Best-known wines Liqueur Muscat
Grape varieties Chardonnay, Sauvignon Blanc, Riesling,
Muscat, Marsanne, Pinot Gris
Style Huge variety
Quality/Price **⋯⟩*****/££⋯⟩£££££

South Australia may produce more wine, but Victoria has more wineries than any other state in Australia – 322 of them, in fact, at the start of 1999. If many of them are not better known, it is probably because more than half make fewer than 4,000 cases of wine a year. Victoria does have its high-volume producers around Mildura in the northwest of the state, where the Murray River provides plentiful water for irrigation. As over the border in South Australia's Riverland, quality is admirable given the quantities concerned.

More interesting are the many smaller wineries dotted about the state. Rutherglen, in the northeast, is the most famous district, best known for its astonishing Liqueur Muscats and Tokays. It's hot here – baking hot – but you don't have to travel too far south to find much cooler pockets of land around Wangaretta, where some surprisingly elegant Chardonnays can be found. Indeed, to look at a map of Victoria, it seems as if someone has taken a bag of wineries and scattered them willy-nilly, a few here, a few there, with only the Yarra Valley receiving a healthy sprinkling.

Generally speaking, the further south the region, the cooler it is. The Mornington Peninsula, Gippsland, Geelong, the Yarra and the Macedon ranges are the cool spots, although conditions are far from uniform within these regions. The vineyards of Bendigo, the Pyrenees, the Grampians and the Goulburn Valley are generally warmer, although again, there is variation.

Victoria has a great history for sparkling wines, with the town of Great Western having produced it since the 1860s. Irvine's White (Ondenc) and Chasselas were the grapes used for many years, but now Pinot Noir and Chardonnay are the preferred varieties.

Chardonnay is also grown widely throughout the state for impressive still wines. Sauvignon Blanc is less popular, although the success of Taltarni and a few others with the grape shows that this is only for want of trying. Riesling can be excellent, although again, it is not exploited to the full. Some lovely wines are made from Pinot Gris, Verdelho and Gewürztraminer. In addition, the Goulburn Valley, home to Chateau Tahbilk and Mitchelton, has extensive plantings of Marsanne which dwarf those of the Rhône.

The Victoria taste Chardonnay covers all shades of the spectrum, from light and fruity in Mildura to rich, oaky and definitely Aussie. The best, which seem to come from wherever a winemaker sets his or her mind to make fine Chardonnay, are complex, thrilling wines.

Marsanne has a light, honeysuckle and peach flavour in its youth, but over five to ten years it develops more honeyed and resinous, gum-like flavours, with a rich, sweet scent like jasmine. Some of the sparkling wines (Hanging Rock) think they're Bollinger, but most are in the elegant style of Australian: forward and fruity, but with toasty, yeasty hints.

The quirkiest fizzes are those made from the red Shiraz variety, which are throaty and packed with sweet, spicy liquorice and berry fruit. They last for ages as well: when Seppelt's 1946 was last teasted it was still going strong. But, the big question is... should this style really be included in a book about white wine?

Where next? Range around **Australia** for equal value and interest, and across to **Western Australia** in particular. See also specific entries for **Liqueur Muscat and Tokay** and **Yarra Valley**.

Vin Doux Naturel

What's *Naturel* about it?
Region Southern France (mostly)
Grape varieties Usually Muscat
Style Heady marmalade, occasionally floral
Quality/Price **⋯⟩****/£££⋯⟩££££

Vin doux naturel (VDN) is France's answer to the fortified wines of Spain and Portugal. The French wines are not as famous, but they are made in a similar way. Fermentation is stopped by the addition of alcohol (grape spirit), so the wine has a high strength; its sweetness comes entirely from the unfermented grape juice that remains in it.

The Mediterranean coast and the Rhône Valley are the centres of production. Some *vins doux naturel* are based on the red Grenache grape, but the best known are made from Muscat. Foremost among these is the light, flowery Muscat de Beaumes-de-Venise from the Rhône Valley. Those from the Mediterranean are weightier and usually not quite as subtle.

Muscat de Frontignan, from the town of that name along the coast from Montpellier, is the pick of the Mediterranean bunch, with those of Lunel, Mireval and Rivesaltes close behind. Most are made with the superior Muscat Blanc á Petits Grains, although Muscat de Rivesaltes can also be made from

Muscat of Alexandria, which produces a heavier, coarser wine. Wines labelled Rancio come from casks that have been kept in warm conditions in order to impart a certain flavour to the wine.

A variation on the VDN theme is *vin de liqueur* (VDL), which involves the grape juice being "muted" by alcohol before the fermentation has a chance to get going. These are usually sweeter and simpler wines, but the fresher fruit taste can be welcome. Pineau des Charentes, which comes from over near the Atlantic coast, is made in this style, but with Cognac rather than just plain grape spirit.

The Vin Doux Naturel taste If you can imagine a cross between the taste of Asti Spumante (without the froth) and white port, then fortified Muscats are something like that. If you can't, then crack open a bottle.

In the Mediterranean wines, you will find flavours of honey, raisins and slightly cooked citrus fruit – like marmalade or candied orange peel. *Rancio* wines have a nutty edge and more intense flavours. Pineau des Charentes is sweet and grapey, and best drunk well chilled as an *apéritif*.

Where next? The strong, sweet Moscatel de Setúbal of JM da Fonseca is produced in a similar way to VDNs (*see* **Portugal**). Muscat of Samos (*see* **Greece**) and Moscato di Pantelleria (*see* **Sicily**) are other fine Mediterranean **Muscat**s.

Vin Santo

Holy, holy, holy
   Region Mainly Tuscany, also Trentino-Alto Adige, Umbria,
   Veneto, the Marches
      Grape varieties Malvasia, Trebbiano
      Style Intense and sweet, with marmalade, nuts,
      apricots and creamy notes
         Quality/Price **⋯⟩*****/£££⋯⟩£££££

Italy's "holy wine" is a rich, sweet, earthy concoction that was traditionally made by hanging bunches of grapes to dry from the beams of smoky country kitchens before fermentation. Today, the grapes are dried on straw mats before vinifying, and the "real thing" still has high status in Italy, especially in Tuscany. Unfortunately, there are quite a few wines that claim to be the real thing and are not. The best are made from Malvasia, perhaps with a small amount of Trebbiano (rather than the other way around). They are aged in barrels called *caratelli* and are sometimes kept under the roof-tiles for as many as eight years in order to develop their characteristic nutty, marmalade and apricot flavours.

Other good *vin santo* is made outside Tuscany in the Marches region, the Gambellara area of the Veneto, in Trentino-Alto Adige and in Umbria; in fact, the wine is made all over Italy on an *ad hoc* basis for family use.

The Vin Santo taste The best *vin santo* starts as gold and ages to deep bronze, developing a spicy richness together with flavours of dried apricots, citrus peel, honey, apples, barley sugar, caramel and more. Yum.

Where next? Old-fashioned **Tokáji** bears a certain resemblance, although it is always sweet. Other Mediterranean wines such as **Málaga** and Moscato di Pantelleria offer similar tastes.

RECOMMENDED PRODUCERS
Avignonesi
Capezzana
Castello di Cacchiano
Il Poggiolo
Isole e Olena
Le Pupille
Pieve Santa Restituta
San Giusto a Rentennano
Selvapiana
Tenuta di Salviano
Tenuta Sant' Agnese

Vinho Verde

Everything's gone green!
Region The Minho, northwest Portugal
Grape varieties Loureiro, Alvarinho, Trajadura, Paderña, Azal, Avesso
Style Light and lemony, with high acidity and hints of apples
Quality/Price *---⟩***/££---⟩£££

RECOMMENDED PRODUCERS
Casa de Sezim
Palacio da Brejoeira
Quinta da Aveleda
Quinta de Azevedo
Quinta da Franqueira
Solar das Bouças

Vinho Verde, the "green wine" of northern Portugal, does not look green; in fact, more than half of it is red. It is not named after the lush countryside where the grapes are grown, although the vigorous foliage does contribute to the overall effect. Nor is it grown organically, although vines here are traditionally manured by cows rather than by bags of chemicals. It is called green wine because it is made to be drunk young.

This is Portugal's largest demarcated wine region, stretching nearly 160 km (100 miles) from just south of Oporto and the River Douro up to the Minho River. Vinho Verde was, and for some producers still is, a cottage industry, with vines being planted around the edges of fields, climbing up trees or slung between posts, leaving room for maize, tomatoes, cabbages and kiwi fruit underneath.

Traditionally, the wine was bottled so soon after fermentation that it underwent a secondary, or malolactic, fermentation in bottle, producing carbon dioxide which dissolved in the wine. This is why, when the bottle is

Portugal's
Costa Verde is
home to
"green" wine
and traditional
winemaking

opened, it produces a very light sparkle, or *pétillance* – a slight prickle on the tongue that enhances the wine's refreshment value.

Faced with wider demand, growers and winemakers modified their methods, planting proper vineyards and standardising carbon dioxide levels. This has made for greater consistency, but something of the creamy quality of traditional Vinho Verde has been lost in the process. It was also sweetened to reduce its searing tartness for the "international palate".

Today, some producers have recognised that modernisation may have gone too far, particularly with regard to sweetness. There are now drier Vinho Verdes available internationally, some from single estates, which are closer to the original style. Most wines are blends of different grapes, but Alvarinho and Loureiro sometimes appear as varietal wines.

The Vinho Verde taste In Portugal, white Vinho Verde is dry, low in alcohol (typically nine per cent) and, because of its very high acidity, almost tear-jerkingly refreshing. It is pale in colour, light and lemony, and varies in perfume according to the grapes used. The freshness of flavour recalls grass, apples and mint. Wines made from Alvarinho are rich and more perfumed, with delicate, spicy, nutty fruit.

Where next? If high acidity is the attraction, then try a young **Chenin Blanc** from the **Loire**. If the acidity is too much, consider **Muscadet** or **Gaillac**. See how Alvarinho performs as **Albariño** in **Rías Baixas**.

Viognier

Spice up your life
Style Richly perfumed and honeyed, with nuts, musky pears and apricots
Grown in The Rhône, southern France and California, but now appearing all over the world

In the past, if you wanted to taste Viognier, there was only one place to go: the northern Rhône Valley, home of Condrieu and Château Grillet. But when the Syrah-based reds of the regions began to become more popular, outsiders began to take more notice of this most exotic of grape varieties. Growers in other parts of the world began to experiment with it, and the result is that it's currently one of the trendiest grape varieties around. Some people are even suggesting that it could be the next Chardonnay.

It won't be, however, and here's why. The word "capricious" is often used by the wine world to describe the nature of Viognier. It doesn't give its best 'till the vines are perhaps 15 years old; it's prone to diseases; it yields sparsely and it ripens irregularly. Put simply, it's a sod to grow, and that's why some growers in Condrieu often end up pulling up all their vines and becoming civil servants.

But capricious doesn't end there. In order to make decent Viognier, the grapes need to be ripe enough for the development of that exotic, musky perfume, yet not so ripe that sugar levels have soared while acidity has all but disappeared. In the winery, a small amount of skin contact (*see* **Chardonnay**) enhances that perfume, but too much makes the wine bitter. Malolactic fermentation properly handled can add richness, while in the wrong hands, the wine becomes a buttery caricature. Just enough oak, whether for fermentation or for ageing, can be beneficial. Too much can spoil a fragile equilibrium. Yet when a grower gets Viognier right, there is nothing else like it. The Rhône and California get it right most often. Southern France sometimes manages, but the grapes are usually picked before the flavours have fully developed, leaving a "nothing" of a wine. Australia and South Africa produce the odd version. There's even a little bit near Rome used to buoy up the Frascati of Castel de Paolis.

The Viognier taste The flavour should be rich and redolent of dried apricots, peaches and pears, with perhaps a dollop of honey. Above all, this most aromatic of grapes should have a heavenly scent. "Seductive", "heady" and other such adjectives of the senses usually come to mind. It's like Gewürztraminer in silk stockings.

Where next? Nothing beats great Viognier for over-the-top perfume. However, **Albariño** in **Rías Baixas**, **Gewurztraminer** and **Pinot Gris** in **Alsace** and elsewhere, and **Argentina**'s Torrontés provide attractive nasal assaults. The occasional high-alcohol Mâcon **Chardonnay** can also be wonderfully spicy.

Vouvray

RECOMMENDED PRODUCERS
Des Aubuisières
Clos Baudoin (Poniatowski)
Bourillon Dorléans
Marc Brédif
Didier Champalou
Du Clos Naudin
Gaudrelle
Huet

The versatility of Chenin Blanc
Region The Loire
Grape varieties Chenin Blanc
Style Apples, nuts, honey and wet wool
Quality/Price *·····⟩*****/££·····⟩£££££

All Vouvray is white, and all of it is made from the Chenin Blanc grape. There are no distractions from red or rosé – not even some Sauvignon to break the monotony. With two millennia to practice, you would expect this small French town upstream from Tours to be good at making wines by now, even from the pig of a grape that Chenin can often be in the Loire. And providing you pick your producer with care, you'd be right. Cheap Vouvray tastes worse than cheap, but great Vouvray is really great, and usually doesn't cost all that much more.

Vouvray can be dry, medium or sweet, still or sparkling. The sweetness level depends largely on weather conditions. Given a warm, dry summer and a long, sunny autumn, the grapes will ripen fully, and in a particularly good year they will be affected by botrytis. In such years, the harvest can continue into November, with the pickers making a number of *tries* (see **Sauternes**) through the vineyards. The rich, sweet, full-bodied, honeyed *moelleux* wines that result are the best that Vouvray produces, with a characteristic refreshing streak of Chenin Blanc acidity. Some producers only make this style of wine in such a vintage, while others will bottle *demi-sec* and dry versions as well. In lesser years when the grapes don't ripen as well, hardly any sweet wines are possible, so Vouvray tends to be dry. Fruit from such a vintage is also often used to make *méthode champenoise* sparkling wines, as the sharp, green acidity is ideal for fizz. While some of these can be excellent, the producers are far happier in the *moelleux* years.

The Vouvray taste As with all great Chenin Blanc from the Loire, Vouvray needs plenty of time in bottle to show its full class. The *moelleux* versions may be wonderfully opulent, with apricotty, botrytis character in their youth, but you only have to try a 20- or 30-year-old bottle to see what you're missing. They are beautifully balanced between soft richness and firm freshness, with flavours of honey and hazelnuts piling on to the pears and quince.

Even dry Vouvray benefits from a decade in bottle. Younger wines are crisp and appley, but definitely not telling the full story. Then with a little more age, the acidity begins to loosen its grip, and a gently nutty flavour emerges in the wine. Vouvray *demi-sec* is that rarity in the wine world: neither dry nor sweet, but a true medium wine. From a good producer, *demi-sec* Vouvray will develop the delicate and juicy fruit tastes of pears and quince. And it still has a streak of clean, refreshing acidity, even after the 15 or 20 years you have waited for it.

The sparkling wines, labelled Vouvray *mousseux* or Vouvray *pétillant* (for less fizzy versions), are at their best full-bodied, honeyed, toasty and appley, and are excellent value. Like all Vouvrays, they are also all the better for bottle age, both on the lees before disgorgement (*see* **Sparkling Wine**) and afterwards in the cellar.

Where next? Try the other **Chenins** of **Touraine** and **Anjou-Saumur**.

Washington State

Watch out, California
Grape varieties Chardonnay, Sémillon, Sauvignon Blanc, Pinot Gris, Riesling, Gewürztraminer
Style California meets France
Quality/Price **⋯⟩****/£££⋯⟩£££££

Washington Merlots and Cabernet Sauvignons are already on a par with all but the best California has to offer, and are getting better and better. However, the state's modern wine

RECOMMENDED PRODUCERS
Canoe Ridge
Château Ste-Michelle
Chinook
Columbia Crest
Columbia Winery
Covey Run
De Lille
Hogue
Kiona
L'Ecole 41

industry was founded on white grapes, and these still outnumber the reds. Riesling was the first to show any form, and still makes some of the finest wines. However, today it is Chardonnay and Sémillon that are proving the most popular and to which the producers are devoting the most effort.

Washington's vineyards lie mostly on the eastern side of the Cascade mountain range which runs down the west coast of North America. The Columbia Valley AVA (*see* **US**) covers the whole of the wine-growing region, taking in the smaller districts of Yakima Valley and Walla Walla. It is a climate of extremes, with hot, dry summers and winters where temperatures can dip to below -20 °C (-4 °F) for a fortnight or more. It would be impossible to grow vines if there were nothing to temper such a climate. Fortunately, the Columbia River and some of its tributaries flow through the area, warming the temperatures, providing irrigation water and making it possible to grow grapes. Even so, many vineyards are hit by severe frosts every few years. There would probably be far more vineyard development in the region but for the fact that you have to have rights to use irrigation water, and obtaining these is difficult – not to mention costly.

On the opposite side of the Cascades, vintners in the Puget Sound, near Seattle, have the opposite problem – too much water. Some producers make fair

Young vines in Washington's Yakima Valley are fed water by irrigation, with orchards growing alongside

Müller-Thurgau, but the damp climate is not ideal for growing grapes, and the region represents less than one per cent of Washington's total wine output.

The Washington taste Washington whites are seldom over the top in the way that California wines can sometimes be. Chardonnay is ripe but tangy, with apple and pear fruit and well-integrated oak. Gewürztraminer and Riesling are full of varietal flavour and always seem to have the right amount of balancing acidity, whatever the sweetness.

Sémillon can be excellent, pithy, lemony and slightly herbaceous on the nose, but followed by a lovely fat, waxy richness on the palate. Old examples simply don't exist, but it should age very well.

Where next? Head south to **California** and **Oregon**, or north to **Canada's British Columbia**.

Western Australia

Happy hunting ground
Best-known wines Margaret River Chardonnay
Grape varieties Riesling, Chardonnay, Muscat, Verdelho, Sauvignon Blanc, Semillon, Chenin Blanc
Style Wide range, but usually restrained, by Aussie standards
Quality/Price **⋯⟩****/££⋯⟩£££££

RECOMMENDED PRODUCERS
Alkoomi
Capel Vale
Chateau Barker
Chatsfield
Evans & Tate
Forest Hill
Goundrey
Houghton/Moondah Brook
Howard Park
Plantagenet
Salitage
Sandalford
Wignalls

It's as far from Perth, state capital of Western Australia (WA), to Sydney as it is from London to Moscow. The leap in mind-set is not as vast, but it does exist, and this means that the WA winemakers will do their best to outdo their eastern relations. Production makes up a small part of the national total, but some of Australia's finest wineries can be found here.

Margaret River in the southwest corner is the prime source of these, but not the only one. Roughly 242 km (150 miles) away on the south coast lies the Great Southern region, which takes in the towns of Albany, Denmark, Frankland and Mount Barker. The Chardonnay and Riesling from here can be as good as anything from Australia. There is also decent Sauvignon Blanc and some delicious, lightly sweet Muscat (from Plantagenet). Between these two regions lies Pemberton, not yet a household name, but a district in which many of Australia's largest companies are investing heavily and which already boasts a superb Chardonnay from Salitage.

Wineries are few and far between along the coast heading north from Margaret River to Perth, but Capel Vale in Bunbury shows that the region can make decent wine. The Swan Valley to the east of Perth is the nearest WA gets to large-scale production. Chenin Blanc and Verdelho perform very well here, given the hot conditions. This is where one of Australia's most famous wines originate. In order to cater for export markets, they've created names for this Chenin Blanc-based blend such as Supreme, but to Australians, it will always be Houghton's White Burgundy.

The Western Australia taste Conditions differ widely around the state, so the range of flavours is also wide. However, two styles do stand out. Swan River Chenin Blanc can be surprisingly tight in its youth, with peachy, lemon-lime fruit, but it ages remarkably well, developing a nutty, honeyed, honeysuckle character. Fifteen-year-old bottles can be a revelation. Great Southern Riesling is tight and pithy, not as citric as the best South Australian examples, but just as age-worthy.

Where next? The smaller wineries of **Victoria** are similarly widespread and quality-minded. See also **Margaret River**.

Yarra Valley

RECOMMENDED PRODUCERS
De Bortoli
Coldstream Hills
Chandon
Seville Estate
St Hubert's
Tarrawarra
Yarra Ridge
Yarra Valley Hills
Yarra Yering
Yeringberg

Good and getting better
Grape varieties Chardonnay, Sauvignon Blanc, Riesling, Marsanne
Style Tight yet full-flavoured Chardonnay
Quality/Price ***·····⟩****/£££·····⟩£££££

This beautiful region, about one hour out of Melbourne, was famous in the 19th century for its wines, but it only began to come alive again in the late 1960s, when a clutch of small wineries was established, and then later in the early 1980s.

The main problem the wines have had is in living up to the hype surrounding them. It was sometimes difficult for a visitor to Australia in the 1980s to comprehend how the locals could ignore the pleasures of a gutsy South Australian Shiraz in favour of a pleasant, but ultimately simple, Yarra Valley Chardonnay at three times the price. However, as the vines mature, and as the winemakers become more sensitive to their grapes, the quality is matching the publicity. And having seen the success of the small fry, the big guys such as Mildara-Blass and Penfolds are now investing in the region.

Chardonnay is the favoured variety by the wine producers here, but Sauvignon Blanc is also popular. A few wineries used to make excellent botrytis Riesling, but these days, it's rare. So, too, is Marsanne, although

Yeringberg makes a lovely version. If you needed proof that this was good sparkling-wine territory, you need look no further than the Domaine Chandon winery and vineyards.

The Yarra Valley taste The finest Yarra Chardonnay is richly textured, with restrained fruit flavours, lovely creamy hints and great length. Sparklers get better with each vintage, with the fruit again toned down but not extinguished, and the toasty/biscuity hints played up. The rosé versions have an attractive strawberry character.

Where next? **Victoria** has many small wineries in cool areas, albeit not as densely clustered as in the Yarra. See what is happening in the **Adelaide Hills** and **Margaret River** as well.

Zinfandel (White)

An exercise in colour blindness
Region California
Grape varieties Zinfandel
Style Banana and bubblegum to sweet berries
Quality/Price *⋯⟩***/£⋯⟩££

RECOMMENDED PRODUCERS
Beringer
Monterey Vineyard

It was one of the marketing successes of the 1980s. People didn't want to be seen buying anything called rosé, and Zinfandel, of which California has oodles, wasn't too popular. However, put the word "White" on the label, and, said the marketeers, it would race out of the door – especially if you made it quite sweet. They were right, too. Sales were enormous and everyone was happy.

Then came the 1990s and a rise in the popularity of red wine The Zinfandel vines were suddenly needed for their intended purpose, and anyone with a taste bud in their head breathed a sigh of relief. White Zinfandel is still big in the US, but many Americans are now getting their kicks from another sweetish wine which can justifiably call itself white – Chardonnay.

The White Zin taste The best are crisp and refreshing. Sweet, yes, but also with pleasant raspberry and blackberry fruit. The worst are stale, bland and best avoided.

Where next? Look at the **Rosé** section for several suggestions (or simply try Red Zinfandel).

White wine by country

France

The Boss
Best-known wines Champagne, Burgundy, Sauternes, Sancerre, Condrieu...

If imitation is the sincerest form of flattery, France should feel flattered indeed. With the exceptions of sherry, Tokáji and German Riesling, all the world's great white-wine styles originated in France, and it is still to France that we look in most cases for the finest examples. Le Montrachet is the best Chardonnay, no other sparkling wine can touch Champagne, Château d'Yquem represents the summit of sweet wine. French Pinot Gris, Viognier, Gewurztraminer and Chenin Blanc have yet to be bettered, and although the competition is stiffer when it comes to Sauvignon Blanc, Sémillon and Muscat, the best versions from France can still hold their own.

Move away from such mainstream varieties and there are other, less famous grapes that are no less interesting: Marsanne and Roussanne in white Hermitage, the Manseng family in the underrated Jurançon. Then there is an under-class of grapes which, while not as noble, can create fascinating wines. In the southwest, for instance, are Mauzac, Ondenc and Len de l'Elh, making sharp Gaillac; there is Jaquère in Savoie, and Savagnin in the Jura, making the

FRENCH WINE LAW

French wine law splits the country's wines into four categories.

• Largest, best known and theoretically best is the *appellation d'origine contrôlée*, known as AOC or simply AC. The AC does not guarantee quality, but it does (or should) guarantee that a wine comes from where the label says it does, is made from certain grapes and is produced in a certain way.

• Below this are *vins délimités de qualité supérieur* (VDQS), with similar controls to AC but for separate regions. This category has all but

disappeared as most have been promoted to AC.

• Less strictly controlled, *vin de pays*, or country wines, say on the label where they come from and (if the producers choose) what grapes they are made from. Vary from simple to modern classics.

• *Vin de table*, the everyday plonk of the working man, can be made from more or less any grapes, grown nearly anywhere; indeed any indication of such things on the label is strictly forbidden.

sherry-like *vin jaune*. They are not the sort of grape varieties anybody would rush off and plant in Oregon, but they are part of the richness of French life.

Of course, the French have always known that they made the best wine in the world, but in the 1970s, it seemed as though some upstarts in California and Australia were proving otherwise. Introspection in many of France's major wine regions had resulted in wines that did not live up to their historic billing – even if their prices did. Developments since then have been interesting. The good guys began to respond to the competition – not by imitation, but by cleaning up their vineyards and wineries, often as a result of a trip to see how they did things on the other side of the world. Their wines improved and continue to improve. Meanwhile, their neighbours persisted in their stagnant ways. Burgundy used to be the place of which it was said that the name of the producer was, if anything, more important than the vineyard from which the grapes came. The same is increasingly true in some other major regions.

Then there has been the renaissance in the south. Grapes have been grown in Languedoc-Roussillon for donkey's years, but the wines made from them were, in nearly all cases, crude and charmless; no one was too concerned that they never left the region. The introduction of the *vin de pays* category in 1973 changed that. Producers could now rip up their inferior vines and replace them with better varieties. The advent of new technology – and, in particular, temperature-controlled, stainless-steel tanks – meant they could turn out crisp, fresh whites which were far better than the turgid wines of old. Prices were lower, too. Of course, the successful versions created a bandwagon on which many rather less impressive wines have jumped.

That is France today. It displays greatness more often than any other country, it has more interesting grape varieties than anywhere else, yet there are still too many wines which do nothing to enhance its reputation. And, it is still the most fascinating country on earth for white wines.

Where next? See the specific entries on French wine styles and grapes: **Aligoté, Alsace, Anjou-Saumur, Bergerac, Blanquette de Limoux, Bordeaux, Burgundy, Chablis, Champagne, Chassagne-Montrachet, Condrieu, Côte Chalonnaise, Côte de Beaune, Coteaux du Layon, Côtes de Gascogne, Entre-Deux-Mers, Gaillac, Graves, Jura and Savoie, Jurançon, Languedoc-Roussillon, Loire, Mâconnais, Meursault, Monbazillac, Muscadet, Muscat de Beaumes-de-Venise, Pessac-Léognan, Pouilly-Fuissé, Provence, Puligny-Montrachet, Rhône, Sancerre and Pouilly Fumé, Sauternes and Barsac, Touraine, Vin Doux Naturel** and **Vouvray**.

Italy

Room for improvement
Best-known wines Asti, *vin santo*

In Sangiovese and Nebbiolo, Italy has two grapes that rank in the top ten red varieties from around the world. Several other of the country's red grapes are more than capable of staking claims for greatness. All of which means that it would be fair to assume that Italy would have a hoard of white varieties capable of challenging Chardonnay and Co. Well, yes. Absolutely. Of course. Well, *no* – actually.

Take away Muscat, which is hardly an Italian exclusivity, and there isn't a lot left. Sure, there are several component varieties, such as Cortese, Arneis, Favorita, Malvasia, Garganega, Verdicchio, Fiano and Greco do Tufo, but only the most patriotic of Italians would dare to suggest that they make the finest white wines in the world. Having the lacklustre Trebbiano as the most widely planted white variety speaks volumes, when neighbouring France usually thinks of it (as Ugni Blanc) as being suitable only for distillation. Even when the Italians get their hands on more interesting grapes – be they imported

varieties such as Chardonnay or Sauvignon Blanc, or indigenous ones – many seem to find it difficult to make a decent wine. A typical Italian white is pale in colour, crisp, dry and neutral. If you're lucky, it may have a slight nutty bite and some texture to it, but if you want anything else (flavour, for instance), then you're asking too much. "Ah, but they come into their own with food," you might say. Perhaps, but only because something so devoid of character could never clash with anything.

Part of the problem stems from the way the wines are made. Yields are high, so the flavours are less concentrated. In the warmer climates (and often in cool ones as well), the grapes are picked early while the acidity is still prominent and the flavours have not fully developed. Methods of production concentrate on accentuating squeaky-cleanness rather than character. In some cases, a prickle of carbon dioxide is left in the wine to make it appear fresher.

Of course, to demand high quality at all levels is unrealistic. Yet it is realistic to demand high quality at the highest level, and here Italy lets us down. It is almost as if the producers have expended so much effort in getting character into their red wines that they have hardly anything left for their whites.

In addition, the DOC system (*see* below) doesn't help those who want to produce good wines, or those who are looking for them. In areas best suited for white production, there is no equivalent of the Burgundian appellations to distinguish between which are the *premier* and *grand cru* vineyards. If DOCG is supposed to represent the summit of white wine, why does all Asti come into this category, and why, oh why, are Vernaccia di San Gimignano and Albana di Romagna DOCG? Naturally, there are exceptions. When producers in northern Italy (especially in Friuli-Venezia Giulia) set their minds to it, they can produce something spectacular. Many red wine estates in Piedmont and Tuscany have increasingly impressive whites in their portfolio, often made from Chardonnay. Flying winemakers, especially in southern Italy, have also made palatable Chardonnay, and in addition have alerted the outside world to the potential of varieties such as Greco di Tufo and Grillo.

Italian sparklers can also be interesting. Asti is the most famous, Lambrusco the most infamous. Good Lambrusco can be found, but it is dry and red rather than white or pink, and comes with a proper cork rather than a screw-top. If

ITALIAN WINE LAW

The DOC system, introduced in the mid-1960s, is an attempt to impose some sort of order on thousands of individualists. Originally, all wines fell into one of three categories:

• *Denominazione di origine controllata e garantita* (DOCG), supposedly the peak of vinous perfection, of which there are currently 14. The regulations stipulate means of production, grape varieties and origin, and Garantita, in theory, guarantees quality.

• *Denominazione di origine controllata* (DOC) is the next step down, DOCG minus the guarantee: there are over 250 DOCs.

• Other words you might see on DOC and DOCG wines are – *classico*: theoretically the best wines the region has to offer; *superiore*: generally a wine with slightly higher natural alcohol, although it, too, may refer to the area of production; *riserva*: which applies to higher-quality wines of a DOC or DOCG that have been aged for longer than usual.

• *Vini da tavola*, or table wine, is officially the lowest of the low. However, from the 1960s onwards, several producers, especially in Tuscany,

decided that they wanted to make wines which did not fit into the framework of the DOC laws.

Although these soon became some of Italy's finest and most expensive wines, they could only be called *vini da tavola*. New legislation in the 1990s has meant that from the 1996 vintage onwards, *vini da tavola* are forbidden to state their origins, grape varieties and vintages.

This latest development has given the producers of the *vini da tavola* two options. They can change to DOC status, either within an existing district where the laws regarding grape varieties and other issues have now been relaxed, or they can apply for their own DOCs. Alternatively, they can be classed as...

• *Indicazione geografica tipica* (IGT), the equivalent of the French *vin de pays*. Many of the *vini da tavola* now come under the IGT Toscana, for example.

you're after dry white fizz, look for wines from Franciacorta, the only DOCG specifically for sparking wines, and the only Italian fizz which must be made by the *méthode champenoise*.

Italy's greatest whites remain the sweet wines. Botrytis-affected versions can be found, but you're more likely to encounter wines made in the *passito* style. This involves drying grapes to concentrate their flavours before they are pressed, and it manages to instil some rich, raisiny flavour even into the humble Trebbiano. One step beyond is *vin santo* – literally "holy wine" – where a *passito* wine is fermented and aged in barrels for several years, acquiring a fabulous nutty, marmalade taste in the process. It is expensive to make, so beware of anything that seems cheap. Tuscany has the best versions.

Where next? See specific entries: **Asti**, **Emilia-Romagna**, **Frascati**, **Friuli-Venezia Giulia**, **Gavi**, **Lombardy**, **Marsala**, **Orvieto**, **Piedmont**, **Sardinia**, **Sicily**, **Soave**, **Trentino-Alto Adige**, **Tuscany** and **Vin Santo**.

Germany

Still in need of a Doktor
Best-known wines Liebfraumilch, Piesporter Michelsberg, Niersteiner Gutes Domtal

If the three wines listed above are Germany's best known outside the country, the Germans have only themselves to blame. One hundred years ago, connoisseurs in Britain and other parts of the world were prepared to pay as much for a bottle of hock or Mosel as they were for first-growth claret. Today, certain of the country's sweet wines are still priced at similar levels and higher, but demand for them is largely confined to the Germans themselves. Elsewhere, Germany is associated with bland, sugary fluids, the most famous of which is Liebfraumilch. The saddest aspect is that the country's great Rieslings, which can be the stuff of legend, are now associated with Lieb and Friends.

Yet this state of affairs was all very well for a while, as sales were buoyant, but then along came the New World. Chardonnay from all over the globe became the new Liebfraumilch, and Germany was suddenly *passé*. Lieb sales are still significant in countries such as Britain and the US, but each year sees other wine styles pinch market share. The Germans are aware of this, and have taken steps to redress the situation, but many of those steps have been sideways and even backwards. Campaigns to re-establish the reputation of the country's wines have largely ignored the very wine that made that reputation in the first place, focusing instead on developing alternatives at Lieb level.

There is very much an element of "if you can't beat 'em, join 'em" about these new wines. They are not packaged in the green or brown flute bottles;

they're dry; they're simply labelled; and they often have names that would not look out of place on wines from Australia, South Africa and elsewhere: Bend in the River, Devil's Rock, Fire Mountain and so on. As for flavour, in some instances it's a case of "*What* flavour?" It seems as if the producers – usually large co-operatives – are trying to make wines that taste like New World wines. Without the ripeness of fruit that is the New World hallmark, they are not succeeding. Most are perfectly pleasant – a definite improvement on the average Lieb – but they're not going to have drinkers flocking back for more.

Even if they do, those drinkers will come in for a shock when they realise that these new products are not at all representative of Germany's great wines, most of which are made from Riesling. Quite what style German Riesling should be is currently a matter of often heated debate. Some say that the wines should be dry, while others prefer sweetness to some degree. The latter is derived either from adding unfermented grape juice, known as *süssreserve*, to a finished wine in order to boost the sugar level, or from arresting the fermentation while there is still some unfermented (residual) sugar. Both camps maintain that theirs is the "traditional" style of wine.

For an outside observer, the argument boils down to one of balance. Riesling is a variety whose acidity is difficult for novices to accept. Something is needed to counter this acidity. With grapes from high-yielding vineyards, where the flavour is not huge and the grapes will often be less than fully ripe, sweetness is certainly the best way of balancing acidity, although the wines will never be great. If such a wine is fermented to dryness, its searing acidity will be the most prominent feature throughout the wine's life. However, if someone in a good vineyard exercises care with his vines, he will harvest riper grapes with more concentrated flavours, and the acidity could be lower as well. This is the person who is able to make balanced wines whether they are dry, medium or sweet – which is partly why many growers do indeed make a wide (and often confusing) variety of wines.

Unfortunately, German wine law makes it impossible for a consumer to know which are the best vineyards. This law says that all vineyards are created equal, regardless of the quality of wine they produce. Quality, in German terms, is measured by how much sugar the grapes have when they are harvested. There is some sense in this, as the best vineyard sites should be able to ripen

GERMAN WINE LAW

Germany's top wine grade is *Qualitätswein mit Prädikat* (QmP), which relates to one of the following six categories of ripeness, and means that the grapes were made into wine without any further addition of sugar (*süssreserve* is permitted, although its use in increasingly less widespread).

• *Kabinett* is made from ripe grapes.

• *Spätlese* is made from late-picked, and therefore riper, grapes.

• *Auslese* is made from specially selected bunches of particularly ripe (sometimes nobly rotten) grapes.

• *Beerenauslese* is made from individually selected, extra-ripe and nobly rotten grapes.

• *Trockenbeerenauslese* is made from dried, specially selected single grapes infected with noble rot.

• *Eiswein* is made from fully ripe grapes that have been left on the vine until they freeze. The ice crystals concentrate the sugars in the remaining juice.

Qualitätswein bestimmter Anbaugebiete (QbA) is the next grade down and must come from one of the 13 designated wine-producing regions and be made from must of a certain minimum weight.

Qualitätswein is subject to official testing, although with over 90 per cent of all wines achieving this level or the higher QmP in a typical vintage, the testing must not be very demanding.

Landwein, the equivalent of French *vin de pays*, is a cut above *tafelwein*, introduced in 1982 for wines of distinct regional character.

Deutscher Tafelwein, or German table wine, is made from a blend of grapes with added sugar to give a semblance of ripeness. The *deutscher* means the grapes must be grown in Germany; plain *tafelwein* can come from anywhere in the EU.

grapes more successfully than others. However, when a wine harvested with a potential alcohol level of 5.9 per cent can call itself a quality wine (as it can in some German regions), there is something wrong with the system.

There are moves afoot to establish a more meaningful classification of the finest vineyards, but these have come largely from conscientious growers and as yet have no official recognition. Given the influence the co-operatives and other major producers are able to exert on the government, it is hard to see such a classification passing into law in the near future. In the meantime, Germany should be approached in a similar fashion to Burgundy: the grower is more important than the quality level shown on the bottle. Those wishing to further their German education should seek out a specialist wine merchant.

There are 13 wine-producing regions, or *Anbaugebiete*: Ahr, Baden, Franken, Hessische-Bergstrasse, Mittelrhein, Mosel-Saar-Ruwer, Nahe, Rheingau, Rheinhessen, Pfalz, Saale-Unstrut, Sachsen and Württemberg. These are divided into *Bereiche* (districts), such as Bernkastel in the Mosel-Saar-Ruwer, and Nierstein in Rheinhessen. A further subdivision into around 160 *Grosslagen* (collective sites) describes vineyards that are grouped together by a supposed similarity of style, such as Gutes Domtal. Smallest of the subdivisions are the 2,600 *Einzellagen*, or individual vineyards, which together make up Grosslagen. The labels give no indication whether you are getting a potentially excellent wine from an *Einzellage*, or something from a (usually) more mediocre *Grosslage*.

The German taste   Baden, Franken, Liebfraumilch, Mosel-Saar-Ruwer, the Nahe, Rheingau, Rheinhessen, Pfalz and Sekt all have entries in this book. Wines from Germany's other growing regions are seen less often outside the country. The Mittelrhein (Middle Rhine) is the place to go for a *Rheinfahrt* (Rhine River cruise) and see the picture-postcard castles clamped to craggy Wagnerian cliffs high above the Rhine Gorge. Between Bingen (on the edge of the Rheingau) and Koblenz (where the Mosel joins the Rhine), Riesling from the slatey slopes is crisp and firm. Most Ahr wine is red, but what little white there is can be good; the best producers are Deutzerhof and Meyer-Näkel.

The Hessische-Bergstrasse is a warm region off the Rhine near Heidelberg; the best producer is the Staatsweingüt Bergstrasse. Württemberg is considered red-wine country, although Riesling is the most widely planted variety. In the former East German districts of Saale-Unstrut and Sachsen, Müller-Thurgau reigns. Lützkendorf in the former and Zimmerling in the latter are considered the best producers.

Where next?   See the specific entries on German wine regions and styles: **Baden, Franken, Liebfraumilch, Mosel-Saar-Ruwer**, the **Nahe, Rheingau, Rheinhessen, Pfalz** and **Sekt**.

Spain

Mañana was yesterday
Best-known wines Sherry, Rioja, Cava

Spain's best wines have been, are and always will be its reds. When it comes to white grapes, it has been dealt something of a duff hand. And until comparatively recently, the winemaking also erred on the duff side – which meant, of course, that many of the white wines were duff to the power of duff. An occasional Malvasia-based Rioja would manage to slide past its oaky exterior to show a bit of class. A Galician wine or Cava from the cooler north would display a modicum of freshness. And of course in Jerez, that outpost of excellence on the south coast, the sherries have always been impressive.

However, with these and a handful of other exceptions, the typical Spanish white was flat, lifeless, dull and oxidised, without any fruit flavour. In the intense heat, it was difficult to grow grapes with enough acidity to keep the wines tasting fresh. Once in the wineries, it was impossible to regulate temperatures in those picturesque but totally impractical Ali Baba jars (called *tinajas*). The occasional decent fortified or sweet wine made in these conditions would sometimes surface, but it was more by accident than by design.

SPANISH WINE LAW

Spain's wine classification is similar to that of Italy or France.

• *Denominación de origen calificada* (DOCa) is a comparatively recent introduction used to denote the superior DOs, and is equivalent to Italy's DOCG.

• *Denominación de origen* (DO) specifies the source, grape varieties and means of production, much as France's AC and Italy's DOC do.

• *Vino de la tierra* is more flexible than a DO, and is roughly equivalent to the French *vin de pays de zone* (subcategory of *vins de pays*).

• *Vino comarcal*, or "regional wine", applies to wine made in 21 *comarcas*, or regions, which show some individual regional character. It is roughly equivalent to the French *vins de pays de région* (subcategory of *vins de pays*).

• *Vino de mesa*, supposedly the lowest level, is equivalent to *vin de table* in France, but some producers make excellent wines in this category.

It was only after producers in similarly torrid climates such as California's Central Valley or Australia's Murray River had been making interesting and fruity wines for several years that it dawned on the Spanish that there might be an alternative. Slowly at first, but then with gathering momentum, they set about rectifying the situation. Just by picking the grapes earlier in the year, before the acidity plummeted, and fermenting at cool temperatures in stainless-steel tanks, enormous strides were made and continue to be made. In the 1970s, Miguel Torres in Catalonia was the first to show that Spain could produce decent dry wines, but now people throughout the country are in on the act. Even baking-hot spots such as La Mancha now routinely trot out sprightly quaffers with ease.

There remains, however, the problem of Spanish white grapes. For the most part, Airén, Viura (Macabeo), Parellada and other native varieties are not packed with powerful fruit, or aromatic pungency, or bright individuality, or any of the things we look for in a really classy wine. Improved winemaking can make them zippier, but it cannot add flavour that wasn't there in the first place. Apart from Muscat, which is used to varying degrees of effect throughout Spain, only Verdejo in Rueda and Albariño in Rías Baixas show any great strength of character. It is no surprise, then, to see foreign varieties (Chardonnay especially) making inroads. Sometimes these are used to spice up the local varieties, but the most successful wines are unblended.

In the north, Rioja, Navarra, Penedès, Rías Baixas and Rueda produce the best white wines, as does up-and-coming Somontano – home to the fine Viñas del Vero and Enate *bodegas*. Further south, the wines tend to be more simple, although increasingly well made. Exceptions to this rule are either sweet or fortified. The fragrant Moscatel de Valencia is one of the world's wine bargains, while Málaga gives a different slant on the same grape. And then there is sherry – now copied by various countries – demonstrating that it is Spain's greatest wine.

Where next? See the specific entries on Spanish wine styles: Catalonia, Cava, Málaga, Montilla-Moriles, Navarra, Rías Baixas, Rioja, Rueda and Sherry.

Portugal

More than Mateus and Madeira

Best-known wines Vinho Verde, Mateus Rosé, Madeira

Joining the European Union in 1986 was a turning point for Portugal's wine producers. Thanks to EU grants, several grape growers who used to send their grapes to the local co-op have been able to begin bottling their own wines, and many vineyards and cellars have also been totally refurbished. The improvement in red wines as a result of these initiatives has been huge, but the rise in standards of the white wines has been no less dramatic. Previously, the only Portuguese white of any renown was Vinho Verde. Now, increasingly skilled winemakers are turning out bright, zippy wines using both indigenous and imported varieties, especially Chardonnay.

As in Italy, the star grapes of Portugal are all red, but there are a number of interesting local white varieties, some with synonyms such as Dog Strangler, Ewe's Tail and Fly Droppings. Fernão Pires, also known as Maria Gomes, is the most widely planted white grape, producing peppery dry wines in Estremadura, Ribatejo and the Bairrada regions. Bical is grown mainly in Bairrada, Dão and Beiras, and has a spicy, lemon-and-ginger character with fresh acidity; older versions can develop some of the petrolly character of aged Riesling. Perhaps the finest variety is Arinto, the main grape of Bucelas where it must make up at least 75 per cent of the blend. Malvasia Fina, or Vital as it is sometimes known, is one of the grapes of white port, and a few Douro producers also use it for making fine table wines.

RECOMMENDED PRODUCERS

Bela Fonte
Caves Velhas
Herdade do Esporão
Fuiza Bright
Fonseca (Dom Prior)
José Maria da Fonseca
Luis Pato
Quinta de Gaivosa
Quinta da Murta
Quinta das Pancas
Quinta da Romeira
Quinta de Saes
Quinta Dom Carlos
Sogrape
JP Vinhos

PORTUGUESE WINE LAW

Portugal's wine classification shows many similarities to that of France.

• *Denominação de origem controlada* (DOC) specifies the source, grape varieties and means of production, much as France's AC does (*see* **France**).

• *Indicação de proveniência regulamentada* (IPR) is the equivalent of VDQS wines, which one day may become full DOCs.

• *Vinho regional* (VR) is a more flexible classifiction than a DOC, and is equivalent to *vin de pays*.

• *Vinhos de mesa* is the equivalent to the French *vin de table*.

No one region has yet emerged as Portugal's great white hope. Vinho Verde, especially with its Alvarinho-based wines (*see* **Albariño**), would seem to be the obvious candidate, but quality remains erratic, a common problem throughout Portuguese whites. Bucelas, just north of Lisbon, is the only DOC exclusively for white wines, but the number of decent producers remains small. Good whites come from places where good winemakers decide to make them.

Port and Madeira are the best known of the fortified wines, but Portugal has another gem up its sleeve. Setúbal, made from Muscat of Alexandria, is a fortified wine of 15 to 16 per cent alcohol whose fermentation is stopped by the addition of spirit, leaving natural grape sugar to provide the sweetness. The wine, a speciality (and indeed, exclusivity) of JM da Fonseca, is livened up by maceration on the grape skins for several months before transferring it to barrel for ageing. There are two principal versions: a vintage wine and a 20-year-old, which takes on the raisiny taste and makes it more intense and concentrated, like a smoky Liqueur Muscat.

Portugal's most famous rosé – indeed, its most famous table wine – is Mateus. A bottle of Mateus Rosé may not be as fashionable as it once was (either as a drink or as a table lamp), but it can still be rather pleasant in a simple, sweet and slightly sparkling way. Other rosés are scarce, although Sogrape's Nobilis from Bairrada shows the potential for the style. Sparkling wines are also hard to find, and are often not that great when you do uncover them. Luis Pato's from Bairrada are notable exceptions.

Where next? Portugal, like **Spain**, **Italy** and **Greece** is more predisposed to red wines, but see how these countries' winemakers are progressing with whites. See also the specific entries on **Madeira**, **Port** and **Vinho Verde**.

Switzerland

As fresh as the Alpine air, with about as much flavour
Best-known wines Chasselas, Fendant, Arvine/Petite Arvine, Silvaner

If you were designing a vine-growing country on the back of an envelope, you might place it somewhere between France, Italy and Germany, making sure to give it a cool climate. You would hope for wines with Burgundy's class,

Piedmont's character and perhaps the Mosel's delicacy. Instead, you get Swiss wines. They can be light and wonderfully fresh – no doubt about it – but the Swiss are handicapped by the fact that their most important grape variety is Chasselas, a table grape the French barely ever bother to make into wine. Give it a little *pétillance*, or slight sparkle, from bottling *sur lie* like Muscadet, and its youth and freshness constitute most of its appeal. It does best in the French-speaking part of Switzerland, particularly under the name of Fendant in the Valais, and also as Dorin in the Vaud, and as Perlan in Geneva and Neuchâtel. Good winemakers, with good sites, can persuade Chasselas to make some fine and age-worthy wines, but we're not talking white burgundy, even if the price tags suggest as much.

Johannisberger, the local name for Silvaner, can have more character, as can Petite Arvine from the Valais; indeed, approval for the latter variety has come from further down the Rhône Valley in France, where Chapoutier now has some experimental plantings in its vineyards. Chardonnay is appearing with some success, while Pinot Gris can make attractive sweet wines, in which case it is labelled as Malvoisie.

Most of the vineyards are in the western, French-speaking part of the country, where two-thirds of the vineyards are planted with white grapes, most of it Chasselas. Reds dominate the Italian-speaking sector. The wines of eastern Switzerland (the German-speaking part) can be good, but you will have to visit the country yourself in order to find them.

The Swiss taste The Swiss say that their grape varieties are extremely sensitive to soil and situation. A cynic would say that their flavour vanishes, whatever the situation. The best wines are juicy, with some texture, and can display flinty notes. Arvine, especially the superior Petite Arvine strain, makes

quite rich wines with hints of lime and grapefruit. Chardonnay is usually fresh and breezy with peachy fruit, and can have similar traits to the wines made in northern Italy.

Where next? **Austria** has the Alpine freshness and bite, but also a wider range of tastes and lower prices. **Savoie** does a French version of Swiss wine – again, at more sensible prices.

RECOMMENDED PRODUCERS

Willy Bründlmayer
Franz Hirzberger
Sattlerhof
Manfred Tement
Fritz Weingärtner Wachau
Fritz Wieninger
Winkler-Hermaden
Franz Xavier Pilcher

Austria

The most underrated wine country in the world

Best-known wines Hardly anything – yet

Talk about clouds and silver linings. In the mid-1980s, some producers were caught sweetening their wines with diethylene glycol, also known as anti-freeze. The whole of the country's wine industry was tarred with the "anti-freeze" brush, and what exports there were plummeted. In some countries, even sales of *Australian* wine suffered! The effect this had on Austria's wine authorities was to make them increase the standards required of the wines and to be more vigilant in policing them. It also galvanised producers into a corporate effort to re-establish the reputation of their wines.

The result is that today, Austria produces some of the finest white wines in Europe; the Rieslings and sweet wines in particular are world class. And with Grüner Veltliner capable of yielding everything from easy-drinking *Heurige* wines to serious, fleshy wines of real substance, Austria has a characterful grape of its very own.

Niederösterreich (Lower Austria) is the largest region producing powerful, long-ageing, dry Rieslings and Grüner Veltliner.

KAMPTAL   WEINVIERTEL
KREMSTAL
WACHAU
TRAISENTAL   DONAULAND
    Danube   VIENNA   ○ Vienna
                   CARNUNTUM
      THERMENREGION
            NEUSIEDLERSEE
                   Neusiedler See
      NEUSIEDLERSEE-HUGELLAND
                  MITTEL-
  Mur   BURGENLAND

            SUDBURGENLAND

WEST STYRIA
      SOUTHEAST STYRIA

  STYRIA

The Austrian taste The green-tinged stuff poured from a jug in an Austrian *Heurige*, or tavern, is most likely to be Grüner Veltliner. At this level, it will be light, fresh and crisp and at its best if it comes from the most recent vintage. Move up to the more ambitious versions from the Wachau and Kamptal-

Donauland regions of Niederösterreich, and the flavours become exotic and complex. Riesling is usually fermented to dryness and can be on the severe side, rather like the dry wines of the Rheingau. But like those wines, if the intensity of flavour is sufficient to balance the acidity, they are splendid, and capable of lasting for decades. Grauer Burgunder (Pinot Gris), Weissburgunder (Pinot Blanc) and Chardonnay (aka Morillon or Feinburgunder) are also used for good, dry wines. Styria specialises in Sauvignon Blanc, although the frequently rasping style will not appeal to all.

With sweet wines, it seems that every available white variety (plus the occasional red) is being pressed into service. Often the character of each variety is hidden behind massive amounts of apricotty botrytis, while the use of new oak adds sexy layers of creamed-coconut flavour.

Where next? Austrian **Riesling** has similarities with the wines of the **Rheingau**. Grüner Veltliner is grown in some Eastern European countries, but never with as good results; **Alsace Pinot Gris** and **Pinot Blanc** are better bets. With the sweeter wines, head for anywhere where botrytis is given full reign: **Germany**, **Sauternes**, Alsace SGN wines and anything nobly rotten from the New World. See **Burgenland**.

> ## AUSTRIAN WINE LAW
> Austria classifies its wine in much the same way that Germany does, with *Tafelwein*, *Landwein*, and *Qualitätswein* from *Kabinett* to *Trockenbeerenauslese* (TBA; *see* **Germany**). It adopts a similar scale of natural grape-sugar level or "must-weight", but the minimum Oechsle levels are higher. An extra category, *Ausbruch*, comes mid-way between *Beerenauslese* and TBA and has an affinity with the *Aszú* wines of Hungarian Tokáji.

Hungary

Slow but steady progress
Best-known wines Tokáji

Take Tokáji and Bull's Blood out of Hungary, and there's not much vinous life left. But the bit that does remain is growing and getting better. Hungary was one of several countries invaded by flying winemakers, and the most successful of these have been Kym Milne with the Balatonboglár winery and Hugh Ryman at Gyöngyös. Perhaps the most encouraging development is that, having seen what the flying winemakers did, some of Hungary's winemakers decided that they would like to

have a go by themselves. First and still foremost among these has been Akos Komocsay at the Neszmély winery; his impressive efforts have encouraged others to follow suit. Chardonnay and Sauvignon Blanc have provided the best wines so far, but Szürkebarát (a variant of Pinot Gris), Irsai Oliver and other local grapes have also been put to good use. We are still talking about wines governed by winemakers rather than *terroir*, but regions such as Lake Balaton, Mór and Azar-Neszmély may very well make an impression in the future.

Where next? See Tokáji and any Eastern Europe flying winemaker's wine.

Bulgaria

An uphill struggle
Best-known wines Khan Krum Chardonnay

When Bulgaria sprang onto the scene in the 1980s, its was the country's reds that captured the attention of wine-lovers. The few whites which did appear were typically dreary and best avoided. Khan Krum Chardonnay occasionally stirred a taste bud or two, but often for its levels of oak rather than for any flavours derived from the grapes.

Since then, white winemaking has improved immeasurably. Spurred on by visiting consultants, winemakers have cleaned up their wineries and invested in new technology, with the result that today's whites are fresher and better made than ever. Unfortunately, the raw materials from which they are made are worse than ever.

Following the end of the communist era, the nation's vineyards were returned to their previous owners – regardless of whether they wanted them or not, or whether they lived 200 miles away. As yet, the wineries own hardly any vineyards, so they have little or no control over the quality of the grapes they receive. Until this situation changes, it's hard to see where further improvements can be made.

The Bulgarian taste It's difficult to put your finger on anything defiantly Bulgarian in many of the wines, largely because of the aforementioned problems with grape supplies. Even when there are good batches of wine, they often disappear in the blending vat, so what remains is the influence of the winemaker. Chardonnay can impress, although enthusiastic oaking remains a problem. Other whites based around aromatic varieties such as Traminer, Riesling (usually Welschriesling), Misket and Muscat Ottonel can be fragrant, easy wines for summer days, but they seldom scale great quality heights.

Where next? Some of the best **Chardonnays** evoke memories of **Mâconnais** wines. However, given that the main reason for choosing Bulgarian wines remains their price, look for varietal wines from other Eastern European countries such as **Romania** and **Hungary**.

Slovenia

Vast, untapped potential
Best-known wines Lutomer Laski Rizling

The disintegration of the former Yugoslavia left Slovenia as a fairly wealthy nation with the bulk of the vineyards, but so far the Slovenians have progressed little from the communist era. The vineyards are situated in two regions: in the west, just across the Italian border from Friuli-Venezia Giulia, and in the northeast abutting Austria's Styria. The latter location is the one with the higher potential. The best-known wine from this region is the Lieb-look-alike Lutomer Laski Rizling (made from Welschriesling) which, despite a fall in popularity, is still a big seller. Even so, Sauvignon Blanc, Gewürztraminer and Chardonnay from Lutomer are rather better.

Where next? Cross the Austrian or Italian frontiers to see what could be done.

Romania

Frustratingly erratic
Best-known wines Cotnari

In an ideal world, Romania would be turning out truckloads of fine and sensibly priced wines, together with a few world-class examples. The country's climate is excellent for wine growing. The vineyards contain a mix of international varieties such as Chardonnay, Pinot Gris, Sauvignon Blanc and Gewürztraminer, alongside interesting local grapes such as Grasa, Tamaiîosa,

Romaneasca and Feteasca Alba. Yet, the average quality remains frustratingly low. Flying winemakers are able to turn out reasonable varietal wines, but the conditions in most wineries are primitive, and no money is forthcoming from either inside or outside the country to invest in new equipment.

The sweet, honeyed Cotnari – a blend of Grasa, Frîncusa, Tamaiîosa, Romaneasca and Feteasca Alba from the Moldavia region – is Romania's best-known wine and the occasional bottle can still be excellent. Indeed, the most impressive Romanian whites available in recent years have been releases of mature vintages of the country's dessert wines dating back to the 1960s, their sweetness more than enough to cover up basic winemaking faults. Dry whites seldom impress, although the occasional Pinot Gris and Gewürztraminer from Tîrnave in Transylvania can be good.

The Romanian taste Lack of freshness is a problem in many dry wines, but the best display their varietal make-up faithfully, especially the lightly spicy, rose-petal-infused Gewürztraminer. The sweeter wines can be very impressive, as most have acidity underpinning their honeyed sweetness.

Noble rot plays a factor in some vintages, but most wines are made from very ripe, late-harvested grapes. Cotnari is a blend, but many of the wines are single varietals. So if you want to try 40-year-old late-harvest Chardonnay, you now know where to come.

Where next? Compare Romania's dry whites with those of **Bulgaria** and **Hungary**. Try a bottle of **Tokáji** to see to what level **Cotnari** aspires.

Greece

Life after Retsina

Best-known wines Retsina, Muscat de Samos

For many wine people, Retsina's only virtues are that it's easy to spot in blind tastings, and it isn't Chardonnay. Others are more enthusiastic. Drunk young and well chilled with a plate of freshly grilled sardines at an Ionian seaside *taverna*, however, and Retsina can be just what a dusty mouth requires.

Yet there is more to Greek wine than Retsina, although you will have to learn a new language in order to come to terms with it. Yes, you'll find pockets of Chardonnay, but it shares the vineyards with the likes of Moscophilero, Assyritiko, Robola, Rhoditis and Savatiano, (the last being the grape responsible for most Retsina). It makes more sense to talk of good producers rather than good regions; even so, the wines of Mantinia, made with the aromatic Moscophilero, are more consistent, while Robola from Cephalonia can be pleasantly limey and fleshy.

What Greece is good at is sweet wines based on Muscat, many of them originating from islands in the Aegean Sea. Foremost among these – and arguably Greece's greatest wine – comes from Samos, close to the Turkish coast. The basic Muscat is impressive, but the Samos Nectar made from sun-dried grapes is a stunner. Those from Rhodes, Limnos, Rion and Patras are also worth seeking out. The number of producers with the desire to make wines that can compete on export markets is increasing, albeit slowly.

However, small wineries are cropping up throughout Greece, and their efforts are encouraging larger companies to make better wine. The reds are still – and probably always will be – more impressive, but at least Greece does now have flag-wavers apart from Retsina.

Where next? Southern **Italy** and **Portugal** are also making great strides in the the white-wine department, with both indigenous and imported grapes being used to increasingly impressive effect. No one else makes Retsina, although a heavily oaked white **Rioja** is halfway towards it.

RECOMMENDED PRODUCERS

Antonopoulos
Argyros
Boutari
Caliga
Domaine Carras
Gentilini
Gerovassiliou
Kouros
Domaine Kostas Laziridis
Mercouri
Oenoforos
Samos Co-op
Château Semeli
Skouras
Spiropoulos
Strofilia
Tsantali
Tselepos

England and Wales

And did those feet in ancient times...

Best-known wines None as yet, but watch out for the sparklers

A lack of training in either viticulture or winemaking was insufficient to stop several single-minded individuals from establishing vineyards in the UK in the 1960s and 1970s. They often planted the wrong varieties in the wrong places, laying their vines open to the worse effects of the generally unfavourable climate. It came as no surprise to outside observers that the wines were, on the whole, dreadful.

But as commercial realities began to hit home, the owners realised things had to change. Vineyards were pulled up, or replanted with more suitable varieties. Owners concentrated on growing grapes and left the winemaking to those with better training. The Germanic image shifted towards one inspired more by France and the New World. The upshot is that today's English wines (and the few made in Wales) are better than they have ever been.

But is that good enough? The English climate is so erratic that only certain grape varieties will ripen. Names such as Reichensteiner, Schönburger and Huxelrebe are associated with Germany, a country whose image remains tarnished as far as wine is concerned. The labels may be attractive, but they don't feature important words such as Chardonnay and Sauvignon Blanc. Actually, a few do bear the name Chardonnay, and this could be the direction English wine is heading in the future. These wines are not still, they're sparkling. You see, the region with which major parts of southern England has the greatest affinity – both in terms of climate and soil type – is Champagne, in northern France. England has produced sparkling wine from the varieties it uses for table wines since the early 1980s, and with time on the lees and further time in bottle, these can be attractive, if a little coarse. Yet, what many observers consider to be England's best wine comes from Nyetimber, a vineyard planted solely with Chardonnay, Pinot Noir and Pinot Meunier, which only makes fizz.

The English taste The biggest influence on the flavour of most English wines is the vintage. It takes an awful lot of jiggery-pokery in the winery to mask the fact that the grapes didn't ripen, as is often the case. The greenness and raw acidity can make some wines almost undrinkable, and even in good years, the presence of smoky, grapefruit flavours speaks of unripe fruit. When conditions are right, however, the wines are delicately slender yet enchantingly aromatic, and flavours of apples, gooseberries, grass and elderflower appear. When botrytis strikes and the rains hold off, some producers are able to make light but intensely sweet wines. Nyetimber's Champagne look-alike shows the heights to which English sparkling wines can aspire, although most have more in common with the rather green and earthy sparklers of the Loire.

Where next? English winemakers increasingly take their inspiration for still wines from New World countries, although few of these have comparable climates. The **Loire** is rather closer in style. For fizz, it has to be **Champagne**.

United States

Have a nice day
Best-known wines Anything as long as it doesn't come in a carafe

Forty of America's 50 states grow grapes and make wine commercially. Alaska doesn't; Hawaii does. Hawaiian wines, along with those from Kentucky, Tennessee and Utah, will probably never make a great impression on the world stage, but those of California have been doing so for many years.

Take California out of the picture, and the amount of wine produced drops by 90 per cent, but there is still much to look out for. Oregon, Washington State and New York State are each making good wines in sizeable quantities, plus Texas, Virginia, Ohio, Pennsylvania and New Mexico all have wine industries.

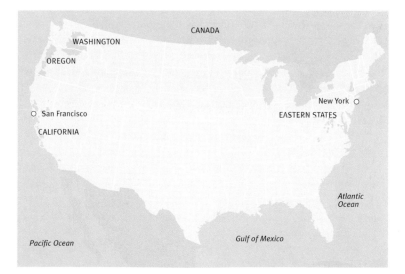

And you can be sure that whichever state you visit, the winemakers there will have a real enthusiasm for their wine. They really care about the wine and the consumer, and will spend time explaining both – hence the proliferation of neck labels, back labels and wine-tasting classes. They also have a certain humility (apart from some precious souls in California) and are always ready to experiment with a wide range of grape varieties and winemaking methods. It is an industry that changes and expands each and every year. Thank you for sharing.

Where next? Try Central Coast styles, and see specific entries on United States wine styles: **Carneros, Monterey and San Francisco Bay Areas, Napa Valley, New York State, Oregon, Sonoma** and **Washington State**.

Canada

Professional hobbyists succeeding in the not-so-frozen north
Best-known wines Icewine

It's Canadian, it comes in a small bottle, and it's very sweet. No, it's not maple syrup, it's Icewine. The Germans may have the edge in these sweet wines in quality terms, but where quantity is concerned, Canada leads the world. The Japanese go wild for this concentrated nectar, usually made from either Riesling or Vidal, and the Europeans would do the same – only the bureaucrats in Brussels won't allow it to be imported. But, while Icewine may be the country's best vinous ambassador, Canada is capable of producing other wines, some of them excellent.

Quebec and Nova Scotia have tiny wine industries, but Ontario and British Columbia are currently the only states whose wines are of more than local interest. Poor advice in the past has meant that inferior Germanic varieties have been planted, but as producers come to terms with their vineyards, Chardonnay, Pinot Blanc, Sémillon and others are already impressing. And come a world Riesling revival – ETA 2043 – Canada could become a very important wine producer.

Where next? Other fledgling wine industries with similar climates include **New York State** and **England**. If you can find – and afford – Icewine, line it up against a German example. See also specific entries for **Ontario** and **British Columbia**.

Argentina

Still-slumbering giant
Best-known wines Torrontés, Catena Chardonnay

Fifth-largest wine producer in the world it may be, but Argentina has much to improve upon before it ranks as highly in terms of quality – especially where white wine is concerned. The Italian influence that exists in the country's red wines is not mirrored in its whites. Indeed, with the exception of Torrontés, the grape which can't make up its mind whether it wants to be Gewürztraminer or Muscat, it is hard to find anything which smacks of Argentinianity. That is not to say that there are no other decent white wines, just not many with any character. Chardonnay has so far been the most successful, with the excellent Catena winery leading the pack. Chenin Blanc, Sauvignon Blanc, Sémillon, Riesling, Viognier and even Pinot Gris have also been pressed into service to provide wines for the export markets (as opposed to wines for domestic consumption which, for the most part are, shall we say, bucolic). However, the warm, dry climate combined with enthusiastic irrigation ensures that while the grapes are plump and healthy, the wines are usually dilute and characterless.

At present, it is more important to look for the name of a producer than that of the region. There may come a day when some of the cooler, higher parts of the sprawling Mendoza region come into their own for whites – but it isn't here yet. Further to the north, Salta is actually cooler because of the altitude, and produces the best Torrontés. Many feel that the provinces of Neuquén and Río Negro in the south may one day provide excellent whites, but it's still far too early to get excited.

The Argentina taste Um, yes. "International" is the best description, as most could have come from anywhere. The Catena Chardonnays made by Californian Paul Hobbs can stand proudly alongside anything else from the New World, but they're still winemaker's wines rather than *terroir* wines. The exception is Torrontés, which rises above its Galician origins to make exotic and friendly wines infused with a grapey spiciness.

Where next? Torrontes, **Viognier**, **Muscat**, **Gewürztraminer** and **Albariño** all offer similar aromatic styles. Try **Chile** and **South Africa**.

Brazil

You'll always be better at football, lads
Best-known wines Err...

Hot? Yes. Humid? Yes. Yet Brazil ranks third in the South American wine-production league behind Chile and Argentina. Virtually all the wine comes from the state of Rio Grande del Sul in the south of the country, particularly in the Sierra Grande and Frontera regions. While hybrid vines dominate, the number of *vinifera* vines is on the increase, although the damp conditions can mean that ripening these is a problem. Perhaps when Chile and Argentina have been more fully exploited, we'll see a few more wines appear. In the meantime, those that are exported usually come from the Aurora co-operative, often with the help of a flying winemaker.

Where next? Staying in South America, try **Chile** and **Argentina** for a view of quite how much progress Brazil needs to make. For a closer companion, seek out the few wines from Peru and **Uruguay** which never leave the continent.

Chile

RECOMMENDED PRODUCERS
Casa Lapostolle
Concha y Toro
Cono Sur
Errázuriz
Mont Gras
San Pedro
Santa Monica
Terra Noble
Valdivieso
Veramonte
Villard
Viña Carmen
Viña Casablanca
Viña de Larose
Viña Gracia
Viña Porta
Viña La Rosa
Viña Santa Carolina
Viña Santa Rita

Could do better
Best-known wines Casablanca Sauvignon, Chardonnay

Chile, so the people who should know about these things have been saying since the 1970s, is a viticultural paradise. In the regions where wine grapes are planted, as opposed to the places you find grapes destined for the rather addictive national spirit Pisco, Chile certainly is paradise.

It hardly ever rains here, yet sea breezes blowing though the gaps in the coastal mountain ranges prevent the temperatures from getting too hot. This means that there are none of the fungal diseases which affect vines in muggier climes. Of course, a vine needs water to survive, and the Chileans have plenty at their disposal, in the form of melting snow from the towering Andes. All a grower needs to do is turn on a tap and his vineyards are flooded with water. Flood irrigation is rather a primitive operation, but there's no denying that the vines love it. From the fruit of these vines, Chile's increasingly adept winemakers make increasingly competent wines. For great wines however, plump, happy grapes are a no-no.

Irrigation is being reduced, but the Chileans face other problems. After several years of growing Chardonnay, there should be more high-quality wines. Those from Casablanca can impress, but what about elsewhere?

With Sauvignon Blanc, the situation is worse still. If you've been unable to find much varietal character in Chilean versions, it is because most of what is grown is the inferior Sauvignonasse variety, a grape that yields at best a wine which struggles to last a year in bottle. Even in Casablanca, where producers have gone out of their way to procure true Sauvignon vines, many are finding that there's some Sauvignonasse mixed in as well. To speak of regions apart from Casablanca is still rather premature. Regions such as Curicó and Maule have promising pockets for whites, but

they are surrounded by less favourable land. Given the stringy shape of the country, there should, in theory, be something suitable for any grape variety going – but it's early days yet.

The Chilean taste Enthusiastic irrigation still means that intensity of flavour is not a hallmark of most Chilean whites. Chardonnay is light, with melon and pear fruit; oaking is (thankfully) sensitive. The best Sauvignons have zippy gooseberry flavours and are very good, but most versions have little going for them apart from a vague herbaceous impression. Wines such as Santa Monica Riesling, Viña Casablanca Gewürztraminer and Viña Larose Sémillon show the potential for these varieties, but they are very much isolated examples.

Where next? Over the Andes to **Argentina**, across the Atlantic to **South Africa**, or round the world to southern France.

Uruguay

Why not?
Best-known wines Make one up yourself

Thirty years ago, Chile, Argentina, Australia and New Zealand were on no wine-lover's shopping list. Will Uruguay feature on the list 30 years from now? The Chardonnay, Sémillon, Gewürztraminer and Viognier made by flying winemakers with local wineries suggest that it is not impossible.

Where next? Stay in South America for the wines of **Chile**, **Argentina** (widely available); **Brazil**, Peru, Bolivia and Venezuela (harder to find).

Australia

The land that launched a thousand Chardonnays
Best-known wines Chardonnay, Jacob's Creek, more Chardonnay...

Open the 'fridge in an Australian student house and one of the first things you're likely to see is a four- or five-litre cask of wine. Not *grand cru* burgundy, but it's at least OK – more than can be said if you'd done the experiment with similarly sized containers on sale elsewhere in the world. This is perhaps Australia's most important legacy to the wine world – the virtual elimination of bad white wine and the establishment of a high standard of reliability.

"Ah," the critics say. "Old World whites are far more complex. Just wait 'till those folks realise that Australia is all in-yer-face fruit with nothing to back it up except half an oak tree. Then we can all get back to drinking proper wine and use proper words such as 'austere' and 'breed' rather than 'wheelbarrows of ugli fruit'." Such criticisms are partially valid. The majority of Australian wine *is* simple. But so, too, is the majority of wine in any country. The question is whether you would rather have something simple and tasty or something simple and nasty.

In reply, the Australians are showing a willingness to get more character into their whites. At one time, Chardonnay would be fermented in stainless-steel tank, filtered and only then put into new oak barrels. The resulting wine served as both beverage and toothpick. Today, ambitious producers are more likely to ferment in barrel and then leave it to age on the lees, and the wines are a big improvement. Many are also experimenting with wild yeast fermentations.

There has always been experimentation with different grapes, but today's producers are far more focused in their trials. Viognier, Pinot Gris and Verdelho are never going to be mainstream, but they have enjoyed some success in recent years. The Great Australian Public are also discovering the pleasures of Riesling and Semillon. However, the area where the biggest strides have been made, and will continue to be made in the future, is with regard to that dirty word, *terroir*. Today's producers are more interested in locating the best sites for their preferred varietals, and thus letting the vineyards have a say in their wines' flavours. Of course, the influences of *terroir* have been apparent for several years to those who could see past the tide of Chardonnay to the great Rieslings of Clare and Eden Valley, and the Semillons of Hunter Valley.

The grapes for the wine casks (and for millions of cheaper, bottled wines) often did not come from single vineyards, varieties, regions or even states. Thanks to enthusiastic planting of certain varieties in recent years, it is likely that the multi-regional blended wines of tomorrow will be based on Chardonnay and Sauvignon Blanc rather than on Palomino and Sultana. But, whatever's in them, may they always be cheap and always cheerful.

SOUTH
AUSTRALIA

NEW SOUTH WALES

WESTERN AUSTRALIA
o Perth

Adelaide o

VICTORIA   o Sydney
o Melbourne

TASMANIA
o Hobart

The Australian taste While the various regions of Australia can now claim individual styles for their own wines, the large number of multi-regional blends does mean that it makes sense to talk of a country-wide style, especially at the cheaper end of the market. A wine labelled "Southeast Australia" basically means that the grapes didn't come from the west coast. Price is sometimes the only indication of whether it will be an everyday quaffer or something rather more ambitious.

Indeed, for most mass-market wines, ripeness of fruit and lushness of texture are the main characteristics, almost regardless of the varietal. Oak handling is rather more sensitive than it once was, although don't think that wines labelled "oak-aged" have seen the inside of a barrel. It is just as likely that the winemaker fermented and/or aged the wine in contact with oak chips or planks – "staves" in winespeak. And when the results are indistinguishable from the real thing, who cares? Riesling maintains its citric identity, although it is often concealed behind a rather bland name such as Australian Dry White.

Australia's skill at making good, basic whites is duplicated with sparkling wines. More ambitious producers will insist on cool-climate fruit and even single-vineyard wines, but for everyday drinking, regional blends such as Seppelt's Great Western, Yalumba's Angas Brut and Seaview Brut have few competitors in the realm of the fizzy. They're usually produced by the transfer method rather than full *méthode champenoise*, and are made from a wide range of different grapes, with ripe fruit flavours to the fore. Thanks to the pioneering work of Piper's Brook's Andrew Pirie, Tasmanian fruit, with its crispness and natural acidity, is particularly prized – both on the mainland and for local fizz, such as Jansz.

Where next? See the specific entries on Australian wine styles: **Adelaide Hills, Barossa, Clare, Coonawarra, Hunter Valley, Liqueur Muscat and Tokay, Margaret River, McLaren Vale, New South Wales, South Australia, Victoria, Western Australia** and **Yarra Valley.**

RECOMMENDED PRODUCERS

Chard Farm
Felton Road
Giesen
Kumeu River
Pegasus Bay
Rippon
Rongopai
Sandihurst
Waipara Springs
Waipara West

New Zealand

A green and pleasant land
Best-known wines Marlborough Sauvignon Blanc

Look at a map of the world, and New Zealand appears as a couple of small blobs to the east of Australia. Look a little closer and you realise that from tip to toe, it is actually rather large. In terms of climate there is nothing around it but the sea and its different currents. The coldest of these comes from the southeast, so there are no wine regions on New Zealand's dramatic but wet and chilly west coast. Most (but not all) of the winegrowing areas are situated in sheltered spots on, or close to, the east coast. Rainfall is less frequent here than in the west, but it can still conspire to wreck a vintage.

Today, New Zealand is best known for its Sauvignon Blanc, but that has not always been the case. The modern revival of the industry was initially based on the apparently sound idea that since the climate was so similar to parts of Germany, then German grapes would perform best. It wasn't long before New Zealand was making the finest Müller-Thurgau in the world. Unfortunately, this was at a time when wine-lovers in the rest of the world were turning on to Chardonnay. Today, Chardonnay has taken hold in the vineyards and is the most widely planted variety (a position held by Müller-Thurgau until as recently as 1994).

However, most people associate New Zealand with Sauvignon Blanc, due largely to its success in Marlborough. Nearby sunny Nelson has a diversity of *terroirs* and makes some great Sauvignons and Rieslings (especailly the Neudorf winery); as do Martinborough, Hawke's Bay and Gisborne (*see* specific entries for further information).

One of the fastest-growing wine areas in New Zealand is Canterbury, around Christchurch on the South Island. In particular, wineries in the Waipara district have shown that they can make Chardonnay, Riesling and Sauvignon Blanc capable of standing alongside New Zealand's finest. The most southerly area – and arguably the most stunning wine region in the world – is Central Otago. In conditions not dissimilar to those found in many fine German vineyards, Riesling thrives here, but Chardonnay, Gewürztraminer, Sauvignon Blanc and Pinot Gris have also yielded some fine wines.

At the opposite end of the country, some of the vineyards north of Auckland yield excellent Chardonnay. Slightly further south is the small Waikato region, the highlight of which is the range of botrytised wines made by Rongopai.

The New Zealand taste For many people, the crisp, gooseberry, asparagus-and-grass style of Marlborough Sauvignon Blanc is New Zealand wine in a nutshell. However, line up a Marlborough Sauvignon next to a Martinborough and Hawke's Bay example of the same grape variety, and there will be a noticeable difference in style. The further south the vineyard, the more likely you are to find greener, herbaceous flavours, instead of ripe citrus fruit.

Chardonnay varies from a simple, unoaked, tropical fruit-cocktail style to creamy and complex, with the producer, rather than the region, usually dictating the style. The situation is similar with Riesling, which some would argue yields better wines on average than Sauvignon Blanc. The wines vary from simple and slightly sweet with a touch of citrus fruit to quite powerful, steely, dry styles that could be mistaken for Alsace wines. Pinot Gris, Chenin Blanc and Gewürztraminer are all being used to create fabulous wines, but again, it is up to the producer to plant those varieties and make the wines well.

Still, *terroir* is beginning to talk in New Zealand. The Gimblett Road area of Hawke's Bay and the Awatere Valley in Marlborough are putting their thumbprints on wines from those regions, and certain parts of Canterbury and Central Otago already seem to be more highly regarded than neighbouring plots. If there is any criticism of the New Zealand wine industry, it is its uniformity of style.

A lot of Marlborough Sauvignon does taste as if it has come out of the same vat, and the same could be said of Chardonnay, regardless of the source. As many of the winemakers have been to the same schools for their training, either in New Zealand or Australia, the similarity in styles should come as no surprise – especially for such a young industry. However, there are producers now working hard to put an accent on more than mere fruit in their winemaking.

Where next? See specific entries on New Zealand wine styles: **Gisborne**, **Hawke's Bay**, **Martinborough** and **Marlborough**.

South Africa

Cape of Good Wine?
Best-known wines Constantia

A typical South African winemaker is like a large ocean-liner – it takes a lot of time and energy to make him (they are usually "hims") alter his chosen course. When South Africa emerged from the apartheid years and began to look at overseas markets, many producers were surprised by the lack of foreign enthusiasm for wines which had been so well received by the partisan audience at home. Since then, progress has been steady but slow, and the quality of the best wines still lags behind that of New Zealand, Australia and California. The QE2 mentality means that those who do decide to change course are only doing so slowly. There are, of course, a number of notable exceptions – forward-looking people who are showing the potential for Cape wines – but there should be more.

A typical Cape winery is usually well-equipped with plenty of modern technology and oak barrels. Fine and dandy. However, before and after the winemaking are the areas where improvements are really needed. The vineyards are generally neglected, and the grapes are often picked before their flavours have fully developed. This is fine for wines at the cheap-and-cheerful level, but not for anyone with higher ambitions.

After the wines have been made, many are still sent away to external facilities for bottling. What's the problem with that? Filtration. Some wines may go through three sets of filters before they are eventually bottled – once before they leave the winery, once on arrival at the bottling plant and then a final bout before actual bottling. Each filtration succeeds in removing some flavour, and the wine that eventually hits the bottle is undoubtably clean, but often a shadow of what it was. Vineyards are being spruced up, grapes are being picked riper, on-site bottling lines are being installed, but – remember the QE2 – only slowly. A further handicap for South Africa is that although it has plenty of vineyards, most were planted with a view to catering for the needs of the vast brandy industry and few contain the fashionable varieties. Chenin Blanc takes up over a quarter of vineyard area, but is usually consigned to the role of cheap and cheerful. It is sometimes blended with Colombard, another widely grown grape. Muscat is a common variety, used mainly for dessert wines, some of which are impressive. Constantia is the best and best known – try Klein Constantia's Vin de Constance.

Much of what the South Africans call Riesling is actually Crouchen. Pockets of true Riesling are few and far between, but some decent wines have appeared, especially from Constantia. Chardonnay has been around for many years, and some of the wines are excellent, having the ripe fruit of the New World along with an element of Old World restraint. However, enthusiastic use of oak remains a problem in some wineries. Slightly more Sauvignon Blanc than Chardonnay is planted. It is often picked early to retain acidity, with the result that the wines, though crisp, lack flavour. Sémillon and Viognier are newcomers, but early results suggest they could have a good future.

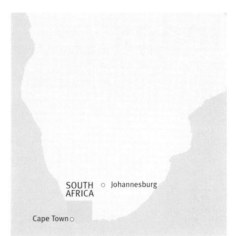

Highlighted section shows where the key wine areas are: Olifantsrivier, Piketberg, Swartland, Tulbagh, Paarl, Durbanville, Worcester, Constantia, Stellenbosch, Robertson, Swellendam, Klein Karoo, Overberg

The initials "MCC" in South Africa stand for *méthode cap classique* – in other words, *méthode champenoise*. While many remain in the still-wine-with-bubbles phase, some of the wines made from Pinot Noir and Chardonnay can be excellent and are attractively priced. Unfashionable as they are, some of South Africa's finest wines are its fortifieds, either in the style of sherry or as something called Jerepigo, where brandy is added to grape juice before fermentation begins.

The finest regions for whites tend to be near the coast, such as Walker Bay (try the crisp, elegant wines from Hamilton Russell and Bouchard-Finlayson), Constantia and the southern reaches of Stellenbosch. Some of the higher districts of Paarl can also offer fine conditions for white varieties. Swartland stretches north from Paarl, and is hot and dry. Towards the coast, in the cooler regions around the town of Darling, a few estates are making promising wines. Tulbagh lies east of Swartland. Further north still, Vredendal has another fine co-op, whose production is usually around the same as the whole of New Zealand. The huge Worcester region has over 20 per cent of South Africa's vineyards, most dedicated to producing bulk wines, while slightly further inland, growers in Robertson make some fine Chardonnay in hot conditions.

Where next? **Chile** is South Africa's closest competitor on the shop shelves. **Australia** does a far better job with similar conditions. Look for wines from **Constantia**, **Paarl**, Robertson, **Stellenbosch** and Walker Bay.

Index

PICTURE CREDITS:

Front cover, Steven Morris Octopus Publishing Group Ltd;
Joe Cornish p.11, 34, 46, 48, 106; James Johnson 7, 9, 19, 37, 39, 55 bottom, 72 bottom, 87, 101, 102, 112, 121, 124, 138, 140, 145, 148, 151, 157; Jason Lowe 69; Richard McConnell 2–3 bottom, 14, 66, 120; Steven Morris 4, 32, 65, 70, 79, 88, 115, 117, 152; Alan Williams

2 top, 2–3 top, 13, 15, 29, 30, 49, 52, 53, 55 top, 68, 72 top, 77, 81, 82, 83, 90, 91, 100, 111, 114, 126, 128, 130, 131, 134, 142, 144, 154

And many thanks to Seagram UK and the ICEP Portuguese Trade and Tourism Office for their kind contributions. Seagram UK 17, 60, 75, 132; ICEP Portuguese Tade and Tourism Office 104, 150